Learning by Design and Second Language Teaching

Learning by Design and Second Language Teaching establishes theoretical, research, and practice connections between the multiliteracies framework *Learning by Design* and L2 teaching and learning.

A comprehensive introductory chapter presents the theoretical tenets of the approach and is followed by four chapters devoted to the establishment of connections between the framework and L2 instruction, information on evidence-based pedagogical practices and suggestions for their implementation, and task examples that can be adapted for use in a variety of educational contexts. Each chapter links theory and research to practical steps instructors can take to select authentic materials and create tasks in each of the framework's knowledge processes with the objective of developing L2 students' performance in the interpersonal (speaking), interpretive (reading and listening), and presentational (writing) modes of communication. A selection of guidance charts, figures, templates, and extra digital resources are included within the text to support learning and teaching.

The book will be of interest to graduate students and in-service and future L2 teachers at all levels of instruction.

Dr. Gabriela C. Zapata was born in Rosario, Argentina. She received her MA in TESOL and PhD in Spanish (Linguistics track) from The Pennsylvania State University. She is Professor of Hispanic Linguistics in the Department of Hispanic Studies at Texas A&M University. Dr. Zapata's research foci are *Learning by Design* and second (L2) and heritage language (HL) pedagogy, multimodal social semiotics, and teacher education. She is also involved in the development and implementation of inclusive open educational resources for the teaching of Spanish as an L2 and HL and Spanish for the Professions.

Learning by Design and Second Language Teaching
Theory, Research, and Practice

Gabriela C. Zapata

LONDON AND NEW YORK

Cover image: enjoynz via Getty Images

First published 2022
by Routledge
4 Park Square, Milton Park, Abingdon, Oxon OX14 4RN

and by Routledge
605 Third Avenue, New York, NY 10158

Routledge is an imprint of the Taylor & Francis Group, an informa business

© 2022 Gabriela C. Zapata

The right of Gabriela C. Zapata to be identified as author of this work has been asserted in accordance with sections 77 and 78 of the Copyright, Designs and Patents Act 1988.

With the exception of Chapter 1, Chapter 2 and Chapter 3, no part of this book may be reprinted or reproduced or utilised in any form or by any electronic, mechanical, or other means, now known or hereafter invented, including photocopying and recording, or in any information storage or retrieval system, without permission in writing from the publishers.

Chapter 1, Chapter 2 and Chapter 3 of this book are available for free in PDF format as Open Access from the individual product page at www.routledge.com. They have been made available under a Creative Commons Attribution-Non Commercial-No Derivatives 4.0 license.

Trademark notice: Product or corporate names may be trademarks or registered trademarks, and are used only for identification and explanation without intent to infringe.

British Library Cataloguing-in-Publication Data
A catalogue record for this book is available from the British Library

Library of Congress Cataloging-in-Publication Data
A catalog record has been requested for this book

ISBN: 978-0-367-61734-9 (hbk)
ISBN: 978-0-367-61733-2 (pbk)
ISBN: 978-1-003-10625-8 (ebk)

DOI: 10.4324/9781003106258

Typeset in Goudy
by Deanta Global Publishing Services, Chennai, India

This book is dedicated to Drs. Mary Kalantzis and Bill Cope, and to my past and present mentors, Prof. Malena Botto, Dr. Margarita Pillado, Dr. Karen E. Johnson, Dr. A. Jacqueline Toribio, and Dr. María Irene Moyna.

Contents

List of figures	x
List of tables	xi
Preface	xii
Acknowledgments	xv

1 Introduction to *Learning by Design*   1

Learning by Design: *Theoretical and Pedagogical Bases*   1
Learning by Design: *Principles and Components*   6
Learning by Design: *Knowledge Processes*   9
    Experiencing   9
    Conceptualizing   11
    Analyzing   12
    Applying   13
Learning by Design: *Recent Theoretical Developments*   14
Summary   15
    Experiencing   17
    Conceptualizing   17
    Analyzing   17
    Applying   17
Notes   17
References   18

2 *Learning by Design* and Second Language Education   20

Second Language Teaching and Learning in Today's World:
    Frameworks, Perspectives, and Foci   20
Learning by Design *and Second Language Teaching and*
    Learning   29
Summary   33
Notes   34
References   34
    Works Cited   34
    Instructional Resources Cited   38

viii Contents

3 *Learning by Design* and Second Language Teaching Practices 39

Learning by Design's *Reflexive Pedagogy* 39
Second Language Instruction Based on Universal Design for Learning
  and Learning by Design 44
  Pedagogical Planning 45
  Instructional Moves 49
Everyday Practices for Second Language Instruction Grounded in
  Learning by Design 57
  Presentation of Learning by Design's Knowledge Processes 57
  Instructional Objectives 58
  Collaborative Learning 61
  Checkpoints and Assessment 67
Summary 69
Notes 70
References 70
  Works Cited 70
  Instructional Resources Cited 74

**4 Genre- and Project-Based Instruction Grounded in
  Learning by Design** 75

Genre-Based Instruction 75
Project-Based Learning 83
Summary 90
Note 90
References 90

5 Sample Second Language Tasks Grounded in Learning by Design 92

  1. Community Development: Talk to an Expert 93
     Instructional Information and Guidance (Task Idea Inspired by
       NEA, 2011, p. 15) 93
  2. Endangered, Threatened, or Vulnerable Flora and Fauna:
     Expository Texts and Infographics 98
     Instructional Information and Guidance (Task Idea Inspired by
       NEA, 2011, p. 20) 99
  3. Fan Fiction 103
     Instructional Information and Guidance (Task Idea Inspired by
       Sauro & Sundmark, 2016) 104
  4. Identity Texts 107
     Instructional Information and Guidance (Based on Zapata &
       Ribota, 2021a) 108
     Other Formats 111
     Related Topics 113

5. Media Collection (Critical Analysis)   117
   Instructional Information and Guidance (Task Idea
      Inspired by Cameron, n.d.)   117
   Memes (Based on Beucher et al., 2020 and Domínguez
      Romero & Bobkina, 2021)   122
6. Multimodal Stories   124
   Instructional Information and Guidance   124
7. Podcasts and Vodcasts   129
   Instructional Information and Guidance
      (Based on Moyna, 2019)   130
8. Recipes and Other Procedural Texts   133
   Instructional Information and Guidance   134
9. School Brochures   138
   Instructional Information and Guidance (Task Idea Inspired by
      Zammit, 2019)   139
Final Recommendations   143
Summary   147
Notes   147
References   149
   Works Cited   149
   Instructional Resources Cited   154

Appendix A: Template Questions and Foci for the Analysis of Multimodal Texts	155
Appendix B: Recommended Websites and Digital Tools	159
Appendix C: Multimodal Product Assessment	163
Index	166

Figures

1.1	Instruction based on *Learning by Design*	10
1.2	Instruction based on *Learning by Design* and metafunctions	16
2.1	An L2 social reading task grounded in *Learning by Design*	32
4.1	Relationship between genre-based instruction's instructional sequence and *Learning by Design*'s knowledge processes and metafunctions	83
4.2	Relationship between project-based learning's instructional phases and *Learning by Design*'s knowledge processes and metafunctions	86
5.1	Example of a persuasive infographic. Note: Infographic: which kind of activist are you? By developmenteducation.ie and Dóchas as part of the European Year for Development, licensed under CC BY-SA 4.0. https://bit.ly/3Cyaluk	144
5.2	Materials development cycle relying on open resources	147

Tables

1.1	Comparison between the Pedagogy of Multiliteracies and *Learning by Design*	7
2.1	21st Century Skills in the L2 Classroom	22
2.2	Summary of Social Justice Standards and Outcomes	28
3.1	Criteria for Measuring *Learning by Design*'s Knowledge Processes Outcomes	51
3.2	Design Template	54
3.3	Guiding Questions for L2 Students on *Learning by Design*'s Knowledge Processes	59
3.4	Sample Form for Group and Self-Assessment	63
3.5	Interpersonal and Small-Group Collaborative Skills	64
3.6	Criteria for Discussion in Group Processing	65
4.1	Genre-Based Instruction Activities Grounded in *Learning by Design*	80
4.2	Sample Project Grounded in *Learning by Design*	87
5.1	Activities for *Learning by Design*'s Knowledge Processes	94

Preface

In the past five years, I have been invited to offer workshops for second language (L2) teachers on the multiliteracies framework *Learning by Design* (Kalantzis et al., 2005, 2016, 2019) and its application to L2 and heritage language learning. On every occasion, I have made an effort not only to provide theoretical and existing-research information but also to incorporate sample tasks and practical tips. Yet, by the end of my workshops, almost without fail, I face the same questions from attendants: "What do I do first?" "What do I do to create activities?" "How do I organize my students?" "What tools do I use?" Clearly, instructors still have doubts about the pedagogy and its implementation. Also, I often see a disconnect between what I am suggesting and their vision of L2 education.

This volume was born out of these experiences. Even though excellent books have been written on multiliteracies-based approaches to L2 learning (e.g., Kumagai et al., 2016; Paesani et al., 2016), I felt there was still a gap in the literature, particularly when it came to *Learning by Design* (Kalantzis et al., 2005, 2016, 2019) and L2 education. In this book, I have tried to fill this gap. My path has been guided by the questions I have gotten from instructors throughout the years; my experience as an L2 researcher, educator, teacher trainer, and materials developer; and the need that I see for concrete connections between theory, research, and practice. To establish these connections, my discussion in the book moves from the most general theoretical perspectives and existing research to pedagogy, classroom practices, and concrete sample tasks.

In **Chapter 1**, I first discuss the tenets of the multiliteracies pedagogy proposed by the New London Group (NLG) (1996), and I introduce the framework of focus, *Learning by Design* (Kalantzis & Cope, 2022; Kalantzis et al., 2005, 2016, 2019). I then draw parallels between the NLG's original ideas and the changes introduced by Kalantzis, Cope, and their colleagues, which gave birth to a new pedagogical vision. I also describe the principles and components of Kalantzis et al.'s framework and its most recent theoretical developments.

The focus of **Chapter 2** is L2 learning. Specifically, I begin to trace the relationship between current L2 teaching and learning and *Learning by Design*. To achieve this goal, I examine the L2 frameworks, perspectives, and foci (in terms of themes and language use) that, based on existing research, I deem most relevant for our profession and that I believe exhibit theoretical and instructional similarities with the pedagogy developed by Kalantzis et al. (2005, 2016, 2019). I also make reference to L2 critical approaches and teaching for social justice. Finally, in the last part of the chapter, I provide an introductory example of an L2 task grounded in *Learning by Design*.

In **Chapter 3**, I center my discussion on pedagogy and everyday classroom practices. In the first part of the chapter, I describe *Learning by Design*'s reflexive pedagogy (Kalantzis & Cope, 2012) and I relate it to the instructional principles and practice guidelines in *Universal Design for Learning* (UDL-IRN, 2011) and the vision of L2 teaching and learning presented in Chapter 2. The second part of the chapter is devoted to the examination of pedagogical moves that I consider essential for the successful adoption of Kalantzis et al.'s (2005, 2016, 2019) framework in L2 classes.

Chapter 4 offers information on two instructional models that are theoretically and instructionally compatible with Kalantzis et al.'s (2005, 2016, 2019) pedagogy—*genre-based instruction* (Hyland, 2014) and *project-based learning* (PBLWorks, 2021). Each of them is discussed in detail, and suggestions for implementation, grounded in *Learning by Design*, are also provided.

In **Chapter 5**, I synthesize the theoretical and evidence-based pedagogical information offered in the four previous chapters, and I embed it in specific tasks that can be adapted for L2 learners in diverse educational contexts. In each example, I offer information about existing research and whom the task is most appropriate for. Additionally, I provide detailed steps for classroom implementation, including activities for students to work in each of *Learning by Design*'s knowledge processes (Kalantzis & Cope, 2022; Kalantzis et al., 2005, 2016, 2019). The sample tasks are complemented with three appendices. **Appendix A** and **Appendix C** are devoted to the provision of templates and foci to guide students' analysis of multimodal texts and to assess their multimodal artifacts. In **Appendix B**, I have compiled the web addresses of the digital tools, platforms, and resources I refer to in the sample tasks, and I have described each of them briefly.

I see the content I have created for this volume as an attempt to offer comprehensive answers to the questions I have gotten from teachers over the years and that have not been possible to answer solely through workshops. I hope the information I provide in the five chapters of this book will result in a more in-depth understanding of *Learning by Design* and what it can offer to L2 education, inspire L2 practitioners to incorporate authentic multimodal texts in their classes, and, above all, encourage them and their students to create materials that can be shared with others.

References

Hyland, K. (2014). *Genre and second language writing*. The University of Michigan Press.
Kalantzis, M., & Cope, B. (2012). *New Learning: Elements of a science of education*. Cambridge University Press.
Kalantzis, M., & Cope, B. (2022). After language: A grammar of multiform transposition. In C. Lütge (Ed.), *Foreign language learning in the digital age: Theory and pedagogy for developing literacies* (pp. 34–64). Routledge.

Kalantzis, M., Cope, B., Chan, E., & Dalley-Trim, L. (2016). *Literacies* (2nd ed.). Cambridge University Press.

Kalantzis, M., Cope, B., & the Learning by Design Project Group. (2005). *Learning by Design*. Victorian Schools Innovation Commission and Common Ground Publishing.

Kalantzis, M., Cope, B., & Zapata, G. C. (2019). *Las alfabetizaciones múltiples: Teoría y práctica*. Octaedro.

Kumagai, Y., López-Sánchez, A., & Wu, S. (Eds.). (2016). *Multiliteracies in world language education*. Routledge.

Paesani, K., Allen, H. W., & Dupuy, B. (2016). *A multiliteracies framework for collegiate foreign language teaching*. Pearson.

PBLWorks. (2021). *Project based learning handbook for elementary schools*. Buck Institute for Education.

UDL-IRN. (2011). *UDL in the instructional process* (version 1.0.). UDL-IRN. https://www.learningdesigned.org/sites/default/files/UDL%20Instructional%20Planning%20Process.pdf

Acknowledgments

The completion of this volume would not have been possible without the Faculty Development Leave awarded to me in fall 2021 by Texas A&M University and the funding I received from the institution's Office for Diversity, for which I am deeply grateful. I would also like to thank my research assistant at Texas A&M University, Ms. Ewurama Okine. ¡Muchas gracias, Ewurama!

1 Introduction to *Learning by Design*

Learning by Design: **Theoretical and Pedagogical Bases**

The global crisis brought about by the COVID pandemic affected all aspects of our lives, including the way in which we communicate, work, teach, and learn. In 2020, the majority of our activities were carried out virtually, and most of us were forced not only to learn how to use a myriad of digital tools, but also how to create a variety of new kinds of texts. This was particularly true in education, where both educators and learners needed to adapt to new instructional environments with different expectations, forms of communication, and overall ways of doing things. Of course, we had lived in this technology-based, new media world for at least two decades (Green & Beavis, 2013), but the health crisis exacerbated our reliance on digital forms of interaction and action. Another crucial aspect of our recent social experience was the civic movements, such as Black Lives Matter, that once more brought to light the realities faced by countless minoritized communities, and the effects of systemic racism and discrimination on people's lives. These movements reminded us that we all have a role to play in making this world more inclusive and equitable, and that the diversity of our societies should be celebrated and valued, and be the norm in all aspects of our lives. Everyone should have a seat *and* a voice at the table, and opportunities and conditions should be present for this to happen. And this cannot be truer than in education, a crucial site for societal change (Kalantzis et al., 2016, 2019).

In the mid-1990s, a group of scholars anticipated what we experienced in the past two years, though I am quite sure they could not have predicted the COVID crisis or envisaged the extent to which their predictions would hold true. The scholars belonged to the New London Group (NLG)—ten international educators who met in New London, New Hampshire, in 1994 (Cope & Kalantzis, 2006, 2009; NLG, 1996) with the purpose of focusing on literacy. Based on current trends in globalization and technology at that time, the NLG posited that the traditional concept of literacy, tied to the printed medium and to "a single, official, or standard form of language" (Cope & Kalantzis, 2015, p. 1), and the way in which it was taught, were inadequate for a generation for whom learning already involved much more than the printed, "official word." The NLG believed that what was needed was a pedagogy that would encompass not just printed language, but also other modalities of communication present in the everyday reality in which the new generation was growing. In addition, this new approach would have to address and incorporate learners' diverse identities and life experiences (Kalantzis et al., 2005). For the NLG scholars, it was evident we were living in a diverse, globalized world, and we were becoming both multimodal and multilingual meaning-makers. The traditional concept of "literacy" was no longer relevant. We needed

> a kind of learning which [would] facilitate [learners'] active engagement with new and unfamiliar kinds of [multimodal] texts, without arousing a sense of alienation and exclusion, [and would focus on the] increasing complexity and inter-relationship of different modes of meaning.
> (Cope & Kalantzis, 2006, pp. 37–38)

To refer to this new type of educational approach, the NLG introduced the concept of *multiliteracies*.

But what exactly did the NLG scholars (1996) have in mind when they coined this term? What does the *multi* in *multiliteracies* refer to? Broadly speaking, the term *multiliteracies* makes reference to the multiple ways in which we create and convey meaning. These encompass two dimensions of meaning-making: The *social* (context/function) and the *modal* (form) (Kalantzis et al., 2016, 2019). The first one is connected to the diverse social contexts in which communication takes place, which shape what and how we communicate. The social *multi* might comprise the personal experiences, cultural or "community setting[s], social role[s], interpersonal relations, identit[ies], subject matter, etc." that are "significant to the ways in which we make and participate in meaning" (Kalantzis et al., 2016, pp. 1–2). The second dimension, the *modal*, refers to the variety of communication modes or semiotic systems to which we might resort to create meaning, such as the linguistic (written and oral), visual, gestural, or auditory. These modes are directly connected to the new media (and the tools and practices associated with them) which we experience daily, and which we have come to rely on in today's world. Lister et al.'s (2009) characterization of *new media* denotes this current *multimodal* nature of meaning, and it encompasses the following (also embedded in the concept of multiliteracies):

> *New textual experiences*: new kinds of [genres][1] and textual [multimodal] forms, entertainment, pleasure, and patterns of media consumption (computer games, simulations, special effects cinema).
> *New ways of representing the world*: media which … offer new representational possibilities and experiences (immersive virtual environments, screen-based interactive multimedia).
> *Computer-mediated communications*: email, chat rooms, avatar-based communication forums, voice image transmissions, the World Wide Web, blogs, [vlogs and vodcasts], etc., social networking sites, and mobile telephony.

New ways of distributing and consuming media texts characterized by interactivity, [multimodality] and hypertextual formats.

A whole range of transformations and dislocations of established media (in, for example, photography, animation, television, journalism, film, and cinema).

(pp. 12–13)

When applied to educational contexts, the concept of *multiliteracies*, which encompasses both *multis*, the social and the modal, entails the need to establish educational contexts that allow learners to understand, create, and be able to appropriately and effectively participate in multimodal meaning-making involving new media in a multiplicity of diverse social contexts (Anstey & Bull, 2006; NLG, 1996). Thus, a pedagogy whose goal is to develop students' multiliteracies relies on students' exposure to and work with multimodal texts and technologies reflective of a variety of social and literate practices. Based on their existing body of work (e.g., Anstey, 2009; Anstey & Bull, 2006), Bull and Anstey (2019) posit that instructional approaches based on the notion of multiliteracies need to prepare learners to:

- Be strategic, creative and critical thinkers who can engage with new texts in a variety of contexts and audiences.
- Understand that … texts that have differing purposes, audiences and contexts will require a range of different behaviors that draw on a repertoire of knowledge and experiences.
- Understand how social and cultural diversity affect literate practices.
- Understand, and be able to use, traditional and new communication technologies.
- Be critically literate … to determine, [in every literate practice], who is participating and for what reason, who is in a position of power, who has been marginalized, and what is the purpose and origin of the texts being used and how these texts are supporting participation in society and everyday life.

(p. 7)

Though not articulated precisely in Bull and Anstey's (2019) terms, these goals were present in the NLG's (1996) proposal for a *pedagogy of multiliteracies*.

This new instructional approach was theoretically grounded in Halliday's (1985) Systemic Functional Linguistics (SFL). This theory's overarching principle is that language is a semiotic system that cannot be separated from its social function, as it expresses meaning according to the different social contexts in which it is used. That is, SFL "treats linguistic systems and structures as intrinsically organized with respect to the … kinds of meaning they construe, enact, and compose" (Martin, 2016, p. 44). Language use in specific social contexts can be analyzed in terms of the three aspects present in all meaning-making: The *field*, the *tenor*, and the *mode*, or, simply put, "what is happening [subject-matter, situation]; who is taking part [participants]; and what it is that the participants expect language to do for them [language form, communication channel]" (Halliday & Hasan, 1985, p. 12). These aspects of meaning will be realized through language, fulfilling three types of semantic functions (or *metafunctions*)—the *ideational* (or *experiential*), the *interpersonal*, and the *textual*. That is, the *field* or what we are experiencing/noticing in the world will be expressed through the *ideational* metafunction; the *tenor* or aspects of our communication with others (e.g., emotions, attitudes, type of relationship, etc.) will be expressed through the *interpersonal* metafunction; and the *mode* or the way in which we structure/organize/ express our message will be expressed through the *textual* metafunction (Halliday & Hassan, 1985; Martin, 2013).

In the *pedagogy of multiliteracies*, SFL's three situational features and metafunctions are first embedded in the importance that the approach bestows upon the connections among language, sociocultural context (including participants), meaning, and text. Nevertheless, the pedagogy goes beyond a focus on only language, to include other modalities of communication, as they are realized in different multimodal meaning-making manifestations beyond printed texts and speech (Cope & Kalantzis, 2006). Additionally, the multiliteracies approach guides learners in the understanding of the how and why of meaning-making based on the analysis of what is communicated (the *field*—*ideational* metafunction), who is participating in the social situation (the *tenor*—*interpersonal* metafunction), and what semiotic resources (or modalities) the participants are using to create and convey meaning (the *mode*) and how they are organized/expressed (*textual* metafunction), and why this is the case.

So how are these foci and goals materialized in the classroom? The NLG (1996) proposed four main pedagogical moves—*Situated Practice, Overt Instruction, Critical Framing*, and *Transformed Practice*—to integrate the multiliteracies pedagogy into educational contexts. Not all of the moves need to be part of the instructional sequence, nor there is a particular order in which they should be enacted, but each of them is crucial for the development of students' multiliteracies (Cope & Kalantzis, 2006). Regardless of which move is chosen and included in educators' practice, the point of departure is always the learner. That is, the NLG scholars believed that for instruction to be relevant and to reflect the diversity of life experiences learners bring to the classroom, curricula must establish connections with their "different subjectivities and with their attendant languages, discourses, and registers, and use these as a resource for learning" (p. 72). Thus, students' personal contributions become part of the *Available Designs*, or existing resources for meaning-making (e.g., language, other semiotic resources, and diverse social discourses), that will be incorporated into the different curricular elements. Through their active involvement in the four pedagogical angles, in a process that the NLG defines as the *Design* (or *Designing*), the instructor and students will collaborate to dissect, use, and transform the curricular Available Designs. This process will result in the *Redesigned*, which can be characterized as new meaning constructions and/or representations (i.e., new knowledge) not only with respect to the Available Designs, but also the meaning-makers themselves. That is, while engaged in *Designing*, both the teacher and learners "transform their relations with each other, [and] themselves, [and also] configurations of subjects, social relations, and knowledges are worked upon and transformed" (NLG, p. 76).

Educators enacting an instructional sequence grounded in the multiliteracies framework might choose *Situated Practice* as their first move. This move relies mostly on the Available Designs students bring to the classroom, which are closely tied to their community and personal and previous academic experiences (NLG, 1996). Connections are established between curricular foci and outcomes, and students' identities and needs. This is also the stage where new, but somewhat familiar, Available Designs are introduced and weaved into what has already been experienced and/or is known (Cope & Kalantzis, 2015). Situated Practice can be followed by *Overt Instruction*, as it is in this pedagogical move that instructors guide learners in the analysis of the semiotic elements in the Designs introduced in the previous move. In Overt Instruction, students learn and work with explicit concepts and metalanguages that they can apply to examine and understand semiotic resources and modes, and how they have been used to convey meaning in the Designs being analyzed. The expected outcome in this "pedagogical angle [is for] students [to] have a way to describe the processes and patterns of [meaning] Design in a meaningful way" (Cope & Kalantzis, 2006, p. 40). Learners' understanding of meaning-making is further developed in the next move, *Critical Framing*. The focus here is on what Kress (1993) defines as the *motivated* aspect of a sign (or Design), i.e., the reasons why it has been created. Students critically explore Designs in terms of their creators' intentions, trying to understand ideological and sociocultural connections with regards to the semiotic resources used, and the message that is being conveyed. The desired result of Critical Framing is for learners to "gain the necessary personal and theoretical distance from what they have learned, constructively critique it, account for its cultural location, [and] creatively extend and apply it" (NLG, p. 87). In the fourth pedagogical move, *Transformed Practice*, students are provided with the opportunity to apply what they have learned or the transformed Available Designs in the creation and use of new ones (e.g., new multimodal texts).

The NLG's (1996) proposal for a multiliteracies pedagogy offered a blueprint for a different approach to education—one that would not only reflect the changes to communication and meaning-making brought about by information technology and the new media, but that would also connect learners' lifeworld and their diverse communities to curricula. Since it was first presented, the framework has guided a myriad of instructional and research projects on a variety of academic subjects, both in the humanities and STEMM, in countless educational contexts around the world. The NLG's work has been cited almost 3,000 times, and a Google Scholar search of "multiliteracies pedagogy" since its inception in 1996 renders close to 17,000 existing articles, web pages, and books. These numbers bear witness to the significance of the approach in current educational settings.

In the year 2000, two of the scholars in the NLG, Mary Kalantzis and Bill Cope, took some of the original ideas in the 1996 proposal, and they reconceptualized them (Cope & Kalantzis, 2015; Kalantzis et al., 2005, 2016, 2019).

6   Introduction to Learning by Design

Kalantzis and Cope's goal was to reframe the concepts in the NLG's (1996) pedagogy of multiliteracies, so that it would be easier for both instructors and students to understand them, and make sense of the instructional path of which they were part. Additionally, the researchers and the team of educators with whom they worked (Kalantzis et al., 2005) introduced new pedagogical conceptualizations. These and the reframed NLG's ideas would become the framework *Learning by Design* (*L-by-D*), the focus of this book. In the next section, each component of this pedagogy will be discussed in detail, and throughout this volume, they will be presented in connection with second language (L2) learning. However, before we do so, we will examine some of the similarities and differences between the NLG's pedagogy of multiliteracies and *L-by-D*, and we will delve into the framework's tenets.

Learning by Design: Principles and Components

The emphasis that the NLG's (1996) pedagogy of multiliteracies places on learners' identities and personal and community experiences as learning resources is also a crucial aspect of *L-by-D*. Indeed, one of the main premises of the framework is the need for the integration of *informal* and *formal* learning. The first type of learning refers to what students learn endogenously and tacitly in their personal, everyday lives: It is a reflection of knowledge based on their lifeworld experiences. The second kind of learning is academic: It is connected with schooling, and can be characterized as systematic and designed. Kalantzis and her colleagues (2005, p. 41) believe that the most effective formal learning experiences are those that incorporate informal learning into curricula, by "engag[ing] with the learner's experiential world and apply[ing] what is learnt in that world." This is particularly important in today's globalized and technology-based society, where, through their interaction with and use of new media and digital tools and their participation in virtual communities, students have more diverse learning opportunities in their everyday lives than in school settings (Green & Beavis, 2013; Zammit, 2010). Also, Kalantzis et al. (2005) posit that learners might prefer this type of learning because they might consider it more appealing and more closely related to their personal lives. It is, therefore, imperative that informal learning be part of students' academic experiences.

The incorporation of informal learning into formal academic experiences is directly connected to the two conditions Kalantzis and her colleagues (2005) have identified as necessary for learning to happen. The first one is *belonging*. This concept emphasizes the importance of establishing instructional environments to which learners can connect at a deep, personal level and to which they feel they *belong*, not only in terms of curricular content, but also with regards to the school/learning community and context. Learners' identities and *funds of knowledge*, defined by Moll et al. (1992, p. 133) as "the historically accumulated and culturally developed bodies of knowledge and skills essential for household and individual functioning and well-being," are also crucial aspects of *belonging*. In Kalantzis et al.'s words, "belonging to learning is founded on …

the learning ways [i.e., the learner's identities and learning preferences], the learning content [i.e., curricula], and the learning community [i.e., the learning environment]" (p. 43). The second essential condition for effective learning is that of *transformation*, which makes reference to the life-long changes that can result from students' in-depth involvement in their learning process, and to the instructional elements needed for this to happen. For learning to be transformative, Kalantzis and her fellow researchers believe that instructional paths need to

> take the learner into new and unfamiliar terrains. However ... the journey into the unfamiliar needs to stay within a zone of intelligibility and safety. At each step, it needs to travel just the right distance from the learner's lifeworld starting point.
>
> (p. 51)

In *L-by-D*, if these two conditions are not met, equitable education is not possible.

These two conditions provide the basis for the implementation of instructional moves and the development of transformative curricula that will result in the equitable development of learners' multiliteracies. *L-by-D*'s pedagogical angles are based on those proposed by the NLG (1996). Nevertheless, in the work of Kalantzis, Cope, and their colleagues (Cope & Kalantzis, 2006, 2009, 2015; Kalantzis et al., 2005, 2016, 2019), the multiliteracies dimensions have been renamed, reconceptualized, and expanded. In *L-by-D*, instructional angles are defined as *knowledge processes* or *epistemic moves*. Kalantzis et al. (2016, p. 74) characterize these processes as "foundational types of thinking-in-action or ... things you can do to know." A comparison between NLG's instructional angles and *L-by-D*'s epistemic moves is provided in Table 1.1.

L-by-D's knowledge processes can be said to be somewhat more comprehensive and transparent than the multiliteracies dimensions, because they offer more information about what is expected of teachers and learners. Also, the terminology used is more straight-forward and easier to understand.

Table 1.1 Comparison between the Pedagogy of Multiliteracies and *Learning by Design*

Pedagogy of Multiliteracies	**Learning by Design**
Situated Practice	Experiencing the Known
	Experiencing the New
Overt Instruction	Conceptualizing by Naming
	Conceptualizing with Theory
Critical Framing	Analyzing Functionally
	Analyzing Critically
Transformed Practice	Applying Appropriately
	Applying Creatively

8 *Introduction to* Learning by Design

L-by-D's eight knowledge processes mirror those that are present in informal learning. In formal or academic learning, they are embedded in the following instructional moves, which allow students to:

1) experience known and new meanings by departing from known concepts and experiences and by moving forward to explore new situations and/or information;
2) conceptualize meanings by grouping into categories, classifying, defining, and by formulating generalizations, establishing connections among concepts, and developing theories;
3) analyze meanings functionally by focusing on the structure and function of semiotic resources and by establishing logical connections, and critically by evaluating different perspectives, interests, and motives; and
4) apply meanings appropriately by engaging in real-life applications of knowledge, and creatively by applying new knowledge in innovative and creative ways. (Kalantzis & Cope, 2010, 2012a)

Cope and Kalantzis (2015) see learning based on the incorporation of these epistemic moves to instruction as "a process of 'weaving' backwards and forwards across and between [them]" (p. 4).

In *L-by-D*, the "weaving" of the eight knowledge processes can constitute a blueprint for the establishment of a *transformative curriculum*—one that will "[take] students from their lifeworld experiences to deep [and new] knowledge, understandings and perspectives" (Bruce et al., 2015, p. 82). However, it is important to emphasize that *L-by-D* does *not* provide prescriptive information on how to develop curricula, what activities to use in the classroom, or in what order to implement them. Instead, the framework offers guidelines on possible types of tasks and ways in which they can be used (Cope & Kalantzis, 2015). This is the case because, above all, *L-by-D* bestows utmost importance upon the idea that if productive learning is to happen, it cannot be based on a one-fits-all model: It has to be *designed* according to each individual learning situation and for each specific group of students. This means that the choice of knowledge processes and/or the order in which they are instructionally organized will depend on who the learners are and the educational context in which learning is taking place.

Regardless of which epistemic moves are chosen and how they are enacted in practice, what is important is the development of a *transformative curriculum*. For Kalantzis and her colleagues (Kalantzis et al., 2005), this type of curriculum incorporates learners' diverse lifeworlds into instruction with the goal of setting and achieving "comparable learning outcomes without prejudice to difference, [so that] the effect[s] … are pluralism—a community of productive diversity—[and] equity" (p. 64). Such a curriculum encompasses the following elements:

- Dialogical, collaborative teaching and learning
- *L-by-D*'s knowledge processes

- Instructional sequences, outcomes, multimodal content, and tasks based on subject matter and learners' academic and personal needs
- Curricular connections with learners' diverse identities, personal experiences, and community (i.e., funds of knowledge [Moll et al., 1992]) (*belonging and transformation*) (Kalantzis et al., 2005)
- Engaged, critical citizenship

In practice, such a curriculum provides opportunities for students to be exposed to and actively work with different multimodal texts that are connected to their lifeworld experiences and those of their families/communities. Curricular materials include different kinds of genres and non-linguistic ensembles[2] associated with a variety of subjects (depending on specific academic content, outcomes, and learners' needs). Tasks are based on *L-by-D*'s knowledge processes, and they allow students to critically analyze meaning-making in terms of social function, structure, and linguistic/non-linguistic semiotic resources. Learners develop their own personal projects, collaborating with their classmates and expressing their identity and newly gained knowledge in what Cope and Kalantzis (2007, p. 78) defined as the "re-voicing, and not replication" of that knowledge. Kalantzis et al. (2005, p. 66) describe the successful outcome of a transformative curriculum as follows:

> First, the learner has, notwithstanding the uniqueness of their identity, belonged in the curriculum. They have been part of the curriculum, and the curriculum has been part of them. Second, the learning has taken them into a new and unfamiliar place, changed their view of the world, and changed them in some incremental way into a person whose horizons have been broadened. [The result has been] productive learning—both purposeful and transformative.

Instruction based on *L-by-D*'s principles and components is summarized in Figure 1.1. In the next section, we will explore each knowledge process in depth.

Learning by Design: Knowledge Processes

Experiencing

Even though Kalantzis, Cope, and their colleagues (Cope & Kalantzis, 2015; Kalantzis et al., 2005, 2016, 2019) do not prescribe an order in which the knowledge processes can be weaved into curricular content, I envision *experiencing* as the point of departure in our teaching practice. For example, in *experiencing the known*, instructors can *situate* students in the specific context of a new learning experience by facilitating connections between academic content and learners' informal learning, lifeworlds (including funds of knowledge), and previous educational experiences. Activities such as recalling, retrieving, and reflecting

10 *Introduction to* Learning by Design

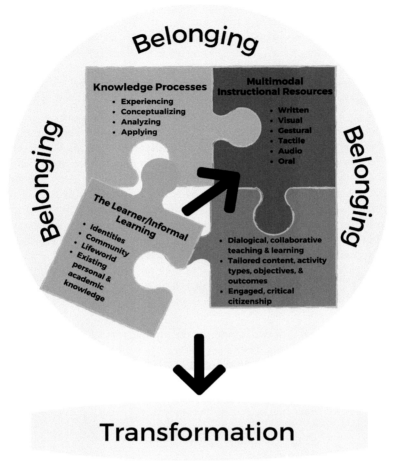

Figure 1.1 Instruction based on *Learning by Design*.

on memories/events in their lives/communities and identifying personal preferences/interests (e.g., through tasks like *show and tell*, class/group surveys, Socratic dialogue) allow students to "introduce their invariably diverse experiences into the classroom, [and] teachers and other learners also begin to get a sense of each student's prior knowledge" (Kalantzis et al., 2016, p. 77). *Experiencing the known*, therefore, can scaffold instructional moves, and can undoubtedly prepare learners for what's to come.

Once existing schemata (Carrell, 1984; Rumelhart, 1980) have been activated, and personal connections have been established in *experiencing the known*, instructors can start to introduce new academic content in *experiencing the new*. This can be achieved in different ways, but in L2 learning, the focus of this book, it can be done through the use of multimodal texts. New texts will take students into the realm of new knowledge and target language use. However, it is crucial to remember that novel content always needs to exhibit some type of connection to the learner to the extent that the new makes enough sense for learning to occur. Also important is the need to scaffold students' work (I discuss this instructional aspect in more depth in Chapter 3) within this process (and, of course, others). Archetypal tasks in this move may include those that involve students' collaboration in the completion of comprehension and interpretation activities that might take the form of jigsaw group work, Think-Pair-Share, spider maps, comparison and contrast between known and new experiences, summarizing, retelling, etc. (Zapata, 2017; also see Table 5.1 on page 94).

Cognitive/learning process dimensions: Retrieving, recognizing, identifying, recalling, general understanding of message (Kalantzis et al., 2005)

Conceptualizing

To describe the processes of *conceptualizing by naming* and *conceptualizing with theory*, we will continue with the text example I introduced in the previous section. When learners are working with a text, their work in these two epistemic moves will first center on its design elements (e.g., the organization and classification of information). That is, in *conceptualizing by naming*, students might

> draw distinctions [e.g., through a focus on what type of information different parts of the text convey]; identify similarities and differences [e.g., through comparisons among different textual elements]; and categorize with labels [e.g., through the development of concepts that identify textual elements such as *hyperlinks*].
>
> (Cope & Kalantzis, 2015, p. 19)

In order to facilitate this kind of work, instructors might rely on tasks that allow students to make connections, classify (or cross-classify), find common patterns, define, and give examples, all of which could be achieved through the use of instructional tools such as affinity diagrams, comparison charts or matrices, concept organizers, information text pyramids, and/or Venn diagrams (Zapata, 2017; also see Table 5.1 on page 94).

Once learners have developed new concepts, in *conceptualizing with theory*, they make connections "to explain how a kind of text works to make meaning, in general terms" (Kalantzis & Cope 2012a, location 7403). That is, students synthesize the functional and theoretical links found among concepts, and they arrive at generalizations or theoretical definitions that can be applied to similar conceptual relationships within a particular discipline, or in our case, other texts. For example, generalizations could be made about specific academic genres such as reports, or about multimodal ensembles such as vlogs (e.g., how they are organized, semiotic resources used, etc.). As a result of their work in this epistemic move, learners are able to "uncover implicit and underlying realities which might not be immediately obvious from the perspective of lifeworld experience" (Kalantzis et al., 2005, p. 77). Tasks that can promote students' analytic synthesizing and theorizing include those that incorporate pedagogical tools such as cause and effect pattern organizers, flow diagrams, mind maps, and/or taxonomies of generalization (Zapata, 2017; also see Table 5.1 on page 94).

Cognitive/learning process dimensions:
- Interpreting (also clarifying, paraphrasing, representing, translating)
- Exemplifying (also illustrating, instantiating)
- Classifying (also categorizing, subsuming)
- Summarizing (also abstracting, generalizing)
- Inferring (also concluding, extrapolating, interpolating, predicting)
- Explaining (also constructing models) (Kalantzis et al., 2005, p. 82)

Analyzing

In the two *analyzing* epistemic moves, learners first explore functional aspects of meaning-making. This is *analyzing functionally*. For example, if students are working with a linguistic text, they might focus on the language structures that are used to convey certain meanings, paying attention to the relationship between meaning and form. If working with multimodal texts, learners' work "may involve examining the choices [i.e., semiotic resources] made by creators in the design of their texts, and the effects of these choices in the representation of meanings" (Cope & Kalantzis, 2015, p. 20). In other words, the process of analyzing functionally, regardless of the ensemble on which students are focusing, rests on finding the answers to the questions *what* and *how* with respect to the semiotic elements present in it. To achieve this goal, teachers can develop tasks that allow learners to compare and contrast, connect, deconstruct, infer, and interpret (Zapata, 2017; also see Table 5.1 on page 94).

The *analyzing critically* epistemic move provides students with the opportunity to explore the reasons why the ensemble they are examining has been created. In this stage of the learning process, learners establish connections between the meaning-maker (i.e., the author/creator) and the ensemble, trying to discover motivations and sociocultural connections, as well as the voices that might be represented or silenced. These goals are achieved through the critical analysis of the semiotic resources used in connection to the author's/creator's identities and their and their text's sociocultural/sociohistorical context, with the purpose of "interrogat[ing] the world of subjectivity—human agency, interest, and intent" (Cope & Kalantzis, 2015, p. 21). To carry out their critical examination, students might appraise, argue, assess, critique, deconstruct, infer, and interpret through tasks such as debates, polling, point of view interviews, and comparison of perspectives and/or ensembles on similar topics (Zapata, 2017; also see Table 5.1 on page 94).

Cognitive/learning process dimensions:

- Differentiating (also distinguishing, focusing, selecting)
- Organizing (also finding coherence, integrating, parsing, structuring)
- Attributing (also deconstructing)
- Checking (also coordinating, detecting, monitoring)
- Critiquing (also judging) (Kalantzis et al., 2005, pp. 82–83)

Applying

Work in the two *applying* knowledge processes, *applying appropriately* and *applying creatively*, involves students' application of their new knowledge in the creation of their own ensembles. In *applying appropriately*, learners might develop products with characteristics similar to the ones found in the texts on which they have been focusing. For example, if students have been analyzing reports, they might create one. It is important to remember, however, that even though student-produced artifacts reflect what their creators have learned in the educational environment and they are tied to classroom work, they also need to bear a clear connection to the real world and learners' lifeworlds (Cope & Kalantzis, 2015; Kalantzis et al., 2005). Applying appropriately might also "involve transfer from theoretical understanding to a practical example of that theory in action" (Kalantzis & Cope, 2012b, p. 248). The form that this process will take will depend on the discipline and the particulars of the instructional context.

In *applying creatively*, learners are encouraged to "think outside the box" by developing products that might incorporate modalities, media, and tools they might have not tried before. Also, students' work might "involve taking something out of its familiar context and making it work—differently perhaps—somewhere else" (Kalantzis et al., 2005, p. 78). This implies that applying creatively tasks are expected to be innovative, imaginative, and creative, and can definitely involve not only learners' lifeworlds (e.g., their interests, identities, and lived experiences), but aspects of the informal learning they bring to class. The richness of new media and digital tools in today's world opens up a myriad of instructional options for instructors to consider to fully engage learners in the meaning-making process (see Chapter 5 and Table 5.1 on page 94).

Cognitive/learning process dimensions:

- Executing (also carrying out)
- Implementing (also using)
- Generating (also hypothesizing)
- Planning (also designing)
- Producing (also constructing) (Kalantzis et al., 2005, pp. 82–83)

Throughout the chapters in this book, I explore a variety of pedagogical possibilities based on existing scholarly work on current L2 education. But before I

Learning by Design: Recent Theoretical Developments

As discussed in the first section of this chapter, *L-by-D* is grounded in the tenets of SFL (Halliday & Hassan, 1985; Martin, 2013, 2016). When examining the pedagogical objectives of each of *L-by-D*'s knowledge processes, it is clear that an instructional path that incorporates them provides students with opportunities to explore meaning in terms of *field* (topic/subject—the what), *tenor* (relationship between participants—the who), and *mode* (presentation of meaning—the how), as well as in connection with SFL's three metafunctions—*ideational, interpersonal*, and *textual*. Recently, however, Kalantzis and Cope have expanded SFL's metafunctions (originally tied to the analysis of speaking and writing) from three to five to offer a more comprehensive framework to analyze meaning in connection with multimodal ensembles or those that incorporate only specific modes (e.g., visual, gestural, etc.). The five metafunctions brought forward by these two scholars are characterized as follows in two of their most recent works (Cope & Kalantzis, 2020; Kalantzis & Cope, Forthcoming):

- *Reference* bears similarities with Halliday's *ideational* metafunction, and aims at answering the question **"what's this ensemble about?"**
- *Agency* is similar to Halliday's *interpersonal* metafunction, but Cope and Kalantzis also encompass social action in general with the purpose of answering the question, **"who or what has created the ensemble?"** (i.e., focus on the meaning-maker).
- *Structure* exhibits similarities to Halliday's *textual* metafunction. However, in a broader multimodal view, it answers the question, **"how does the ensemble hang together?"**, with a focus on "the devices used to create internal cohesion, coherence, logic, and boundedness in meanings" (Cope & Kalantzis, 2020, p. 46).
- *Context* is one of the added metafunctions, though it is connected to the concept of the same name in SFL. Cope and Kalantzis, however, have transformed it into a metafunction. The purpose is to "locate meaning in its surroundings [e.g., time and space]" (Cope & Kalantzis, 2020, p. 47) and to answer the question, **"what is the ensemble connected with?"**
- *Interest* is connected to SFL's notion of purpose, but Cope and Kalantzis (2020) have expanded it as a function with the goal of answering the question, **"what is the ensemble for?"** That is, through the analysis of *interest*, we can explore:
    - what emotions, social impulses, and reasoning motivate meaning;
    - how subjectivity and objectivity work … in texts;
    - how interests [are] embodied; [and]
    - how interests [are] served and shaped in the spaces of nature and the constructed environment (p. 48).

These five metafunctions are part of an integrated theory that Cope and Kalantzis (2020; Kalantzis & Cope, 2020) have developed for the analysis of multimodal meaning, which they have named *a grammar of multimodal transposition*. Even though the grammar might not have a pedagogical purpose per se, its five metafunctions bear a theoretical relationship with *L-by-D*'s knowledge processes and overall principles behind the framework, and they expand it. That is, not only are the metafunctions compatible with the type of discovery and work that learners already undertake in each epistemic move (e.g., *context* and *interest* and *analyzing critically*), but they are also clearly connected with the idea of a transformative curriculum. Cope et al. (Forthcoming, pp. 7–8) posit that

> to trace meaning patterns [e.g., by focusing on the five metafunctions they propose] is to see the meaningful coherence of the world, while recognizing the finely calibrated nuances of ceaseless differentiation. It is also to insist on the responsibility of meaning-makers because, in our natures, we are always changing the world.

Clearly, these words mirror the expected outcomes of transformative learning. In other words, by expanding the range of analysis in the eight epistemic moves, the inclusion of the five metafunctions into *L-by-D* allows for the creation of tasks through which learners can delve more deeply into meaning-making in terms of both analysis and action (as meaning-makers themselves). In Figure 1.2, I offer a modified representation of instruction based on *L-by-D*'s principles and components, establishing connections between the knowledge processes and the five metafunctions.

Summary

In the first part of this chapter, I introduced the pedagogical framework from which *L-by-D* evolved, the NLG's (1996) *pedagogy of multiliteracies*. I discussed its theoretical tenets, connected to SFL (Halliday & Hassan, 1985; Martin, 2013, 2016), and I described its four pedagogical moves—*Situated Practice, Overt Instruction, Critical Framing*, and *Transformed Practiced*. I also tied the pedagogy to current sociocultural aspects, including our reliance on new media and the diversity of today's world.

In the second part of the chapter, I examined *L-by-D*, first comparing it with the multiliteracies pedagogy. Once I had established existing parallels between the two approaches, I introduced *L-by-D*'s principles, components, and goals. I offered definitions for key concepts such as *belonging, transformation, knowledge processes*, and *transformative curriculum*. I then presented each knowledge process in detail, describing them in connection to instruction. In the final section of the chapter, I focused on some of the theoretical developments that the creators of the framework, Mary Kalantzis and Bill Cope, have recently introduced in connection with meaning-making. Specifically, I discussed the five

16 *Introduction to* Learning by Design

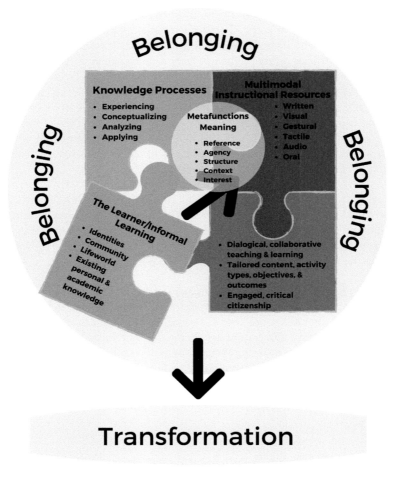

Figure 1.2 Instruction based on *Learning by Design* and metafunctions.

metafunctions in their *grammar of multimodal transposition—reference, agency, structure, context,* and *interest*—and I tied them to *L-by-D*'s epistemic moves. I decided to incorporate these metafunctions as part of this chapter's discussion because I believe they expand the approach, even though they are not directly related to it.

In the next chapter, I examine the connections between *L-by-D* and current L2 education. However, before I move to this topic, I offer a summary of the *L-by-D*'s knowledge processes as "a series of pedagogical principles" (Kalantzis et al., 2016, p. 82). The information presented is adapted from my existing work with Kalantzis and Cope (Kalantzis et al., 2019, pp. 73–74).

Experiencing

- Premise: Human cognition is always situated in a particular sociohistorical and sociocultural context.
- Meaning is intrinsically connected to personal experiences (including funds of knowledge), actions, and subjective interests, and it is grounded in the real world.
- Formal, academic learning is weaved with learners' identities, lifeworld, lived experiences, and informal learning.
- Learners' experiences and the texts they are familiar with are also weaved with novel experiences and texts.

Conceptualizing

- Learners do not merely reproduce concepts. Instead, they are active conceptualizers and theory developers.
- Students transform tacit information into explicit knowledge, and they arrive at generalizations from the connections they establish among concepts.

Analyzing

- Learners develop analytic skills to not only discover, interpret, and articulate functional aspects of meaning in terms of semiotic elements, but also purposes, interests, and motivations in connection with meaning-makers.

Applying

- Learners apply their new knowledge, conceptualizations, and understandings to real-world situations.
- Learners create diverse texts with different communication purposes, resorting to a variety of semiotic resources.

Notes

1 In this book, I adopt Hyland's (2014, p. 4) definition of *genre* as

> a term for grouping texts together, representing how [individuals] typically use language to respond to recurring situations. [The term is] based on the idea that members of a community usually have little difficulty in recognizing similarities in the texts they use frequently and are able to draw on their repeated experiences with such texts to read, understand, and [create] them relatively easily.

I discuss this concept in connection with L2 instruction and *Learning by Design* in Chapter 4 (see pages 75–83).

2 In this volume, the words *text*, *artifact*, and *ensemble* are used interchangeably to make reference to multimodal products. The use of the term *ensemble* is based on Serafini's (2014) work, in which it is defined as "a type of text that [might] combine written language, design elements, [and/or] visual images, [and] utilize[s] various semiotic resources to represent and communicate meaning potentials" (p. 2).

References

Anstey, M. (2009). Multiliteracies, the conversation continues: What do we really mean by "Multiliteracies" and why is it important? *Reading Forum New Zealand, 24*(1), 5–15.

Anstey, M., & Bull, G. (2006). *Teaching and learning multiliteracies: Changing times, changing literacies*. Australian Literacy Educators' Association and International Reading Association.

Bull, G., & Anstey, M. (2019). *Elaborating multiliteracies through multimodal texts*. Routledge.

Bruce, M., Gill, P., Gorman, S., Gorman, S., Henry, P., Kiddy, R., & van Haren, R. (2015). A Learning by Design journey. In B. Cope & M. Kalantzis (Eds.), *A pedagogy of multiliteracies: Learning by Design* (pp. 70–96). Palgrave Macmillan.

Carrell, P. (1984). Evidence of a formal schema in second language comprehension. *Language Learning, 34*(2), 87–112. https://doi.org/10.1111/j.1467-1770.1984.tb01005.x

Cope, B., & Kalantzis, M. (2006). From literacy to 'multiliteracies': Learning to mean in the new communications environment. *English Studies in Africa, 49*(1), 23–45. https://doi.org/10.1080/00138390608691342

Cope, B., & Kalantzis, M. (2007). New media, new learning. *The International Journal of Learning, 14*(1), 75–79.

Cope, B., & Kalantzis, M. (2009). Multiliteracies: New literacies, new learning. *Pedagogies: An International Journal, 4*, 164–195. https://doi.org/10.1080/15544800903076044

Cope, B., & Kalantzis, M. (2015). The things you do to know: An introduction to the pedagogy of multiliteracies. In B. Cope & M. Kalantzis (Eds.), *A pedagogy of multiliteracies: Learning by Design* (pp. 1–36). Palgrave Macmillan.

Cope, B., & Kalantzis, M. (2020). *Making sense: Reference, agency, and structure in a grammar of multimodal meaning*. Cambridge University Press.

Cope, B., Kalantzis, M., & Tzirides, A. O. (Forthcoming). Meaning without borders: From translanguaging to transposition in the era of digitally-mediated multimodal meaning. In K. K. Grohmann (Ed.), *Multifaceted multilingualism* (pp. 1–33). John Benjamins.

Green, B., & Beavis, C. (2013). Literacy education in the age of new media. In K. Hall, T. Cremin, B. Comber, & L. C. Moll (Eds.), *International handbook of research on children's literacy, learning, and culture* (pp. 42–53). John Wiley & Sons.

Halliday, M. A. K. (1985). *An introduction to functional grammar*. Edward Arnold.

Halliday, M. A. K., & Hasan, R. (1985). *Language, context, and text: Aspects of language in a social-semiotic perspective*. Oxford University Press.

Hyland, K. (2014). *Genre and second language writing*. The University of Michigan Press.

Kalantzis, M., & Cope, B. (2010). The teacher as designer: Pedagogy in the new media age. *E-learning and Digital Media, 7*(3), 200–222. https://doi.org/10.2304/elea.2010.7.3.200

Kalantzis, M., & Cope, B. (2012a). *Literacies* (eBook ed.). Cambridge University Press.

Kalantzis, M., & Cope, B. (2012b). *New learning: Elements of science education* (2nd ed.). Cambridge University Press.

Kalantzis, M., & Cope, B. (2020). *Adding sense: Context and interest in a grammar of multimodal meaning*. Cambridge University Press.

Kalantzis, M., & Cope, B. (2022). After language: A grammar of multiform transposition. In C. Lütge (Ed.), *Foreign language learning in the digital age: Theory and pedagogy for developing literacies* (pp. 34–64). Routledge.

Kalantzis, M., Cope, B., Chan, E., & Dalley-Trim, L. (2016). *Literacies* (2nd ed.). Cambridge University Press.

Kalantzis, M., Cope, B., & the Learning by Design Project Group. (2005). *Learning by Design*. Victorian Schools Innovation Commission and Common Ground Publishing.

Kalantzis, M., Cope, B., & Zapata, G. C. (2019). *Las alfabetizaciones múltiples: Teoría y práctica*. Octaedro.

Kress, G. (1993). Against arbitrariness: The social production of the sign as a foundational issue in critical discourse analysis. *Discourse and Society*, 4(2), 169–91. http://www.jstor.org/stable/42888774

Lister, M., Dovey, J., Giddings, S., Grant, I., & Kelly, K. (2009). *New media: A critical introduction* (2nd ed.). Routledge.

Martin, J. R. (2013). Systemic functional linguistics. In Hawkins, M. R. (Ed.), *Framing languages and literacies: Socially situated views and perspectives* (pp. 24–50). Routledge.

Martin, J. R. (2016). Meaning matters: A short history of systemic functional linguistics. *WORD*, 62(1), 35–58. https://doi.org/10.1080/00437956.2016.1141939

Moll, L. C., Amanti, C., Neff, D., & Gonzalez, N. (1992). Funds of knowledge for teaching: Using a qualitative approach to connect homes and classrooms. *Theory into Practice*, 31(2), 132–141. https://www.jstor.org/stable/1476399

New London Group. (1996). A pedagogy of multiliteracies: Designing social futures. *Harvard Educational Review*, 66, 60–92. https://doi.org/10.17763/haer.66.1.17370n67v22j160u

Rumelhart, D. E. (1980). Schemata: The building blocks of cognition. In R. J. Spiro, B. C. Bruce, & W. E. Brewer (Eds.), *Theoretical issues in reading comprehension* (pp. 35–58). Lawrence Erlbaum Associates.

Serafini, F. (2014). *Reading the visual: An introduction to teaching multimodal literacy*. Teachers College Press.

Zammit, K. (2010). The new learning environment framework: Scaffolding the development of multiliterate students. *Pedagogies: An International Journal*, 5(4), 325–337. https://doi.org/10.1080/1554480X.2010.509479

Zapata, G. C. (2017). A match made in heaven: An introduction to Learning by Design and its role in heritage language education. In G. C. Zapata & M. Lacorte (Eds.), *Multiliteracies pedagogy and language learning: Teaching Spanish to heritage speakers* (pp. 1–26). Palgrave Macmillan.

2 *Learning by Design* and Second Language Education

Second Language Teaching and Learning in Today's World: Frameworks, Perspectives, and Foci

In this chapter, my objective is to explore the theoretical and pedagogical connections between *Learning by Design* (*L-by-D*) and second language (L2) teaching and learning in today's world. My work with the framework started almost ten years ago, when I was assigned to teach a Spanish as a heritage language (HL) class at the institution of higher education where I was working. While planning my curricular materials based on my students' needs, I realized that the existing commercial textbooks did not have much in common with my learners' identities, lifeworlds, and communities. Additionally, research at that time (e.g., Potowski et al., 2009) had shown that the methodologies on which these books were based (e.g., processing instruction and output-based approaches) were not appropriate for heritage learners. I looked for a different approach, and I discovered first multiliteracies (NLG, 1996) and then *L-by-D* (Kalantzis et al., 2005). I immersed myself into the framework, and I was inspired by the studies that had incorporated it in Australia, where *L-by-D* had been developed, with English learners belonging to minoritized groups (e.g., Mills, 2010; Neville, 2008; Zammit, 2010). These works not only offered me instructional guidance for the class I was about to teach, but they also changed my path as an HL and L2 instructor, researcher, program director, and materials developer.

I saw a variety of parallels between HL/L2 instruction[1] and *L-by-D*. For example, for me, there was a clear connection between *L-by-D*'s principles of *belonging* and *transformation* (Kalantzis et al., 2005), and Norton's (2010, 2013; Norton & Toohey, 2011) and Pittaway's (2004) work on L2 learner identity and investment. This literature has emphasized the crucial need for L2 pedagogy to not only recognize learners as multidimensional beings but also to engage them with instruction at a personal level, fostering both their investment in the learning process and their own legitimation as L2 meaning-makers (Pittaway, 2004). *L-by-D*'s emphasis on the pedagogical use of a variety of multimodal texts also mirrored L2 researchers' call (e.g., Allen & Paesani, 2010; Byrnes, 2006; Kern, 2000) for a more comprehensive, discourse-oriented L2 instructional approach. These scholars see the need for L2 instruction to move beyond

DOI: 10.4324/9781003106258-2

limited approaches such as Communicative Language Teaching (CLT) to offer L2 instructional contexts that will allow learners to work with and produce a variety of multimodal texts. That is, rather than limiting target language use to just transactional interactions, a common feature of current iterations of CLT, it is essential to create opportunities for students' active use of the target language in diverse social environments through engagement with and production of texts representative of different kinds of genres and incorporating a variety of modes. In other words, in order to be effective meaning-makers in contemporary society (i.e., to become multiliterate), L2 students need to work within the "dynamic, culturally, and historically situated practices of using and interpreting diverse … [multimodal] texts to fulfil particular social purposes" (Kern, 2000, p. 6).

More recently, some of these ideas were incorporated into the framework for language learning and teaching proposed by the **Douglas Fir Group** (2016). Even though this work focuses mostly on SLA research, the framework does address L2 pedagogy. Indeed, through their proposal, these scholars seek to "respond to the pressing needs of additional language users [i.e., L2/HL learners], their education, their multilingual and multiliterate development, social integration, and performance across diverse globalized, technologized, and transnational contexts" (p. 24). The framework integrates, from an ecological perspective (Bronfenbrenner, 1979), three different dimensions or levels of sociocultural/sociohistorical contexts and activities that play a crucial role in the learning process. At the base of the model is, of course, situated human communication, which in today's world can take place in a variety of contexts (including digital environments) and is not limited to language use, but instead might involve other semiotic resources (e.g., images, music, etc.). This is what the group calls the "micro level of social activity." The next component, "the meso level of sociocultural institutions and communities," makes reference to aspects connected to learners' identities, lifeworlds, and the communities and institutions of which they are part (e.g., places of work and worship). In the third level of the framework, "the macro level of ideological structures," the scholars in the group place

> the society-wide ideological structures with particular orientations toward language use and language learning … that both shape and are shaped by sociocultural institutions [level 2] as well as by the agency of individual members within their locally situated contexts of action [level 1].
>
> (p. 24)

The Douglas Fir Group's (2016) framework and *L-by-D* (Cope & Kalantzis, 2015; Kalantzis et al., 2005, 2016, 2019) are not theoretically related. However, they share a similar vision of learning in today's globalized, diverse, and technology-driven society, and the need for students to be "engaged in *learning* semiotic systems [including the L2] and literacies, *using* [them] to learn about other things, and *learning* about how [they] operate and function in our society" (Anstey & Bull, 2004, p. 13, emphasis in original).

22 Learning by Design *and L2 Education*

In recent years, teacher organizations have also offered their vision of L2 learning in the 21st century, and their foci bear similarities to both the Douglas Fir Group's (2016) framework and *L-by-D*'s (Kalantzis et al., 2005) principles and pedagogical vision. For example, in the United States, in 2011, the **National Education Association** (NEA) partnered with the **American Council on the Teaching of Foreign Languages** (ACTFL) in what was called the **Partnership for 21st Century Learning** or **P21** (NEA, 2011) to develop a guide that would help instructors integrate L2 learning with skills that will prepare learners to be part of the future workforce. The result was the *21st Century Skills Map* (Partnership for 21st Century Skills [P21], 2011). Four skills (the Four Cs) were at the center of the proposal—critical thinking and problem solving, communication, collaboration, and creativity and innovation. In Table 2.1, I describe what L2 students are expected to accomplish when these skills are integrated with L2 learning.

Even though I present these skills separately, they are always integrated in the learning process. For example, in today's world, critical thinking and problem

Table 2.1 21st Century Skills in the L2 Classroom

Skills	Expected Learner Outcomes
Critical thinking (and problem solving)	• Exercise sound reasoning in understanding • Make complex choices and decisions • Understand the interconnections among systems • Identify and ask significant questions that clarify various points of view and lead to better solutions • Frame, analyze, and synthesize information in order to solve problems and answer questions
Communication	• Articulate thoughts and ideas effectively using oral, written, and nonverbal communication skills in a variety of forms and contexts • Use communication for a range of purposes (e.g., to inform, instruct, motivate, and persuade) • Communicate effectively in diverse multilingual environments
Collaboration	• Articulate thoughts and ideas clearly and effectively through speaking and writing • Demonstrate the ability to work effectively with diverse teams • Exercise flexibility and willingness to be helpful in making necessary compromises to accomplish a common goal • Assume shared responsibility for collaborative work
Creativity (and innovation)	• Demonstrate originality and inventiveness in work • Develop, implement, and communicate new ideas to others • Be open and responsive to new and diverse perspectives • Act on creative ideas to make a tangible and useful contribution to the domain in which the innovation occurs

Table based on information in *21st Century Skills Map*, by Partnership for 21st Century Skills, 2011, pp. 6–11 (https://www.actfl.org/sites/default/files/resources/21st%20Century%20Skills%20Map-World%20Languages.pdf).

solving might rely on communication, collaboration, and creativity, as much of our work is carried out in teams and might involve working in digital environments with different types of media/digital tools (NEA, 2011). Our current reliance on new, collaborative media and technologies is also recognized by the scholars in P21 (2011). The skills map integrates the Four Cs with information, media, and technology literacy, as well as with the need to develop learners' flexibility, adaptability, initiative, self-direction, leadership, and responsibility. Other crucial aspects of L2 learning included in the P21's document are social and cross-cultural skills, which entail students':

- Working appropriately and productively with others,
- Leveraging the collective intelligence of groups when appropriate, [and]
- Bridging cultural differences and using differing perspectives to increase innovation and the quality of work.

P21 (2011)

When the skills in the *21st Century Skills Map* (P21, 2011) are combined with ACTFL's standards for language learning, delineated in the *World-Readiness Standards for Learning Languages* (The National Standards Collaborative Board, 2015), and the organization's guidelines for performance-based instruction and assessment,[2] described in *ACTFL Performance Descriptors for Language Learners* (ACTFL, 2012), L2 instructional contexts need to incorporate pedagogical elements such as the ones presented in the following list. I have adapted them from the skills map (P21, p. 4), and I have also further developed them taking into account existing literature. In today's L2 classrooms:

- Students learn to use the target language in three modes of communication:
  - *Interpersonal*: Learners interact with other learners in a variety of ways (e.g., orally; in signed, written, or multimodal conversations in contextualized, socially appropriate situations [e.g., to share information, express emotions, discuss different viewpoints/opinions, etc., as well as in "collaborative interactions" when using the target language to complete a variety of tasks; e.g., when working in the other two modes of communication; Allen & Paesani, 2019, p. 45]).
  - *Interpretive*: Learners are exposed to and analyze multimodal texts in order to critically understand meaning-making (i.e., in terms of what is communicated, how it is done [language and other semiotic resources; Douglas Fir Group, 2016; Kern, 2000], and why it is done in that way [author's objectives and motivations/ideology, connections to community sociocultural discourses]).
  - *Presentational*: Learners present content (e.g., ideas, information, concepts, etc.) in a variety of multimodal ways (i.e., target language + other semiotic resources) to diverse audiences on topics related to their lifeworlds and/or in connection to curricular subjects.

- Instruction is centered on the learner. The learner's role is that of a *doer* and *creator* (emphasis on active language use). Instructors act as facilitators/collaborators.
- Curricular content is developed following an iterative *backward design* (Richards, 2013; Wiggins & McTighe, 1998) that involves:
  1. The determination of instructional outcomes. Instructors outline curricular priorities in terms of desired
     - Attained performance (i.e., what students will be able to do with the target language in the three modes of communication based on their level of performance—novice, intermediate, or advanced).
     - Knowledge (linguistic, cultural, discipline-specific, and/or multimodal).
  2. The determination of evidence of learning (assessment—what students will be able to do with the target language and other semiotic resources).
  3. The planning and development of instructional moves, materials, activities and tasks, and learning experiences.

     Glisan and Donato (2021) characterize this process as "iterative" because instructors will revisit it and, if needed, modify it, while reflectively assessing their practice and their students' learning experiences.
- Content is based on thematic units and authentic, socially diverse multimodal resources.
- Instructional moves and materials allow learners to critically analyze the relationship among the perspectives, practices, and products of target culture(s).
- New media and digital tools are incorporated into instruction to enhance learning and develop students' multiliteracies, as well as information, media, and technology literacy.
- The target language is used in the teaching of academic content (cross- and interdisciplinary connection).
- Educators create instructional moves that mirror students' diverse ways of interacting and learning, and that answer their personal and academic needs.
- Tasks are connected to both language use in the real world and to learners' lifeworlds.
- Instructors develop opportunities for students' active use of the target language beyond the classroom. Learners share their products with diverse audiences (not just the instructor).
- Instructors discover what students can do with the target language through formative and summative assessment tools.
- Students actively participate in their learning process by having explicit knowledge and in-depth understanding of the ways in which they will be assessed (e.g., by reviewing and discussing assessment criteria with their instructor).

The enactment of practices that integrate these elements can result in the establishment of *meaningful* and *purposeful* pedagogical contexts, two essential aspects for the success of the L2 learning process (Glisan & Donato, 2021). An instructional context is *meaningful* when it is directly related to learners' identities and personal experiences, and it "involves topics and interactions to which [they] can relate and that they perceive as useful to their learning and future use of the target language outside of class" (Glisan & Donato, p. 18). In *purposeful* L2 instruction, learners feel that their learning has a particular authentic (i.e., real, social) objective to be achieved. That is, "students … understand that there is a concrete outcome to their participation in the lesson beyond simply 'getting the right answer'" (Glisan & Donato, p. 18).

One way in which L2 instructors and curriculum developers are currently creating meaningful and purposeful L2 learning environments is by developing materials or adapting existing ones for the specific group(s) of learners they serve. For many L2 educators, these activities are directly connected to **open education** and the creation/adaptation and use of **Open Educational Resources** (OERs). OERs can be defined as instructional materials (e.g., multimodal texts, images, curricular units, etc.) "that are openly available for use by educators and students, without an accompanying need to pay royalties or license fees" (Butcher, 2011, p. 5). There exist clear connections between open education and the utilization of OERs and the kind of L2 instruction we have been delineating in this chapter. For example, the emphasis we have been placing on our students' identities, lifeworlds, and communities is reflected in the definition of open pedagogy offered by Jhangiani and DeRosa (2017, p. 14) as "an access-oriented commitment to learner-driven education." The use of OERs also facilitates the creation or adaptation of socially and linguistically authentic multimodal resources, grounded in pedagogies such as *L-by-D* (as it is shown in Chapter 5 of this volume), with which our students can identify and connect, and which can "foster [both] critical awareness raising and self-reflection" (Blyth et al., 2021, p. 165), and creative uses of the L2 for meaning-making. Existing research on OER and L2 learning (e.g., see studies in Blyth & Thoms, 2021 and in Comas-Quinn et al., 2019) has also shown that incorporating tasks and content that move instruction beyond the one-size-fits-all approach often found in commercial textbooks has the potential to "lead to the creation of a collaborative learning environment where learners … are provided opportunities to co-create and/or co-curate L2 content, which may lead to increasing motivation to learn and/or make use of the L2 in meaningful ways" (Blyth & Thoms, 2021, p. 1).

Another important affordance of open education is the chance to integrate L2 use in tasks connected with issues related to social justice, diversity, equity, and inclusion in both the target culture(s) and learners' community(ies). The social movements awakened in recent years (e.g., the #MeToo and Peoples Climate Movements, Black Lives Matter, etc.) have reminded us of our responsibility to incorporate socially relevant issues in L2 curricula, and to offer students opportunities for what Osborne (2006) characterizes as **critical inquiry**. For Osborne, this approach to L2 teaching entails a cycle of collaborative "exploration [of a sociocultural/sociohistorical issue] that can be entered into by students, community members, and teacher as learners together in their individual contexts" (p.

33). The critical inquiry cycle involves informed cooperative, in-depth investigation of the issue, followed by inductive analysis, tentative conclusion, and mutual critical reflection, where participants "explore [their] own privilege ... power, and powerlessness" (Osborne, p. 35). When considering curricular content, Osborne proposes four thematic areas (which he calls "pillars") that can constitute a first step toward the establishment of L2 teaching for social justice. The proposed pillars are *identity*, *social architecture*, *language choices*, and *activism*, and they include the following sub-themes:

- *Identity*: Identity (Who am I, who are we?); affiliation (Who are we? Who are they?); conflict, struggle, and discrimination; and socioeconomic class.
- *Social architecture*: What we believe: ideology; historical perspectives: to the victors...; school and languages: hidden curricula; and media: entertainment.
- *Language choices*: Beyond manners: Register and political or power relations: Whose culture is whose? Hybridity; media: journalism and politicians; who is in control? Hegemony.
- *Activism*: Law, rights, resistance, and marginalization.

Osborne (2006, p. 62)

Osborne's (2006) work bears similarities to that of other scholars interested in critical L2 teaching and learning. For example, Kubota (2003, p. 84) has posited that, when focusing on target cultures, "teachers and students need to explore multiple perspectives and to critically examine plural ways of representing perceived cultural facts," including those related to learners' own (and local) cultures. This implies that students need to be provided with opportunities to analyze the "why" behind representations of both target cultures and socially relevant issues, focusing on discovering how they have been constructed discursively (through the use of language and other semiotic resources); what political, ideological, and social forces have constructed them; and to achieve what purposes. Nieto (2009) has also embraced this view of L2 teaching and learning by suggesting that

> classrooms should not only simply allow discussions that focus on social justice, but in fact welcome them ... These discussions might center on issues that adversely and disproportionately affect disenfranchised communities—poverty, discrimination, war, the national budget—and what students can do to address these problems. (pp. 77–78)

Both the democratizing, equity, and social justice ideals embedded in open education (Zawacki-Richter et al., 2020) and the development of OERs can facilitate the practices and goals that Osborne, Kubota, and Nieto envision for L2 education. That is, instead of relying on the sanitized, homogeneous, main-stream representations of target cultures offered by most mass-produced textbooks, which not only ignore cultural and ethnic diversity (Canale, 2016; Chisholm, 2018; Elissondo, 2001), but also avoid socially relevant issues related to Osborne's pillars (Apple, 2004; Apple & Christian-Smith, 1991), educators can develop or adapt resources that do offer diverse and comprehensive social and thematic representations, and can incorporate a diversity of authentic, inclusive voices.

When developing curricula, units, and/or tasks that integrate topics pertaining to target cultures and issues within Osborne's (2006) four pillars, L2 educators and material developers can also take advantage of existing pedagogical resources offered without charge by non-profit organizations that work on education for social justice. One of the most relevant groups is *Learning for Justice*, founded by the Southern Poverty Law Center in 1991 "to be a catalyst for racial justice in the South and beyond, working in partnership with communities to dismantle white supremacy, strengthen intersectional movements and advance the human rights of all people" (https://www.learningforjustice.org/about). Learning for Justice's instructional materials focus on race and ethnicity, religion, ability, class, immigration, gender and sexual identity, bullying and bias, and rights and activism. To facilitate the incorporation of these topics in educational contexts, the organization provides classroom resources (e.g., lessons, learning plans, tasks, teaching strategies, etc.) as well as professional development opportunities such as workshops, webinars, and podcasts. In 2018, Learning for Justice created a set of social justice standards and learning outcomes to serve as "a road map for anti-bias education at every grade level" (Teaching Tolerance, 2018, p. 2). The proposed standards and outcomes are organized in four different domains—identity, diversity, justice, and action—and even though they apply mostly to K–12 educational contexts, they can also be adapted for use with university students.

Recently, ACTFL identified the Learning for Justice's (Teaching Tolerance, 2018) standards (summarized in Table 2.2) as a resource for L2 educators, and it is clear to see why this was the case. First, language(s) and cultures play a central role with respect to the knowledge, attitudes, and behaviors learners are expected to develop when immersed in instruction based on social justice. Second, Learning for Justice offers grade-level outcomes and scenarios in general terms, which allows instructors to adapt them to address their students' personal and academic needs. Third, the anchor standards (i.e., identity, diversity, justice, and action) are compatible with Osborne's (2006) four pillars and, if enacted, the stages of his critical inquiry cycle could result in the attainment of the outcomes in the Learning for Justice's document. Therefore, it is no surprise that ACTFL has chosen to highlight them as useful for the integration of socially relevant issues into L2 teaching and learning.

My goal for the first section of this chapter was to review what I consider the most important developments, in terms of theoretical perspectives, pedagogical frameworks, and instructional approaches, we have seen in recent years in L2 pedagogy. My next objective is to explore how *L-by-D* fits with the vision of L2 teaching and learning I have delineated.

Table 2.2 Summary of Social Justice Standards and Outcomes

Standards	Expected Learner Outcomes
Identity	Students will: • Develop positive social identities based on their membership in multiple groups in society; • Develop language and historical and cultural knowledge that affirm and accurately describe their membership in multiple identity groups; • Recognize that people's multiple identities interact and create unique and complex individuals; • Express pride, confidence, and healthy self-esteem without denying the value and dignity of other people; [and] • Recognize traits of the dominant culture, their home culture, and other cultures and understand how they negotiate their own identity in multiple spaces.
Diversity	Students will: • Express comfort with people who are both similar to and different from them and engage respectfully with all people; • Develop language and knowledge to accurately and respectfully describe how people (including themselves) are both similar to and different from each other and others in their identity groups; • Respectfully express curiosity about the history and lived experiences of others and exchange ideas and beliefs in an open-minded way; • Respond to diversity by building empathy, respect, understanding, and connection; [and] • Examine diversity in social, cultural, political, and historical contexts rather than in ways that are superficial or oversimplified.
Justice	Students will: • Recognize stereotypes and relate to people as individuals rather than representatives of groups; • Recognize unfairness on the individual level (e.g., biased speech) and injustice at the institutional or systemic level (e.g., discrimination); • Analyze the harmful impact of bias and injustice on the world, historically and today; • Recognize that power and privilege influence relationships on interpersonal, intergroup, and institutional levels and consider how they have been affected by those dynamics; [and] • Identify figures, groups, events, and a variety of strategies and philosophies relevant to the history of social justice around the world.
Action	Students will: • Express empathy when people are excluded or mistreated because of their identities and concern when they themselves experience bias; • Recognize their own responsibility to stand up to exclusion, prejudice, and injustice; • Speak up with courage and respect when they or someone else has been hurt or wronged by bias; • Make principled decisions about when and how to take a stand against bias and injustice in their everyday lives and do so despite negative peer or group pressure; [and] • Plan and carry out collective action against bias and injustice in the world and evaluate what strategies are most effective.

"Anchor Standards and Domains," by Teaching Tolerance, 2020, p. 3 (https://www.learningforjustice.org/sites/default/files/2020-09/TT-Social-Justice-Standards-Anti-bias-framework-2020.pdf).

Learning by Design and Second Language Teaching and Learning

In this part of the chapter, I will examine how *L-by-D* can contribute to L2 teaching and learning. The focus of my discussion will be both theoretical and methodological. However, I offer a variety of concrete examples in Chapter 5. Let's start with the learner. As we saw in Chapter 1, *L-by-D* bestows great importance upon the premise that transformative learning is not possible without the incorporation of students' lifeworlds, funds of knowledge (including informal learning; Moll et al., 1992), personal and academic needs, and communities into the curriculum (Kalantzis et al., 2005, 2016, 2019). This resonates both with the Douglas Fir Group's (2016) model and the P21's (2011) *21st Century Skills Map*. Another point in common between *L-by-D* and these two proposals is the need to provide students with opportunities to be exposed to, work with, and produce authentic multimodal ensembles, making use of the target language *and* other contemporary semiotic resources. This also entails the development of learners' multiliteracies in terms of the effective use of new media and digital tools.

The pluralistic, equitable goals of *L-by-D*'s transformative curriculum are also compatible with the democratizing nature of open education and the goals of organizations such as Learning for Justice. First of all, the use of instructional resources that are freely available can have the "intended equity effect of [a] transformative curriculum" (Kalantzis et al., 2005, p. 63), as all learners, regardless of their socioeconomic background, have access to the same educational opportunities. Second, open practices and OERs often rely on the utilization of multimodal material that can be digitally reused, retained, redistributed, revised, and remixed to answer the needs of specific student populations (Blyth & Thoms, 2021; Wiley & Green, 2012), which mirrors the tenets of *L-by-D*'s principle of *belonging*. A third aspect shared by *L-by-D* and open education is the emphasis that they both place on learners as *active* meaning-makers, and "co-producers on their lifelong learning path" (ICDE, 2011). The use of resources (and, of course, instructional moves and tasks) that directly answer specific learners' needs can result in L2 practices that are both meaningful and purposeful (Glisan & Donato, 2021). Additionally, OERs grounded in *L-by-D* can incorporate socially relevant topics, and the standards for social justice developed by Learning for Justice (Teaching Tolerance, 2018) can be part of the outcomes set for specific instructional units, lessons, or tasks.

Clearly, there exists a number of connections between *L-by-D* (Kalantzis et al., 2005, 2016, 2019), the Douglas Fir Group's (2016) model, the *21st Century Skills Map* (P21, 2011), and open education. However, I believe the most significant link between *L-by-D* and L2 learning and teaching lies in the framework's knowledge processes and the five metafunctions (i.e., reference, agency, structure, context, and interest) recently brought forward by Cope and Kalantzis (Cope & Kalantzis, 2020, Cope et al., Forthcoming; Kalantzis & Cope, 2022; see page 14). These framework components offer a blueprint to enact the type of L2 teaching and learning discussed in the previous section of this chapter. Additionally, they can facilitate the incorporation of the kind of critical inquiry and socially relevant content recommended by Osborn (2006), Kubota (2003), and Nieto (2009), and educational groups such as Learning for Justice. Also, Kalantzis et al.'s (2005) concept of transformative curriculum can inform L2 teachers' iterative process of backward design (Richards, 2013; Wiggins & McTighe, 1998).

Let's take this as our starting point. An L2 educator is designing instruction for a group of L2 students. The first question to be answered is who the learners are, which, for Kalantzis and Cope (2012, p. 139), involves the consideration of the following three dimensions of learner difference, as well as the "identity [that is] shaped from living at the intersection of many group-related experiences." The proposed identity dimensions include:

- Corporeal attributes: Differences of age, sex and sexuality, physical and mental capacities;
- Material conditions: Differences of social class, geographical locale, family, [and community]; [and]
- Symbolic differences: Differences of culture or ethnicity, language [or dialects], gender [identity], affinity, and persona.

Kalantzis and Cope (2012, p. 139)

Also important are learners' existing knowledge (the result of informal and formal learning), their academic (linguistic, and also discipline-specific) and personal needs, and their level of L2 performance (e.g., novice, intermediate, or advanced). These factors will determine the instructional outcomes to be achieved in terms of L2 performance, academic content, and multiliteracies (meaning-making and the use of new media and digital tools). Additionally, the learner difference dimensions will guide the choice of materials to be included in the curriculum and the development of instructional moves that will result in the attainment of outcomes. Of utmost importance is the need to integrate socially relevant issues into the curriculum, remembering that it is essential to always find a personal connection with regards to learners' identities and/or local communities. That is, even when the focus is on target cultures, there needs to exist some type of link to who the students are (e.g., thematic similarities with learners' lifeworlds or lived experiences). The incorporation of socially relevant themes into the L2 curriculum can be guided by Osborne's (2006) cycle of critical inquiry and Learning for Justice's standards and outcomes for social justice (Teaching Tolerance, 2018).

Once curricular content and outcomes have been designed, instructors (and/or curricular developers) can create tasks for students to carry out within each knowledge process, considering also how they will be guided in the analysis and understanding of each meaning-making metafunction (i.e., what the text is about [reference]; who has created it [agency]; how meaning is organized and conveyed [structure]; what it is connected with [context, e.g., social, cultural, historical]; and what its objective is [interest; meaning-maker's motivation and intended audience]). In order to illustrate how this can be accomplished, I will resort to a practical example based on materials Maybel Mesa Morales and I developed for L2 Spanish students in a fourth-semester university class in 2017 (Zapata & Mesa Morales, 2018). At that time, Maybel was a graduate student with a specialization in Latin American literature, and she was teaching in the Basic Spanish Program I was directing. She was passionate about both literature and L2 teaching, and she wanted to create an instructional opportunity that would allow her students to actively and meaningfully use the target language in the three modes of communication—interpretive, interpersonal, and presentational—to critically analyze and produce literary and multimodal texts.

Our point of departure was Maybel's learners. She and I first considered their social identities, lifeworlds, and level of L2 performance, as well as curricular themes and expected outcomes. Based on the information we gathered, we agreed on the topic of environmental pollution and destruction. Maybel chose to develop her instruction around two authentic texts: The multimodal animated short film *Man* by artist Steve Cutts (2012), and the digitally published poem *Bosque…jas* (Ramos Aranda, 2013). The poem became the main instructional text. To facilitate students' collaborative construction of knowledge and their use of the target language in both the interpersonal and interpretive modes of communication, Maybel and I organized learners' work in the open, digital social-reading platform *eComma* (Center for Open Educational Resources and Language Learning, n.d.).[3] Social-reading platforms and tools have become quite popular in both academic and social circles because they allow people to interact virtually, either synchronously or asynchronously, while reading a text (written or multimodal) to comprehend and interpret it. In the case of L2 learning, while participating in social-reading activities, students can help one another gain a deep understanding of the content and language of a given text by using digital annotation tools, and sharing their thoughts, queries, and views with their classmates (Blyth, 2013). For example, based on his research on L2 French and social reading, Blyth (2014) has shown that these kinds of tasks can provide learners with opportunities to "evaluate the meaning of foreign words, reflect upon cultural differences, interpret the meaning of textual features, connect reading to personal experience, and co-construct meaning" (p. 215).

When planning our social-reading instructional move, Maybel's and my work was guided by existing studies with L2 students (e.g., Blyth, 2014; Thoms and Poole, 2017) and on social-reading practices in other instructional environments (e.g., Mendenhall et al., 2011; Wu & Wu, 2017; Zarzour & Sellami, 2017). Once we had chosen the topic, resources, and digital platform to be used, we organized students' work within *L-by-D*'s eight knowledge processes, also incorporating activities that would allow for the analysis of the five meaning-making metafunctions (i.e., reference, agency, structure, context, and interest). In Figure 2.1, I offer a schematic presentation of the tasks we developed for each epistemic move. I also provide information about the modes of communication of focus. The figure illustrates how *L-by-D* can be tied to L2 teaching and learning to facilitate:

32 Learning by Design *and L2 Education*

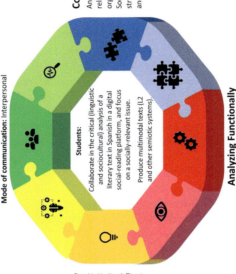

Experiencing the Known
Brainstorming existing knowledge of and personal experiences with local environmental problems and/or those affecting personal communities. Experience with poems. **Mode of communication:** Interpersonal

Experiencing the New
Analysis of ideas presented in short film *Man* and poem *Bosqu...jas*. Focus on meaning (comprehension of main idea and overall message). Comparison with personal experiences, opinions, viewpoints. Social reading. **Mefunctions:** Reference and agency. **Modes of communication:** Interpersonal and interpretive.

Conceptualizing by Naming
Analysis of organizational features of the poem and relationship to content (how the information is organized with respect to each part of the text). Social Reading. **Metafunctions:** Reference and structure. **Modes of communication:** Interpersonal and interpretive.

Conceptualizing with Theory
Based on similarities (in terms of form and meaning) identified in previous epistemic move, students define concepts related to structure of poem (e.g., verse, stanza, rhyme, etc.). Learners also analyze poems as social texts. Social Reading. **Metafunctions:** Reference, agency, structure, context, and interest. **Modes of communication:** Interpersonal and interpretive.

Students:
Collaborate in the critical (linguistic and sociocultural) analysis of a literary text in Spanish in a digital social-reading platform, and focus on a socially-relevant issue.
Produce multimodal texts (L2 and other semiotic systems)

Analyzing Functionally
Focus on language (e.g., verbs, nouns, adjectives). Guiding questions: 1. What kind of meaning is expressed by...? 2. How is meaning expressed by...? 3. What rhetorical devices are used to convey...? 4. What language do we need to convey...? Social reading. **Metafunctions:** Reference, agency, structure, context, and interest. **Modes of communication:** Interpersonal and interpretive.

Analyzing Critically
Focus on meaning maker(s): Purpose, message (reading between the lines), audience, emotional effectiveness, personal and social connections (ideology, community, present and hidden voices). Interpretation. Text comparison. Social reading. **Metafunctions:** Reference, agency, structure, context, and interest. **Modes of communication:** Interpersonal and interpretive.

Applying Appropriately
Collaborative (in pairs) development of a short poem to reflect feelings/emotions about the topic of environmental pollution/destruction or climate change. **Metafunctions:** Reference, agency, structure, context, and interest. **Modes of communication:** Interpersonal and presentational.

Applying Creatively
Collaborative (in groups) development of a multimodal project: Blueprint for a non-profit organization to work on local environmental problems. **Metafunctions:** Reference, agency, structure, context, and interest. **Modes of communication:** Interpersonal and presentational.

Figure 2.1 An L2 social reading task grounded in *Learning by Design*.

- The critical examination of a socially relevant issue connected to learners' lifeworld (in this case, climate change, environmental pollution/destruction).
- Students' collaborative work with authentic L2 texts, and their active use of the target language in the three modes of communication—interpersonal, interpretive, and presentational, including the use of specific L2 terminology and grammatical structures.
- Learners' work with new media and digital multimodal tools.
- Language learning tied to authentic texts and critical inquiry.

Figure 2.1 serves as an introduction to show how *L-by-D* can guide L2 teaching and learning (the activity presented will be discussed in more detail in Chapter 3). In Chapter 5, I delve into this relationship in more depth, presenting a variety of tasks for L2 learners of different ages grounded in Kalantzis et al.'s framework. Before I do so, however, in the next chapter, I discuss pedagogical practices that, based on existing research, I deem essential for the successful integration of *L-by-D* in L2 classes.

Summary

My goal for this chapter was to start exploring the relationship between current L2 teaching and learning and *L-by-D*. To do so, I chose the frameworks, perspectives, and foci (in terms of themes and language use) that I believe are the most relevant for our profession, and that I see as connected to *L-by-D*. Since I live in the United States, and my work as an L2 educator has been guided by evidence-based practices advocated by ACTFL, my discussion only included terminology, standards, and outcomes developed by this organization. The same can be said about my recommendations for the incorporation of socially relevant topics in L2 classes (e.g., Osborne's four pillars), and my reliance on Learning for Justice's standards and outcomes.[4] Based on the discussion I presented (grounded in existing literature), I envision current L2 learning and teaching as entailing:

- L2 learners as legitimate, active L2 users and L2 educators as facilitators and collaborators.
- Curricular connections with learners' diverse identities, personal experiences, and the community/institutions to which they belong.
- Instructional sequences, outcomes, multimodal content, and tasks based on L2 level of performance, specific discipline (when L2 is connected to academic content), and learners' linguistic, academic, and personal needs.
- L2 active use in the three modes of communication—interpersonal, interpretive, and presentational—in diverse social contexts and for diverse audiences beyond the language classroom.
- The development of the Four Cs (critical thinking and problem solving, communication, collaboration, and creativity and innovation) and learners' flexibility, adaptability, initiative, self-direction, leadership, and responsibility.

- The incorporation of socially relevant issues into instruction and the creation of tasks that offer opportunities for the integration of Osborne's cycle of critical inquiry and/or Learning for Justice's social justice standards and outcomes.

In the second part of the chapter, I began to establish theoretical and methodological connections between this vision of L2 learning and teaching and *L-by-D*. I did so by resorting to an example from an L2 Spanish class. In the remaining chapters of this volume, this connection will be made more explicit through the presentation of a variety of examples. To prepare for the ensuing discussion, in the next chapter, I examine some of the pedagogical practices that I consider essential for the successful blending of *L-by-D* and L2 education.

Notes

1 In this book, I center my discussion on L2 teaching and learning. For information on *L-by-D* and HL Spanish learning, see Zapata (2017) and the studies in Zapata & Lacorte (2017).
2 In this volume, my focus will be on L2 *performance*, instead of *proficiency*. That is, my objective is to explore how *L-by-D* can contribute to L2 development in instructional settings, where students are exposed to and use the target language to discuss specific topics related to both their needs and language use in a globalized society (ACTFL, 2012). L2 performance-based instruction can result in proficiency development—a person's ability to use their target language(s) beyond instructional settings, in real-world contexts. However, my interest is in L2 language development and use in the classroom.
3 *eComma* has been recently retired. For instructors who wish to use a free, social-reading platform, I recommend *hypothes.is* (see Appendix B).
4 The information presented in this chapter is also compatible with the descriptors, guidelines, and goals for L2 education developed by the Council of Europe (2001, 2020).

References

Works Cited

Allen, H. W., & Paesani, K. (2010). Exploring the feasibility of a pedagogy of multiliteracies in introductory foreign language courses. *L2 Journal*, *2*(1), 119–142. https://doi.org/10.5070/L2219064

Allen, H. W., & Paesani, K. (2019). Interpersonal writing in the advanced foreign language curriculum: A multiliteracies perspective. In N. Yiitolu & M. Reichelt (Eds.), *L2 writing beyond English* (pp. 42–59). Multilingual Matters.

American Council on the Teaching of Foreign Languages (ACTFL). (2012). *ACTFL performance descriptors for language learners*. ACTFL.

Anstey, M., & Bull, G. (2004). *The literacy labyrinth* (2nd ed.). Pearson.

Apple, M. (2004). Cultural politics and the text. In S. Ball (Ed.), *Routledge falmer reader in sociology of education* (pp. 42–60). Routledge Falmer.

Apple, M., & Christian-Smith, L. K. (1991). *The politics of the textbook*. Routledge.

Blyth, C. (2013). *eComma*: An open source tool for collaborative L2 reading. In A. Beaven, A. Comas-Quinn, & B. Sawhill (Eds.), *Case studies of openness in the language classroom* (pp. 32–42). Research-publishing.net. http://research-publishing.net/publication/chapters/978-1-908416-10-0/Blyth_108.pdf

Blyth, C. (2014). Exploring the affordances of digital social reading for L2 literacy: The case of eComma. In J. Guikema & L. Williams (Eds.), *Digital literacies in foreign and second language education* (pp. 201–226). Computer Assisted Language Instruction Consortium.

Blyth, C. S., & Thoms, J. J. (Eds.). (2021). *Open education and second language learning and teaching: The rise of a new knowledge ecology*. Multilingual matters. https://www.multilingual-matters.com/page/detail/?k=9781800411005

Blyth, C. S., Warner, C., & Luks, J. (2021). The role of OER in promoting critical reflection and professional development: The foreign languages and the literary in the everyday project. In C. S. Blyth & J. J. Thoms (Eds.), *Open education and second language learning and teaching: The rise of a new knowledge ecology* (pp. 158–179). Multilingual matters. https://www.multilingual-matters.com/page/detail/?k=9781800411005

Bronfenbrenner, U. (1979). *The ecology of human development: Experiments by nature and design*. Harvard University Press.

Butcher, N. (2011). *A basic guide to open educational resources (OER)*. Commonwealth of Learning.

Byrnes, H. (2006). Perspectives: Interrogating communicative competence as a framework for collegiate foreign language study. *The Modern Language Journal*, 90(2), 244–266. https://doi.org/10.1111/modl.2006.90.issue-2

Canale, G. (2016). (Re)searching culture in foreign language textbooks, or the politics of hide and seek. *Language, Culture, and Curriculum*, 29, 225–243. https://doi.org/10.1080/07908318.2016.1144764

Center for Open Educational Resources and Language Learning. (n.d.) *eComma*[Computer software]. University of Texas at Austin. https://ecomma.coerll.utexas.edu/

Chisholm, L. (2018). Representations of class, race, and gender in textbooks. In E. Fuchs & A. Bock (Eds.), *The Palgrave handbook of textbook studies* (pp. 225–237). Palgrave Macmillan.

Comas-Quinn, A., Beaven, A., & Sawhill, B. (Eds.). (2019). *New case studies of openness in and beyond the language classroom*. Research-publishing.net. https://doi.org/10.14705/rpnet.2019.37.9782490057511

Cope, B., & Kalantzis, M. (2015). The things you do to know: An introduction to the pedagogy of multiliteracies. In B. Cope & M. Kalantzis (Eds.), *A pedagogy of multiliteracies: Learning by Design* (pp. 1–36). Palgrave Macmillan.

Cope, B., & Kalantzis, M. (2020). *Making sense: Reference, agency, and structure in a grammar of multimodal meaning*. Cambridge University Press.

Cope, B., Kalantzis, M., & Tzirides, A. O. (Forthcoming). Meaning without borders: From translanguaging to transposition in the era of digitally-mediated multimodal meaning. In K. K. Grohmann (Ed.), *Multifaceted multilingualism* (pp. 1–33). John Benjamins.

Council of Europe. (2001). *Common European framework of reference for languages: Learning, teaching, assessment*. Cambridge University Press. https://rm.coe.int/1680459f97

Council of Europe. (2020). *Common European framework of reference for languages: Learning, teaching, assessment - companion volume*. https://rm.coe.int/common-european-framework-of-reference-for-languages-learning-teaching/16809ea0d4

Douglas Fir Group. (2016). A transdisciplinary framework for SLA in a multilingual world. *Modern Language Journal, 100*(S1), 19–47. https://doi.org/10.1111/modl.12301

Elissondo, G. (2001). Representing Latino/a culture in introductory Spanish textbooks. *National Association of African American Studies. Culture Monograph Series, 1*, 71–99. https://eric.ed.gov/?id=ED478020

Glisan, E. W., & Donato, R. (2021). *Enacting the work of language instruction: High-leverage teaching practices* (Vol. 2). ACTFL.

ICDE. (2011). *International conference on data engineering.* http://www.icde2011.org/

Jhangiani, R., & DeRosa, R. (2017). Open pedagogy. In E. Mays (Ed.), *A guide to making open textbooks with students* (pp. 6–21). The Rebus Community for Open Textbook Creation.

Kalantzis, M., & Cope, B. (2012). *New learning: Elements of a science of education.* Cambridge University Press.

Kalantzis, M., & Cope, B. (2022). After language: A grammar of multiform transposition. In C. Lütge (Ed.), *Foreign language learning in the digital age: Theory and pedagogy for developing literacies* (pp. 34–64). Routledge.

Kalantzis, M., Cope, B., Chan, E., & Dalley-Trim, L. (2016). *Literacies* (2nd ed.). Cambridge University Press.

Kalantzis, M., Cope, B., & the Learning by Design Project Group. (2005). *Learning by Design.* Victorian Schools Innovation Commission and Common Ground Publishing.

Kalantzis, M., Cope, B., & Zapata, G. C. (2019). *Las alfabetizaciones múltiples: Teoría y práctica.* Octaedro.

Kern, R. (2000). *Literacy and language teaching.* Oxford University Press.

Kubota, R. (2003). Critical teaching of Japanese culture. *Japanese Language and Literature, 37*(1), 67–87. https://www.jstor.org/stable/3594876

Mendenhall, A., Kim, C., & Johnson, T. E. (2011). Implementation of an online social annotation tool in a college English course. In D. Ifenthaler, P. Isaias, J. M. Spector, P. Kinshuk, & D. Sampson (Eds.), *Multiple perspectives on problem solving and learning in the digital age* (pp. 313–323). Springer.

Mills, K. (2010). What learners 'know' through digital media production: Learning by Design. *E–Learning and Digital Media, 7*(3), 223–236. https://doi.org/10.2304/elea.2010.7.3.223

Moll, L. C., Amanti, C., Neff, D., & Gonzalez, N. (1992). Funds of knowledge for teaching: Using a qualitative approach to connect homes and classrooms. *Theory into Practice, 31*(2), 132–141. https://www.jstor.org/stable/1476399

National Education Association (NEA). (2011). *Preparing 21st century students for a global society: An educator's guide to the "Four Cs".* https://dl.icdst.org/pdfs/files3/0d3e72e9b873e0ef2ed780bf53a347b4.pdf

National Standards in Foreign Language Education Project. (2015). *World-readiness standards for foreign language learning.* ACTFL.

Neville, M. (2008). *Teaching multimodal literacy using the Learning by Design approach to pedagogy: Case studies from selected Queensland schools.* Common Ground.

New London Group. (1996). A pedagogy of multiliteracies: Designing social futures. *Harvard Educational Review, 66*, 60–92. https://doi.org/10.17763/haer.66.1.17370n67v22j160u

Nieto, S. (2009). *Language, culture, and teaching: Critical perspectives for a new century* (2nd ed.). Routledge.

Norton, B. (2010). Language and identity. In N. H. Hornberger, & S. L. McKay (Eds.), *Sociolinguistics and language education* (pp. 349–369). Multilingual Matters.

Norton, B. (2013). *Identity and language learning: Extending the conversation* (2nd ed.). Multilingual Matters.

Norton, B., & Toohey, K. (2011). Identity, language learning, and social change. *Language Teaching, 44*(4), 412–446. https://doi.org/10.1017/S0261444811000309

Osborn, T. A. (2006). *Teaching world languages for social justice: A sourcebook of principles and practices.* Routledge.

Partnership for 21st Century Skills (P21). (2011). *21st century skills map.* https://www.actfl.org/sites/default/files/resources/21st%20Century%20Skills%20Map-World%20Languages.pdf

Pittaway, D. S. (2004). Investment and second language acquisition. *Critical Inquiry in Language Studies: An International Journal, 1*(4), 203–218. https://www.tandfonline.com/doi/pdf/10.1207/s15427595cils0104_2

Potowski, K., Jegerski, J., & Morgan-Short, K. (2009). The effects of instruction on linguistic development in Spanish heritage language speakers. *Language Learning, 59*(3), 537–579. https://doi.org/10.1111/j.1467-9922.2009.00517.x

Richards, J. C. (2013). Curriculum approaches in language teaching: Forward, central, and backward design. *RELC Journal, 44*(1), 5–33. https://doi.org/10.1177/0033688212473293

Teaching Tolerance. (2018). *Social justice standards: The teaching tolerance anti-bias framework.* https://www.learningforjustice.org/sites/default/files/2020-09/TT-Social-Justice-Standards-Anti-bias-framework-2020.pdf

Thoms, J. J., & Poole, F. (2017). Investigating linguistic, literary, and social affordances of L2 collaborative reading. *Language Learning & Technology, 21*(2), 139–156. http://llt.msu.edu/issues/june2017/thomspoole.pdf

Wiggins, G., & McTighe, J. (1998). *Understanding by design* (1st ed.). Merrill Prentice Hall.

Wiley, D., & Green, C. (2012). Why openness in education? In D. G. Oblinger (Ed.), *Game changers: Education and information technologies* (pp. 81–89). EDUCAUSE. https://www.educause.edu/-/media/files/library/2012/5/pub72036-pdf.pdf?la=en&hash=5989BA6C23194520202C84AC54DFAF54209FC44D

Wu L., & Wu, Y. (2017). Adolescents' social reading: Motivation, behavior, and their relationship. *The Electronic Library, 35*(2), 246–262. https://doi.org/10.1108/EL-12-2015-0239

Zammit, K. (2010). The new learning environment framework: Scaffolding the development of multiliterate students. *Pedagogies: An International Journal, 5*(4), 325–337. https://doi.org/10.1080/1554480X.2010.509479

Zapata, G. C. (2017). A match made in heaven: An introduction to *Learning by Design* and its role in heritage language education. In G. C. Zapata & M. Lacorte (Eds.), *Multiliteracies pedagogy and language learning: Teaching Spanish to heritage speakers* (pp. 1–26). Palgrave Macmillan.

Zapata, G. C., & Lacorte, M. (Eds.) (2017). *Multiliteracies pedagogy and language learning: Teaching Spanish to heritage speakers.* Palgrave Macmillan.

Zapata, G. C., & Mesa-Morales, M. (2018). The beneficial effects of technology-based social reading in L2 classes. *Lenguas en Contexto, 9*(Suplemento 2018–2019), 40–50. http://www.facultaddelenguas.com/lencontexto/?idrevista=25#5.40

Zarzour, H., & Sellami, M. (2017). A linked data-based collaborative annotation system for increasing learning achievements. *Educational Technology Research and Development, 65*(2), 381–397. https://doi.org/10.1007/s11423-016-9497-7

Zawacki-Richter, O., Conrad, D., Bozkurt, A., Aydin, C. H., Bedenlier, S., Jung, I., Stöter, J., Veletsianos, G., Blaschke, L. M., Bond, M., Broens, A., Bruhn, E., Dolch, C., Kalz,

M., Kerres, M., Kondakci, Y., Marin, V., Mayrberger, K., Müskens, W., Naidu, S., Qayyum, A., Roberts, J., Sangrà, A., Loglo, F. S., Slagter van Tryon, P. J., & Xiao, J. (2020). Elements of open education: An invitation to future research. *The International Review of Research in Open and Distributed Learning, 21*(3), 319–334. https://doi.org/10.19173/irrodl.v21i3.4659

Instructional Resources Cited

Cutts, S. (2012, December 21). *Man* [Video]. https://www.youtube.com/watch?time_continue=7&v=WfGMYdalClU

Ramos Aranda, G. (2013). *Bosque...jas*. https://www.concienciaeco.com/2014/06/11/el-poeta-defensor-del-medio-ambiente/

3 *Learning by Design* and Second Language Teaching Practices

Learning by Design's Reflexive Pedagogy

In Chapter 1, when I introduced *Learning by Design* (*L-by-D*) (Cope & Kalantzis, 2015, 2020; Cope et al., Forthcoming; Kalantzis & Cope, 2022; Kalantzis et al., 2005, 2016, 2019), I examined the connections between its principles, knowledge processes, and metafunctions, and the enactment of transformative curricula. In this chapter, I explore the second important dimension of education, *pedagogy*, defined by the creators of the framework as "a series of activities consciously designed to promote learning—the creation of knowledge and the development of a generalized capacity to make knowledge" (Kalantzis & Cope, 2012, p. 273). Guided by this definition, I will discuss teaching practices that can facilitate the integration of *L-by-D* in L2 classrooms. My focus will be on L2 teachers' instructional planning and daily actions in connection with Kalantzis and Cope's framework, including the principles of *belonging* and *transformation* and the eight knowledge processes and five metafunctions (see Chapter 1).

The integration of *L-by-D* into L2 instruction is only possible with the adoption of a pedagogy that is *reflexive*. This type of pedagogy "is a more varied and open-ended process of knowledge making, moving backwards and forwards between … knowledge processes. It is a to-and-fro dialogue between learners and teachers, peers, parents, experts, and critical friends" (Kalantzis & Cope, 2012, p. 273). In a classroom where L2 teaching practice is grounded in *L-by-D*'s reflexive pedagogy, it is important to develop learning activities like the ones I discuss below. To do so, I have adapted the instructional moves recommended by Kalantzis and Cope (2012, pp. 273–276), and I have incorporated pedagogical aspects that specifically pertain to L2 learning. Additionally, I use the L2 Spanish social-reading activity I introduced in Chapter 2 (see Figure 2.1 on page 32; Zapata & Mesa Morales, 2018) to exemplify the proposed practices.

L-by-D's **reflexive pedagogy** can be implemented in L2 instruction through tasks that:

- *Position L2 learners as legitimate L2 users and knowledge creators*. Students are agents in the knowledge-making process. They actively use the L2 to make new knowledge that connects broadly applicable discursive (e.g., textual practices connected to different genres) and linguistic concepts (e.g., specific vocabulary and grammatical structures) with issues related to their local realities. In the case of our social-reading example, students utilize L2 terminology (e.g., vocabulary related to poetry and the environment) and structures (e.g., the present subjunctive to express opinions) to critically analyze two authentic texts, to discuss environmental problems in their communities, and to collaborate in the proposal of solutions.

- *Encourage L2 learners to undertake activities that are meaningful and realistically complex.* Reflexive L2 pedagogy is either connected to life or is life-like. The target language is most effectively developed in instructional settings that focus on whole, socially realistic, meaningful, and purposeful tasks, within a socially engaged community of L2 users (in and beyond the classroom) (Allen & Paesani, 2010; Douglas Fir Group, 2016; Glisan & Donato, 2021; Kern, 2000). The social-reading task in Chapter 2 reflects this practice in a variety of ways. First, learners work with an authentic social activity that mirrors current reading practices in both academic (e.g., the popular *Perusall* platform [Appendix B]; also see Chapter 2, pages 31–33) and social contexts (e.g., through apps such as *Bookship*, *Bookself*, and *Glose*; Agarwal, 2019). Second, students are exposed to and produce texts in an academic genre, poetry, that not only is part of the L2 curricular content in their language program but also relies on complex analytic skills. Additionally, poetry engages learners at a deep, personal, and emotional level, which, as Hanauer (2012) has shown, allows them to "learn about themselves, about the presence of others, and the diversity of thought and experience that are so much part of this world" (p. 114). Finally, the tasks that students complete in the *applying knowledge* processes synthesize their new knowledge (linguistic, conceptual, multimodal, and thematic), bring them closer to the community, and give them the opportunity to propose possible solutions to local problems.
- *Challenge L2 learners to develop increasingly sophisticated and deeply perceptive conceptual schemas.* Reflexive pedagogy engages L2 learners as collaborative co-constructors of concepts—as definers of terms, maker of theories, careful analysts, and thoughtful critics. Students work collaboratively within Vygotsky's (1978) *Zone of Proximal Development*: They are provided with a conceptual scaffold, and with their classmates, they can undertake tasks and use the L2 in ways that would not be possible individually. The social-reading example we have been discussing offers learners the opportunity to develop specialized concepts related to the poetry genre, and to understand how these concepts are connected to L2 use and audience, as well as expand their critical understanding of the socially relevant issue of focus. That is, through their collaborative in-depth analysis of the chosen texts (the multimodal animated short *Man* [Cutts, 2012] and the poem *Bosque...jas* [Ramos Aranda, 2013]), students can broaden their perspective and knowledge of a current complex issue and can learn L2 terminology to refer to both poetry and environmental pollution and destruction.

- *Prompt L2 learners to make their thinking or knowledge processes explicit.* Existing research (e.g., National Academies of Sciences, Engineering, and Medicine, 2018; National Research Council, 2000) has shown that in order for learning to be successful, students need to be aware "of their own mental processes (cognitive and affective) and [develop] their ability to monitor, regulate, and direct their thinking to achieve a desired objective" (National Academies of Sciences, Engineering, and Medicine, 2018, p. 70). Therefore, it is important for educators to create opportunities for, for example, the explicit connection between the L2 and the message conveyed in a variety of authentic texts, and to guide students in their understanding of the ways in which they discover those connections. When working within *L-by-D*'s epistemic moves, the L2 students participating in the sample social-reading activity are engaged in a process of guided discovery for which "metacognitive strategies are provided initially by the teacher" (National Research Council, 2000, p. 19). Through their collaborative exploration and the application of the strategies taught, learners unveil meaning-making in terms of the five metafunctions (i.e., what the text is about [reference]; who has created it [agency]; how meaning is organized and conveyed [structure]; what it is connected with [context, e.g., social, cultural, historical]; and what its objective is [interest; meaning-maker's motivation and intended audience]), and the relationship between L2 (and other semiotic resources) and message, and they articulate their thinking process in connection with the results of their work. The incorporation of metacognitive strategies into instruction not only benefits students when completing a specific task but also results in life-long learning that can be applied to other novel academic or personal situations. Indeed,

  > in research with experts who were asked to verbalize their thinking as they worked, it was revealed that they monitored their own understanding carefully, making note of when additional information was required for understanding, whether new information was consistent with what they already knew, and what analogies could be drawn that would advance their understanding. These meta-cognitive monitoring activities are an important component of [the learning process].
  > (National Research Council, p. 18)

- *Incorporate a variety of knowledge media, representing knowledge in many ways.* A focus on the development of L2 learners' multiliteracies implies that tasks should involve exposure to and use of the L2 in the written and oral modes, as well as other representational modes: Visual, audio (linguistic and non-linguistic), tactile, gestural, and spatial. In our social-reading activity, students analyze two texts that incorporate a variety of modes (the animated short—visual, audio, gestural, and spatial) and the L2 in the written mode (the poem). Additionally, learners work in the multimodal environment of the digital social-reading platform *eComma* (Center for Open Educational

Resources and Language Learning, n.d.), using the L2 and other forms of communication through the images, colors, and videos they offer to convey their comprehension and interpretation of the text. When working in the two *applying* epistemic moves, students use the L2 in the oral and written mode (*applying appropriately*), and they also employ other semiotic resources to carry out the *applying-creatively* assignment.

- *Encourage dialogue and group collaboration.* Instructional settings need to reflect the collaborative, social nature of learning and meaning-making that students encounter in their personal lives. That is, an ample body of research has shown that collaboration is the norm in everyday settings, but it is not always the case in formal instructional contexts (National Research Council, 2018). For example, in their analysis of the cognitive aspects of learning, the scholars in the National Research Council make reference to studies that have demonstrated how seemingly individual activities such as piloting a ship, decision making in emergency rooms, or scientific discoveries always depend on team work. In the L2 classroom, it is therefore important to foster dialogue among the class community and to create tasks that rely on collaboration and result in the collaborative construction of knowledge. Learners' cooperative work can be beneficial at the cognitive level because, with their partners, within Vygotsky's (1978) *Zone of Proximal Development*, students can engage in L2 uses that they would not be able to tackle individually. Additionally, cooperation can promote the development of the target language and the Four Cs (NEA, 2011; P21, 2011)—critical thinking and problem solving, communication, collaboration, and creativity and innovation. In the social-reading activity I have been describing, textual comprehension and interpretation are carried out collaboratively. Also, within all knowledge processes, learners work in pairs or groups.
- *Offer a broad variety of tasks to cater to the diversity of learners and create a learning environment that gives continuous feedback on their learning.* In Chapter 1, I stated that the main goal of *L-by-D*'s transformative curriculum is to "achieve comparable learning outcomes without prejudice to difference, [with the] intended effect [of] pluralism—a community of productive diversity" (Kalantzis et al., 2005, pp. 63–64). This implies that instructional environments need to cater to the needs of diverse students, and pedagogical tasks need to be sufficiently open to allow variations in the knowledge created, and the way it is created from one learner to the next. In our social-reading task, we enacted this practice by offering students the opportunity to convey their comprehension and interpretation of the poem's content and language in different ways, depending on both students' level of L2 performance and/or their learning preference. For example, some learners expressed their ideas linguistically (in both their first language [L1] and L2 or a mixture of both), visually (through the use of photos or illustrations), or multimodally (through a combination of modes or through music videos). Since the main focus of the social-reading task

was the development of the L2 in the interpretive mode of communication, the options given to learners were appropriate in terms of the type of task and the students' level of L2 performance. That is, some of the questions posed in the interpretation activities could not have been answered comprehensively in the target language. In current L2 education, the use of the L1 is an accepted practice in tasks that involve critical thinking and the communication of complex ideas (e.g., see p. 31 in ACTFL's *World-Readiness Standards for Foreign Language Learning* [National Standards in Foreign Language Education Project, 2015] and the discussion in Scott & Huntington, 2007).

Another important aspect of reflexive pedagogy is its reliance on constant *formative assessment* during the learning process. This type of assessment allows instructors to offer direct and specific feedback that supports learning in two ways: (1) It identifies areas that might need attention and, as a result, teachers can incorporate those areas in novel instructional moves; and (2) it provides a platform for learners to reflect on and take charge of their learning process. Multiple regular and diverse forms of assessment and feedback are key elements to instruction based on *L-by-D*.

- *Incorporate a mix of activities that represent different knowledge processes.* When I introduced *L-by-D*'s knowledge processes in Chapter 1, I posited that learning entails weaving among the kinds of learning activities associated with each process. In the social-reading task I presented in Chapter 2, it is easy to see how students' work within each epistemic move is connected to what they have done previously, in other moves, and it anticipates what they will do next. For example, learners' comprehension and interpretation tasks in *experiencing the new* are thematically linked to the discussion in *experiencing the known*, and they anticipate the connections between meaning and form to be addressed in the *conceptualizing* and *analyzing functionally* processes.

The enactment of these practices calls for instructors anticipating and understanding students' needs in connection with the three dimensions of learner difference (i.e., corporeal attributes, material conditions, and symbolic difference; see page 30; Kalantzis & Cope, 2012), as well as their funds of knowledge (Moll et al., 1992), informal learning, and of course, linguistic and academic realities.

In order to cater to their specific group of learners, L2 educators' practice can be guided by the principles of evidence-based frameworks such as *Universal Design for Learning* (UDL). UDL originated from studies carried out by scholars in the learning and brain sciences (Rose & Meyer, 2002). Its main premise is that educators need to support "the variability of every learner … [by] implementing instructional practices that include the establishment of clear goals, intentional planning for learner variability, the use of flexible [pedagogical moves] and materials, and maintaining timely progress monitoring" (Nelson & Bashman, 2014, pp. 92–93). Embedded in this definition are three main principles that instructors need to attend to when planning and enacting their practice, namely: (1) *multiple means of engagement*; (2) *multiple means of representation*; and (3) *multiple means of action and expression* (Tobin & Behling, 2018).

The first principle, *multiple means of engagement*, makes reference to the need for practitioners to actively engage students with content by taking into account their motivation, needs, and learning preferences, and by offering diverse paths for academic work, including cooperative learning and opportunities for self-reflection. The second one, *multiple means of representation*, is connected to the various, inclusive formats in which materials need to be offered to learners (e.g., in different modalities—written, visual, oral, etc.), as well as to the enactment of pedagogical moves that will foster belonging and learner investment (Pittaway, 2004). The last principle, *multiple means of action and expression*, refers to the opportunities provided to students to tackle learning and assignments in different ways. This principle is connected to the previous two, but it also entails the need for varied, regular forms of assessment (see page 67 in this chapter) (Tobin & Behling, 2018). Overall, through the incorporation of these principles into their practice, instructors can create "inclusive, learner-centered [instructional settings], accessible education, [and] engage diverse learners [academically, through] learning activities that appeal to the largest number of [students]" (Dyjur et al., 2021, pp. 71 and 73).

Clearly, these UDL principles are compatible with the tenets of Kalantzis and Cope's (2012) **reflexive pedagogy** (which I presented on pages 39–43 of this chapter), the goals of *L-by-D*'s **transformative curriculum** (Kalantzis et al., 2005; see page 8), and the vision of L2 learning and teaching introduced in Chapter 2 (see pages 20–28). In the next section, I will examine how UDL can inform instructional planning for the integration of *L-by-D* in L2 classes.

Second Language Instruction Based on Universal Design for Learning and *Learning by Design*

In addition to the connections that exist between UDL, reflexive pedagogy, and *L-by-D*'s transformative curriculum, UDL is also compatible with the model of iterative backward design (Glisan & Donato, 2021; Richards, 2013; Wiggins & McTighe, 1998) I introduced in Chapter 2 (see page 24). Indeed, in 2011, the organization *Universal Design for Learning Implementation and Research Network* (UDL-IRN) developed five UDL-based steps that teachers can resort to when planning their curricula, units, lessons, and/or instructional sequences/moves using a process of backward design. The objective of these recommendations is to facilitate instructors' establishment of pedagogical contexts that "translate into multiple means of representation, multiples means of action and expression, and multiple means of engagement ... [and] inject as much flexibility as possible in all dimensions of the learning experience" (Fovet, 2021, p. 3). To address our specific needs as L2 educators, I have adapted the UDL-IRN's (2011) recommendations to L2 instruction. I have divided the recommendations into two categories: *Pedagogical planning* and *instructional moves*. Both are presented in the next two sections.

Pedagogical Planning

Pedagogical planning based on both UDL and iterative backward design should incorporate the following:

1. **The establishment of clear outcomes.**
   ***L-by-D* connection: Principles of *belonging* and *transformation*; goals of transformative curriculum; all knowledge processes and metafunctions.**

   It is important for instructors to establish a clear understanding of the goal(s) of the curriculum, unit, lesson, and/or instructional move/sequence and specific learner outcomes in connection to:
   - The desired outcomes and essential student understandings and L2 performance for every learner. (What does L2 learning look like for my students? What will my students be able to do with the L2?)
   - The content (linguistic and thematic and/or discipline-related) learners should come to understand and their alignment to the established standards (e.g., ACTFL and/or grade/discipline-specific) within the program of study. Also important: The development of the Four Cs and learners' information, media, and technology literacy, as well as their flexibility, adaptability, initiative, self-direction, leadership, and responsibility (see Chapter 2, page 22; NEA, 2011; P21, 2011).
   - The potential misunderstandings, misconceptions, and areas where learners may meet barriers to learning.
   - How goals will be clearly communicated to learners (i.e., what is needed for goals to be understandable to all learners).

2. **The anticipation of learner needs.**
   ***L-by-D* connection: Principles of *belonging* and *transformation*; goals of transformative curriculum; *experiencing* knowledge processes.**

   Before they start planning the instructional experience, L2 teachers should have a clear understanding of learners' needs within their educational setting. Understandings should minimally include:
   - Learner strengths and weaknesses specific to established goals for the curriculum, unit, lesson, instructional move/sequence.
   - Learner background knowledge (linguistic and thematic/discipline-specific) for scaffolding new learning, also taking into account informal learning.

- Learner preferences for representation, expression, and engagement (dimensions of learner difference [Kalantzis & Cope, 2012; see page 30], funds of knowledge [Moll et al., 1992]).
- Learner language preferences/needs (L1 and L2, translanguaging [Cope et al., Forthcoming; García & Wei, 2018], dialects, registers, genres).
- Sociocultural relevance and understanding (target and local cultures/communities/institutions; socially relevant issues).
- Curriculum barriers (e.g., physical, socioeconomic, cultural, or ability-level—dimensions of learner difference) that could limit the accessibility to instruction and instructional materials.

3. **The development of measurable outcomes and an assessment plan.**
   L-by-D connection: Principles of *belonging* and *transformation*; goals of transformative curriculum; all knowledge processes (but an emphasis on *applying*) and metafunctions.

   Before they start planning the instructional experience, L2 teachers need to establish how learning is going to be measured. Considerations should include:
   - Previously established goals and learner needs (#1 and #2).
   - Embedding checkpoints to ensure all learners are successfully meeting their desired outcomes.
   - Providing learners with multiple ways and options to authentically engage in the learning process, take action, and demonstrate understanding.
   - Supporting higher-order skills and encouraging a deeper connection with the content (L2 learners as legitimate L2 users; the learning process "facilitates personally meaningful expression" [Hanauer, 2012, p. 106]). (Adapted from UDL-IRN, 2011.)

These three goals (and the practices associated with them) can be achieved in a variety of ways. In order to maximize representation and to ensure the incorporation of learners' lifeworlds into curricula, units, lessons, and/or task sequences/instructional interventions, educators can explore who their students are in terms of the three dimensions of learner difference discussed in the first section of this chapter and in the previous one (see page 30; Kalantzis & Cope, 2012), their funds of knowledge (Moll et al., 1992), as well as their community, and local and institutional ties. This can happen before the start of the academic year (though not all instructors will have access to this sort of data) or in the first week of classes. In her book *This Book Is Anti-Racist Journal*, Jewell (2021) offers a variety of activities that can guide learners to reflect on their identities and sociocultural/sociohistorical ties in a comprehensive, diverse, and inclusive way. The following task, adapted from pages 14–19, could be used as a gateway to students' identities and lifeworlds and could be modified for use with learners of different ages and levels of L2 performance.

WHO AM I?*

Step 1.

Set a timer for five minutes, and write words/phrases defining who you are. You can also use illustrations or videotape yourself expressing your ideas orally (you can add other elements to your video, too, like your favorite music).[1]

Think of your personal identities—parts of you that *you* define, create, name, and frame. Here are some questions you can use as a start. However, don't feel you need to respond to them: You are welcome to include your own perspectives of your identity.

- What do you sound like?
- What is your favorite color?
- What do you like to do? (interests, hobbies, favorite activities)
- How do you feel?
- What is your favorite animal?
- When is your birthday?
- What is your favorite shape?
- Who are your friends?
- What do you like to eat?
- Where is your favorite place to be?
- Your own question:
- Your own question:

Now use the figure below to express your vision of your personal identities. You can write/draw in the figure, or you can create a digital multimodal poster or a video. If you choose the poster or video option, include the link to your work in the figure.

Step 2.

You are also defined by your social identities—parts of you that relate to other people in society. These categories—and the way you define yourself within them—are based on creations that have been historically named, framed, and defined by society. Social identity categories include *race*, *ethnicity, socioeconomic class, gender expression, sexual orientation, age, nationality* (and/or state/geographical ties), *language* (including the varieties of the language(s) you speak/identify with), *religious beliefs* (or lack of), *abilities, education, family structure* (and your role in your family).

Taking these categories into account, add to your previous definition of yourself (i.e., personal identities). Modify your previous work (the figure in Step 1 or your digital artifact/video) to incorporate your new identities.

Step 3.

Now you are going to build a map of yourself. You will show who you are as a whole person. Using a piece of paper or an electronic document (e.g., a Google slide), position your name at the center. Then, all around, place the words, phrases, illustrations, etc., writing, drawing, collaging, painting your many and various identities. You can create connections among different identities to reflect intersections. Build your map however you like. You may want to keep coming back to this to add more details of who you are.

*Activity adapted from Jewell, 2021, pp. 14–19.

L2 practitioners could use the data that originate from this activity to revise previously made decisions on outcomes, materials, instructional interventions, and assessment, and to plan future pedagogical moves. The information gathered might also guide instructors in the inclusion of socially relevant issues, pointing to those that might be of interest to the students (based on their identities) and/or might be connected to local groups/institutions or to those to which learners belong. To kick start the class's critical inquiry (Osborne, 2006), Jewell (2021) suggests focusing on the land where the educational context is located and where students live. She proposes that both practitioners and students explore who the indigenous group(s) who inhabit(ed) the land are/were, and what the original name of the area was. Additionally, since our focus is L2 teaching, it would be important to include linguistic information, for example, what language(s) are/were spoken in the area, what language family(ies) they belong(ed) to, etc. Jewell (p. 7) posits that introducing this kind of content in the classroom

> help[s] us not only to acknowledge the past, but become better stewards (caretakers) so those who come after us will have this earth. Learning about the original names of [our] cit[ies], and what happened to the [local] indigenous tribes when … settlers colonized and dominated the land and people, [can deepen our] understanding of how the work of racism and colonization is not new. It happens everywhere. No place is immune to the effects of racism and colonization.

This first critical focus can open the doors for L2 teaching for social justice, which teachers can materialize through the inclusion of related issues affecting minoritized communities in the country and the target cultures (e.g., those related to Orborne's [2006] four pillars—identity, social architecture, language choices, and activism; see page 26). The activity proposed can also set the stage for reflexive pedagogy, and learners' use of the L2 for critical work in *L-by-D*'s knowledge processes. A further benefit of this task might be that students belonging to underrepresented groups will be able to see how representation and inclusion are essential aspects of their current learning process (which can contribute to *belonging*). In the next section, we will focus on the enactment of L2 instruction that incorporates both UDL and *L-by-D*.

Instructional Moves

Once L2 instructors have determined learning outcomes in connection with curricular content and their learners' identities and personal and academic needs, the next step entails the development of instructional moves (e.g., units, lessons, task sequences, single instructional interventions). In this section, I will discuss ways to achieve this goal, starting with the following practices, adapted from the UDL document created by UDL-IRN (2011):

4. **The establishment of the instructional experience.**
   ***L-by-D* connection: Principles of *belonging* and *transformation*; goals of transformative curriculum; all knowledge processes and metafunctions.**

   L2 teachers establish their instructional sequence. At a minimum, plans should include:
   - Intentional and proactive ways to address the established goals, learner needs, and the assessment plan (see #1, #2, and #3 in the previous section).
   - A plan detailing what instructional materials will be used and how, and what knowledge processes will be integrated into the L2 teacher's practice to overcome barriers, support learner understanding, and maximize L2 use in the three modes of communication—interpersonal, interpretive, and presentational. When selecting resources, there should be a balance "in terms of paper [printed], electronic, and live [texts]; semiotic systems used [e.g., the L2 + other modalities, such as visual, gestural, and auditory]; genre [see Chapter 4] and delivery platform" (Anstey & Bull, 2006, p. 53). In Appendix A, I offer a template with questions and semiotic foci which teachers can employ to guide their students' work with multimodal ensembles.
   - A plan that ensures high expectations for all learners and that the needs of the learners in the margins (i.e., struggling and advanced) are answered, anticipating that a broader range of learners will benefit.
   - An assessment plan based on multiple, diverse forms of formative assessment to provide necessary data for both the teacher and

students. For example, L2 instructors can implement evidence-based L2-performance assessment frameworks such as *Integrated Performance Assessment* (Adair-Hauck et al., 2006, 2013), tied to learners' work in *L-by-D*'s knowledge processes. Another useful resource which L2 teachers can employ to involve learners in self-assessment and reflection are the *NCSSFL-ACTFL Can-Do Statements* (ACTFL- NCSSFL, 2017). These statements are "aligned with ... ACTFL's *Performance Descriptors for Language Learners* [ACTFL, 2012], [and they] reflect the continuum of growth in L2 communication skills through the Novice, Intermediate, Advanced, Superior, and Distinguished levels [of performance]" (https://www.actfl.org/resources/ncssfl-actfl-can-do-statements). When topics related to social justice are included in the curriculum/lesson/unit/instructional sequence/moves, educators can use Learning for Justice's standards for social justice (Teaching Tolerance, 2018) (see page 28) to assess and/or guide learners to self-assess in connection to their knowledge of and attitudes towards the issues discussed.

Additionally, in Table 3.1, I provide a starting point for L2 teachers to develop measurable outcomes in connection to students' work in *L-by-D*'s eight knowledge processes. This information is based on Kalantzis et al.'s (2005) work. The importance that *L-by-D* places on students' collaborative construction of knowledge is reflected in the assessment criteria, which point to the need for instructors to "assess individuals in a group context: the ability to make productive social connections (to texts and people)" (p. 94). Indeed, in the criteria offered,

> the capacity to make and share knowledge with others is considered the most difficult and highest order level of competence because it involves communication, negotiation, and sensitivity, as well as sound knowledge of a subject or familiarity with a task.
>
> (p. 95)

This orientation is compatible with students' L2 (social) use in the three modes of communication—interpersonal, interpretive, and presentational. L2 practitioners can adapt the suggested *L-by-D* assessment categories and the language used in them to serve their instructional needs, and/or they can combine them with other L2 assessment tools (e.g., the *NCSSFL-ACTFL Can-Do Statements*). I will revisit the topic of assessment in the third section of this chapter.

The scholars in the UDL-IRN group (2011) also believe that, when enacting their instructional interventions, teachers need to take into account considerations of how to support multiple means of learner representation, expression and action, and engagement. I have adapted the UDL-IRN's recommendations for application in L2 teaching and learning settings. The integration of both UDL and *L-by-D* presupposes the following:

Table 3.1 Criteria for Measuring *Learning by Design*'s Knowledge Processes Outcomes

Students demonstrate that they:

Level of Performance / Knowledge Processes	Exceed Expectations *Collaborative Competence:*	Meet Expectations *Autonomous Competence:*	Almost Meet Expectations *Assisted Competence:*
	Can work effectively with others, including people with less or different knowledge and expertise than themselves, to produce an excellent piece of work (their own, or a joint piece of work).	Can figure out how to undertake the task or activity by themselves, and complete it successfully (their own work, or a part of a joint piece of work).	Need explicit instruction or support from the teacher or peers to be able to undertake the task or activity.
Experiencing the Known	Are able to demonstrate to others the connections between the learning task at hand, and their own or the other person's lifeworld, lived experiences, identities, communities, previous learning (formal or informal).	Can figure out for themselves the connection between their own lifeworld, lived experiences, identities, communities, previous learning (formal or informal), and the learning task.	Need prompts from the teacher or peers to make the connection between their own lifeworld, lived experiences, identities, communities, previous learning (formal or informal) and the learning task.
Experiencing the New	Are able to engage in and with an unfamiliar text or activity, in such a way that they actively interact with it and/or add meaning based on the connection between their own perspective, knowledge, and experience and the meaning embedded in the text or activity.	Are able to make enough sense on their own of an unfamiliar text or activity to comprehend the main idea/meaning conveyed and offer a general interpretation of the message in the text or activity.	Need scaffolds by the teacher or peers to make sense of an unfamiliar text or activity. Limited comprehension and/or interpretation.
Conceptualizing by Naming	Are able to find patterns and define concepts in terms of other concepts with an accurate simplifying definition and by providing clear examples.	Are able to work out for themselves the meaning of a concept from the context of its use or by looking up its meaning, and then use that concept to make an abstraction.	Once explained to them, are able to use a concept appropriately in context, and make effective, but limited conceptual connections.

(*Continued*)

Table 3.1 Continued

Conceptualizing with Theory	Are able to put concepts together in a theory/generalization and can explain that theory/generalization to others.	Are able to work out for themselves the connections among concepts in a theory/generalization.	Are able to see the connection between two or more concepts and how they might reflect a theory/generalization once this is pointed out to them.
Analyzing Functionally	Are able to work with others to figure out and demonstrate the way they see causal connections (e.g., between meaning and form) to people who might not see them in the same way.	Are able to analyze causal connections (e.g., between meaning and form) for themselves.	Are able to understand, once pointed out to them, the general function or purpose of a particular structure in connection to meaning or other relevant causal connections.
Analyzing Critically	Can corroborate from multiple sources an analysis or develop a group understanding of explicit and implicit motives, agendas, and actions, as well as community, institutional, and/or ideological connections.	Can construct a plausible interpretation of underlying motives, agendas, and interests driving a text, action, or piece of knowledge.	Are able to comprehend, once explained to them, some of the obvious human interests and agendas behind a text, action, or piece of knowledge.
Applying Appropriately	Master a convention or a genre to the point where they become fully fledged members of a new L2 community of practice.	Are able to independently communicate in ways which conform to L2 conventions or textual genres.	Are able, in a supportive and structured environment, to communicate in ways which conform to L2 conventions or textual genres.
Applying Creatively	Can create a hybrid text which involves a genuinely original combination of knowledge, actions, and ways of communicating (including the L2).	Are able to independently put together in a meaningful way a limited hybrid text (including the L2).	Are able, in a supportive and structured environment, to put together in a meaningful way one or two elements of a hybrid text (including the L2).
Multiliteracies	Effectiveness in communication of meaning and use of multiple modes of meaning (e.g., the L2, images, audio, gestures, etc.)		

Adapted from "*Learning by Design*: Criteria for Measuring Learning Outcomes," by Kalantzis et al., 2005, pp. 95–97.

- The L2 teacher purposefully uses a variety of strategies and instructional tools and moves within each knowledge process to present information and content to anticipate students' diverse and unique needs and preferences. **(Representation)**
- Students use a variety of strategies, instructional tools, and methods to demonstrate new understandings. Teachers enact "practices congruent with a metacognitive approach to learning [that] include those that focus on [learners'] sensemaking, self-assessment, and reflection on what worked and what needs improving" (National Research Council, 2000, p. 12). **(Expression and action)**
- A variety of methods are used to engage students (e.g., to provide choice, address student interest, integrate funds of knowledge [Moll et al., 1992], including linguistic practices [e.g., translanguaging; García & Wei, 2018]) and promote their ability to monitor their own learning (e.g., goal setting, self-assessment, and reflection; metacognitive approach). **(Engagement)**

To facilitate the planning, development, and organization of instructional moves (including materials and comprehensive L2 use), I have created a design template for L2 instructors. This resource, presented in Table 3.2, incorporates the pedagogical aspects we have been discussing, and it can be adapted for units, lessons, or tasks in a variety of educational settings. Even though the template includes all epistemic moves and metafunctions, educators can choose only the ones they want to integrate into their practice.

The final essential component of L2 teachers' practice in reflexive L2 pedagogy grounded in *L-by-D* and UDL is the assessment of the teaching practice itself. Instructors' self-reflection can be guided by the following questions:

5. **Instructors' reflection and new understandings.**
   L-by-D connection: Reflection on the attainment of goals in each knowledge process as well as those embedded in the transformative curriculum (including principles of *belonging* and *transformation*).

   L2 teachers establish checkpoints for their own reflection and new understandings. Considerations should include:
   - To what extent L2 learners have achieved the desired outcomes: What data support your inference(s).
   - What instructional strategies (including materials used) have worked well and, if needed, how they can be improved.
   - What tools have worked well, and, if needed, how their use can be improved.
   - What strategies and tools have provided for multiple means of representation, action/expression, and engagement. Evidence of students' *belonging*.
   - What additional tools would have been beneficial to have access to and why.
   - Overall, how you might improve your practice. (Adapted from UDL-IRN, 2011)

Table 3.2 Design Template

Cultural/Social Justice Focus	Approximate Length of Module/Unit/Lesson	_____ minutes _____ days _____ weeks
Genre/Discursive Practice		
Theme/Topic		
Outcomes		
What should learners know and be able to do by the end of the module/lesson/unit?	Linguistic (L2): Thematic/discipline-specific:	
Instructional Moves		
Knowledge Processes and Metafunctions	*Experiencing the known* Instructional materials: Planned activities/tasks: Checkpoint/formative assessment: Modes of communication: ❑ Interpersonal ❑ Interpretive ❑ Presentational Metafunctions: ❑ Reference (what is this about?) ❑ Agency (who or what is doing this?) ❑ Structure (how does this hang together?) ❑ Context (when/where is this connected?) ❑ Interest (why?/what's/who's this for?)	
	Experiencing the new Instructional materials: Planned activities/tasks: Checkpoint/formative assessment: Modes of communication: ❑ Interpersonal ❑ Interpretive ❑ Presentational Metafunctions: ❑ Reference (what is this about?) ❑ Agency (who or what is doing this?) ❑ Structure (how does this hang together?) ❑ Context (when/where is this connected?) ❑ Interest (why?/what's/who's this for?)	

(Continued)

Table 3.2 Continued

Knowledge Processes and Metafunctions	***Conceptualizing by naming*** **Instructional materials:** **Planned activities/tasks:** **Checkpoint/formative assessment:** **Modes of communication:** ☐ Interpersonal ☐ Interpretive ☐ Presentational **Metafunctions:** ☐ Reference (what is this about?) ☐ Agency (who or what is doing this?) ☐ Structure (how does this hang together?) ☐ Context (when/where is this connected?) ☐ Interest (why?/what's/who's this for?)
	Conceptualizing with theory **Instructional materials:** **Planned activities/tasks:** **Checkpoint/formative assessment:** **Modes of communication:** ☐ Interpersonal ☐ Interpretive ☐ Presentational **Metafunctions:** ☐ Reference (what is this about?) ☐ Agency (who or what is doing this?) ☐ Structure (how does this hang together?) ☐ Context (when/where is this connected?) ☐ Interest (why?/what's/who's this for?)
	Analyzing functionally **Structural focus:** **Instructional materials:** **Planned activities/tasks:** **Checkpoint/formative assessment:** **Modes of communication:** ☐ Interpersonal ☐ Interpretive ☐ Presentational **Metafunctions:** ☐ Reference (what is this about?) ☐ Agency (who or what is doing this?) ☐ Structure (how does this hang together?) ☐ Context (when/where is this connected?) ☐ Interest (why?/what's/who's this for?)

(Continued)

Table 3.2 Continued

Knowledge Processes and Metafunctions	*Analyzing critically* **Instructional materials:** **Planned activities/tasks:** **Checkpoint/formative assessment:** **Modes of communication:** ❑ Interpersonal ❑ Interpretive ❑ Presentational **Metafunctions:** ❑ Reference (what is this about?) ❑ Agency (who or what is doing this?) ❑ Structure (how does this hang together?) ❑ Context (when/where is this connected?) ❑ Interest (why?/what's/who's this for?)
	Applying appropriately **Task:** **Deliverables:** **Formative and summative assessment:** **Modes of communication:** ❑ Interpersonal ❑ Interpretive ❑ Presentational **Metafunctions:** ❑ Reference (what is this about?) ❑ Agency (who or what is doing this?) ❑ Structure (how does this hang together?) ❑ Context (when/where is this connected?) ❑ Interest (why?/what's/who's this for?)
Knowledge Processes and Metafunctions	*Applying creatively* **Task:** **Deliverables:** **Formative and summative assessment:** **Modes of communication:** ❑ Interpersonal ❑ Interpretive ❑ Presentational **Metafunctions:** ❑ Reference (what is this about?) ❑ Agency (who or what is doing this?) ❑ Structure (how does this hang together?) ❑ Context (when/where is this connected?) ❑ Interest (why?/what's/who's this for?)

(*Continued*)

Table 3.2 Continued

Multimodal Resources	Digital Tools/Media

The incorporation of the instructional moves presented in the previous sections into L2 educational settings entails the enactment of everyday practices that can facilitate the weaving of *L-by-D*'s processes and the organization and flow of instruction. In the next section, I will examine the ones that, based on existing literature, I consider essential for the success of the learning process.

Everyday Practices for Second Language Instruction Grounded in *Learning by Design*

In this section, I describe everyday teaching practices that, based on existing literature and my experience as an L2 researcher, instructor, language program director, teacher trainer, and materials developer, I believe can result in the success of L2 teaching grounded in *L-by-D*, as well as in the incorporation of the principles of UDL. My focus, however, is limited. For example, I will not discuss high leverage practices (i.e., "the tasks and activities that are essential for skillful beginning teachers to understand, take responsibility for, and be prepared to carry out in order to enact their core instructional responsibilities" [Ball & Forzani, 2009, p. 504]).[2] Rather, my goal is to make reference to small moves that offer an instructional path for both practitioners and students, and that, despite the apparent simplicity of some of them, are crucial in the L2 classroom. Our point of departure is the framework itself.

Presentation of Learning by Design's *Knowledge Processes*

When I introduced *L-by-D* in Chapter 1, I posited that one of its creators' main goals when adapting and expanding the NLG's (1996) pedagogy of multiliteracies was to simplify the terminology so that both instructors *and* students would be able to understand what they were doing to know. Kalantzis et al. (2016, 2019) believe that the terms they have adopted to name their knowledge processes (i.e., experiencing, conceptualizing, analyzing, and applying) should be explained to learners in connection with the work each move entails, and the objectives and outcomes embedded in them. One way to achieve this goal is to elicit this information from students through a process of guided discovery. That is, while working within a particular knowledge process, the teacher can focus learners' attention on the task at hand, and through questions, can facilitate connections between what students are doing and the objectives of the epistemic move. As a result, again by doing, learners can discover what kind of knowledge each process involves in terms of content (what it is about), action (what we do and how we do it), and results (what we learn, what we can do now)—the examination of meaning-making. Sample questions to facilitate this process are provided in Table 3.3.

This knowledge can help teachers legitimize their practice in their students' eyes, and it can offer a theoretical, yet comprehensible, basis to connect expected outcomes (e.g., those similar to the ones presented in Table 3.1), L2 use, and meaning-making.

Instructional Objectives

Besides understanding what work within each knowledge process entails and how it is connected to outcomes, L2 use, and meaning-making, learners need to clearly see how what they are doing with the L2 is relevant for their academic growth *and* lifeworlds. That is, as we saw in Chapter 2 and the first sections of this chapter, it is crucial for L2 learning to be both meaningful and purposeful (Glisan & Donato, 2021). L2 content and use must be connected to who the students are—to their identities, lived experiences, communities, and to the development of their multiliteracies and 21st-century skills (see page 22). Thus, it is imperative for instructors to always explain L2 use in connection with a specific meaning-making purpose relevant to their learners. For example, if students are working with a text belonging to a specific genre and on a socially relevant issue, they must understand how both the genre and issue are connected to their reality, and why they have been chosen by the teacher to be part of the curriculum, unit, lesson, and/or pedagogical intervention.

Additionally, L2 practitioners need to contextualize instruction in terms of purpose (what language is used for), making reference to how language will be used in the eight knowledge processes and embedding the five metafunctions (i.e., focus on different aspects of meaning-making) in learners' L2 use. This means that instructional objectives must never be just linguistic or purely thematic (i.e., the past tense or a particular topic should never be objectives by themselves). Instead,

> students need to be made aware not only of the overarching theme or topic that motivates [L2 use] but also of the nature of the communicative exchanges, the persons with whom they are speaking, the goals and purposes of the interactions, cultural forms, [and textual form].
>
> (Glisan & Donato, 2021, p. 17)

This essential pedagogical aspect will become clearer when I present specific examples of L2 instruction grounded in *L-by-D* in the next two chapters of this volume.

To summarize, when instructional objectives are clearly articulated and they make reference to outcomes and expectations in terms of L2 use, learners should be able to answer these questions:

- What am I supposed to be learning here (e.g., in each knowledge process; outcomes/expectations)?

- What is this lesson/pedagogical move about (i.e., how it is connected to my understanding of/participation in meaning-making [L2 + other semiotic systems])?
- How do I participate in this lesson/pedagogical move (i.e., expected use of the L2 in the interpersonal, presentational, and interpretive modes of communications)?
- Have I been an effective L2 user in this lesson/pedagogical move?
- What do I need to work on based on what I did in this lesson/pedagogical move? (Adapted from Anstey & Bull, 2018, p. 139.)

Table 3.3 Guiding Questions for L2 Students on *Learning by Design*'s Knowledge Processes

Knowledge Processes	Guided Discovery
Preliminary Guiding Questions *Focus on Meaning-Making* *Metafunctions:* Reference (what) Agency (who) Structure (how) Context (where/when) Interest (why/for whom)	1. Understanding meaning-making You want to communicate a message (e.g., a joke, some information to a fellow student, a meme). What is important? Check all that apply. Explain your answers. ❑ What you want to communicate (content) and why (objective) ❑ Who you want to communicate with (audience) ❑ How you want to communicate the message (mode—language/dialect, image, audio, gesture, etc.) ❑ What you are going to use to communicate (e.g., text message, phone call, conversation, etc.) 2. Understanding the "motivated" message. What influences your message? Check all that apply. Explain your answers. ❑ Who you are (your identities, your culture, your language, etc.) ❑ Who you want to communicate with (audience—their identities, culture, language, etc.) ❑ What you want to communicate (content) ❑ Situation (e.g., informal vs. formal context, in-person vs. virtual, etc.) ❑ Your objective (e.g., asking your instructor to give you extra credit vs. participating in a Roblox event) 3. Now, based on your answers, define "meaning-making." What is important? Why do we say that all meaning-making is "motivated"? Is it the same when you use the L1 or L2? Why?/Why not? Explain.
Experiencing the Known	• What are we talking about? • What is the basis of our discussion? • What is this topic related to in our discussion? • How is each student contributing to it? • How is our work connected to the dimensions/analysis of meaning-making, including the use of the L2?

(Continued)

Table 3.3 Continued

Knowledge Processes	Guided Discovery
Experiencing the New	• What topic are we focusing on? • How is this topic connected to our previous work/discussion? • What are we doing now? • How is our work connected to the dimensions/analysis of meaning-making, including the use of the L2?
Conceptualizing by Naming	• What are we doing with the text(s) we are working with? • What are we expected to do/find out in this task? • How is our work related to our previous task(s)? • How is our work connected to the dimensions/analysis of meaning-making, including the use of the L2?
Conceptualizing with Theory	• How is our work related to our previous task(s)? • What are we expected to do/find out in this task? • What kind of information will we get? • How is our work connected to the dimensions/analysis of meaning-making, including the use of the L2?
Analyzing Functionally	• What are we focusing on? • What do we want to know? • How is our work related to our previous task(s)? • How is our work connected to the dimensions/analysis of meaning-making?
Analyzing Critically	• What are we focusing on now? • How is our work related to our previous task(s)? • What are we expected to do/find out in this task? • What kind of information will we get? • How is our work connected to the dimensions/analysis of meaning-making including the use of the L2?
Applying Appropriately	• What are we expected to do? • What is the expected result of our work? • How are we going to accomplish this result? • How is our work related to our previous task(s)? • What dimensions of meaning-making do we need to consider to complete this task, including the use of the L2?
Applying Creatively	• What are we expected to do? • What is the expected result of our work? • How are we going to accomplish this result? • How is this task different from the previous one? • How is our work related to our previous task(s)? • What dimensions of meaning-making do we need to consider to complete this task, including the use of the L2?

Collaborative Learning

Throughout this chapter, I have emphasized the importance of learners' collaborative construction of knowledge in *L-by-D*. Kalantzis and Cope (2012, p. 71) believe that "knowledge sharing and collaborative learning are the glue that binds together collective intelligence," and, thus, it is an essential component of the learning process in both cognitive and social terms. Furthermore, these scholars posit that the development of students' *collaborative competence* should be an instructional goal in itself. In *L-by-D*,

> collaborative competence is a capacity to contribute something of your own experience and knowledge in a group learning context, where the sum of the group knowledge is greater than the sum of the individual parts. Learners make the inside/outside connections, between education and the rest of their lives, and between their lives and other people's lives. Each learner has a sense of their unique perspective and the contribution they can make in the learning context ... They share their knowledge and perspectives with others. They also come to rely on the knowledge of others ... They can work in groups with diverse experiences and knowledge, negotiating in such a way that the differences are the strength rather than a problem ... They can solve problems collectively that could not be solved individually. Collaborative learning, in sum, creates conditions for making social knowledge. Much more than the stuff that's in your head, the key to this kind of knowledge is in the social connections.
>
> (Kalantzis & Cope, 2012, pp. 294–295)

This characterization of collaborative learning is compatible with UDL's principles (UDL-IRN, 2011) because this type of learning can facilitate representation (different perspectives and ways of learning are valued), expression and action (students are able to express their understanding to their peers and construct knowledge with them), and engagement (learners can monitor their own as well as the group's learning). Additionally, when students work together, they can develop their Four-Cs collaboration and communication skills, as well as their critical thinking and problem solving and creativity and innovation (NEA, 2011; P21, 2011). Cooperative work can also promote L2 use in the three modes of communication—interpersonal, interpretive, and presentational—as learners can employ the target language when working within *L-by-D*'s knowledge processes to plan, organize, and present their work (with and to peers), express their perspectives, and complete specific tasks.

A vast body of research (e.g., see meta-analyses by Kyndt et al., 2013; Loh et al., 2020; and Rohrbeck et al., 2003) has provided evidence for the significant beneficial effects that result from learners' working in pairs or small groups. For example, the work of Barron and her colleagues (e.g., Barron, 2000a, 2000b, 2003; Darling-Hammond et al., 2008) and Johnson et al. (e.g., Johnson & Johnson, 1981, 1999; Johnson et al., 1994) has shown that, in individual assessments, students with the experience of working in groups outperform learners that have not done so, and that groups usually do better on learning tasks than individuals. Additionally, these scholars have reported benefits in terms of self-efficacy, negotiation and interactional skills, time on task, and empathy toward peers. Nevertheless, this research (e.g., Johnson et al.'s work) has also stressed the need for organization and structure if collaborative learning is to succeed. That is, students need to be provided with strategies and community rules or norms to ensure respectful and productive interactions and a fair division of labor, and educators need to develop tasks that require equitable collaboration in order to be completed.

Johnson et al. (1994) identify five essential conditions to achieve productive collaborative work. The first one is *positive interdependence*, which refers to the need for group members to understand that success depends on each person's active contribution to the collaborative work, as individual effort benefits individuals as well as the group as a whole. Johnson and his colleagues believe that positive interdependence "creates a commitment to other people's success as well as one's own, which is at the heart of cooperative learning" (p. 9). One way to ensure that this condition is met is to assign unique responsibilities or roles to each member of the group. Depending on the educational context, L2 teachers can take care of this task, or, alternatively, group members can democratically distribute responsibilities and choose members to act as group leaders, materials managers, time keepers, notetakers, presenters, etc.

The second important aspect of collaborative learning is *individual and group accountability*. This entails the need for the group to commit to the successful completion of the assigned activity and to assume collective responsibility for doing or not doing so. The same applies to each individual member, and the task(s) they are in charge of. In order to guarantee that both groups and individual members are accountable for their work, Johnson and his colleagues (1994) recommend establishing clear goals for the completion of the assignment (e.g., checkpoints) and developing criteria to

> measure [the group's] progress towards achieving [their goal(s)] and ... the performance of each individual student [so that] the results [can be given] to the group and the individual, [and they] can ascertain who needs more assistant, support, and encouragement in completing the assignment.
> (p. 9)

Again, depending on the instructional setting, the assessment could be carried out by the L2 instructor or by the members themselves and the rest of the group. In Table 3.4, I provide a sample template for students' group and self-assessment. This resource can be adapted to assess a group's ongoing or finalized work. Also, it could be modified for peer assessment.

The third important element in cooperative learning is *promotive interaction*. This aspect makes reference to the need for members of a group to work together, face-to-face, "promot[ing] each other's success by sharing resources and helping, supporting, encouraging, and praising [each individual's] efforts to learn"

Table 3.4 Sample Form for Group and Self-Assessment

Step 1. Overall group assessment

1. Name three things your group is doing/did well when working together. Be as specific and descriptive as possible. Also, think of examples of these practices that you can share with your group members.
    i. _____
    ii. _____
    iii. _____
2. Name one thing your group could do/could have done even better. Think of specific suggestions.
3. Write down something about each of your group members that has helped/helps the group be effective. Share your views with your group.

Step 2. Self-assessment

Assess your work using the following criteria. Please be fair, honest, and professional.

Criteria

5 points: Excellent work; my contribution was a crucial component to our group's success.
4 points: Very strong work; I contributed significantly to our group.
3 points: Sufficient effort; I contributed adequately to our group.
2 points: Insufficient effort; I met minimal group standards.
1 point: Little or weak effort; my work did not benefit our group.

Categories

1. Showed enthusiasm and interest in the assignment. Assessment: _____
2. Participated in project planning and contributed ideas. Assessment: _____
3. Listened to and respected the ideas of others. Assessment: _____
4. Compromised and cooperated with other group members. Assessment: _____
5. Took initiative, encouraged members' participation, and/or gave the group direction when needed. Assessment: _____
6. Did my share of the workload/tasks and/or fulfilled the role assigned to me. Assessment: _____

Share your self-ratings with your group, and explain why you rated yourself the way you did. Together with your fellow group members, plan any changes that might be needed for your and the group's future work.

The first part of the table has been adapted from information in "Cooperative Learning in the Classroom," by Johnson et al., 1994, p. 98.

(Johnson et al., 1994, p. 10). These interactive exchanges and active collaboration are crucial for members' commitment to one another and the achievement of a common goal. In recent years, however, with the increase of online learning environments, students' face-to-face interaction has proved elusive. Nevertheless, existing literature (e.g., Smith Budhai & Brown Skipwith, 2022) has shown that online settings may be quite conducive to highly interactive collaborative learning, and they might even be essential for the development of a class community. To facilitate promotive interaction when organizing cooperative learning in a face-to-face or online environment, it is important that L2 instructors offer students the opportunity to create a social presence within the group. This can be achieved, for example, by requiring learners to create personal profiles through identity tasks like the one I introduced on pages 47–48, incorporating different modes of communication and/or creating a personal video. These individual presentations can give group members the chance to get to know their peers even before they start working as a group, and to identify shared interests and/or experiences. Additionally, formal opportunities (in terms of specific meeting days and times) should be organized for students to work together.

Johnson et al.'s (1994) fourth condition for cooperative learning is related to the previous one since it entails *the teaching of interpersonal and small-group skills* so that groups can function harmoniously and effectively. These skills include those that allow learners to "provide effective leadership, make decisions, build trust, communicate [respectfully and effectively], manage conflict, and be motivated to do so" (p. 11). To achieve this goal, L2 instructors can develop and provide learners with rules for group community interaction, or they can collaborate with learners to create them. Currently, however, there is a myriad of existing resources with norms for group communication and work, including some which are open, that practitioners can adapt to answer their specific students' needs.[3] As a point of departure, I recommend Bosworth's (1994) *Taxonomy of Collaborative Skills*. I have adapted some of the categories and collaborative actions developed by this scholar in Table 3.5.

The final condition for successful cooperative learning is *group processing*. This component is related both to the previous and second elements discussed

Table 3.5 Interpersonal and Small-Group Collaborative Skills

Skills Category	Types of Skills
Interpersonal Skills	• Exhibit congenial and friendly overall attitudes/behavior • Make clear statements • Listen attentively and non-judgmentally • Address other members of the group respectfully • Avoid making assumptions about people and/or ideas • Make eye contact
Group Building/Management	• Organize work • Keep the group on task • Run a meeting • Participate in group processing • Show empathy
Inquiry Skills	• Ask for or offer clarification • Critique constructively • Probe assumptions and evidence • Probe implication and consequences • Elicit viewpoints and perspectives

Adapted from "Developing Collaborative Skills in College Students" by Bosworth, 1994, p. 27.

because it involves group members in the interactive discussion of "how well they are achieving their goals and maintaining effective working relationships … [carefully analyzing] how members are working together and how group effectiveness can be enhanced" (Johnson et al., 1994, p. 11). To assess how the group is functioning, members can reflect on their work using categories like the ones I have included in Table 3.6. This resource is based on Watson and Michaelsen's (1988) research on the factors that influence effective group performance. Also, L2 instructors can create accountability and/or monitoring roles for students in each group, and assign these learners the task of scheduling, organizing, and documenting group processing sessions. The categories in Table 3.6 could be included in the group's discussion. As with other aspects of learning, however, before carrying out their group self-assessment, students should be provided with specific instructions and guidelines (or criteria), objectives, and expectations.

Table 3.6 Criteria for Discussion in Group Processing

	To a Very Great Extent	To a Great Extent	To Some Extent	To a Little Extent	To a Very Little Extent
We work well together.					
Everyone participates.					
We share high-performance expectations.					
Everyone has a chance to express their opinion.					
We listen to each individual's input.					
Members feel free to make positive and negative comments.					
Member diversity aids group problem solving.					
We organize our time well.					
An atmosphere of trust exists in our group.					
All members are prepared on a daily basis.					
We are comfortable with the roles we have in the group.					
We are on track in terms of achieving our goals and completing the assignment.					

Adapted from "Group Interaction Behaviors That Affect Group Performance on an Intellective Task" by Watson & Michaelsen, 1988, pp. 501–502.

In addition to the five components previously discussed, Johnson and his colleagues (1994) emphasize the need for the incorporation of specific instructional moves to ensure the success of collaborative learning. The following recommendations are based on their work, but also on my experience as an L2/HL instructor and teacher trainer:

Planning: L2 instructors

1. Formulate the reasons why students will be working collaboratively in terms of L2 use and meaning-making, *L-by-D* (work within epistemic moves), and UDL (benefits for all learners).
2. Establish clear objectives, expectations, and outcomes for learners' work, and then tie them to curricular objectives/outcomes and L2 use for meaning-making.
3. Decide what students' work will look like:
    a. Are learners going to work in pairs or small groups? Why?
    b. Are learners going to be assigned roles? If so, which ones? What will each role entail?
    c. What will the outcome of learners' work look like for each learner/for the group?
4. Create specific instructions for the task(s) to be carried out collaboratively, as well as activities and resources (e.g., guidelines, assessment rubrics) that will:
    a. Offer students opportunities for the development of positive interdependence and interpersonal and small-group skills.
    b. Facilitate promotive interaction.
    c. Assist group members in the assessment of individual accountability, personal responsibility, and group processing.
5. Decide when collaborative work will take place (e.g., specific days and times), including instances for group and self-assessment, and how long students will be working in pairs/groups.

Implementation: In class, L2 instructors

1. Articulate the objectives of the collaborative task and the reasons why students are working in groups.
2. Tie these objectives to the overall goals of the lesson/unit/curriculum, as well as L2 use for meaning-making and *L-by-D*'s knowledge processes. The collaborative work should be meaningful and purposeful.
3. Explain to students what the collaborative task will entail, and provide detailed instructions (including length of planned group work), also making reference to what is expected in terms of individual and group work and overall results.

4. Create the pairs/groups. Depending on the type of task, class community, and educational setting, L2 teachers might want to let students form their own pairs/groups.
5. "Monitor students' learning and intervene in the groups to provide task assistance or to increase [learners'] interpersonal and group skills ... [as well as to ensure that] students do the intellectual work of organizing, explaining, summarizing and integrating material into existing conceptual structures" (Johnson et al., 1994, pp. 4–5).
6. Implement checkpoints for individual accountability and group processing.
7. Organize the presentation/sharing of students' work with the class community and/or audiences beyond the classroom.
8. Assess students' collaborative learning in terms of expected outcomes, L2 use, and *L-by-D*'s knowledge processes, and "help [learners] process how well their groups functioned" (Johnson et al., p. 4).

Not all these recommendations will apply to every educational setting and/or instructional sequence, and like *L-by-D*'s epistemic moves, not all of these steps need to be included in L2 teachers' practice. However, they might offer an evidence-based blueprint for the implementation of cooperative learning as envisioned by Kalantzis and Cope (2012).

Checkpoints and Assessment

As discussed in previous sections of this chapter, both *L-by-D* (Kalantzis & Cope, 2012; Kalantzis et al., 2005, 2016, 2019) and UDL (UDL-IRN, 2011) scholars recommend the inclusion of regular and diverse forms of formative assessment in teachers' practice. Additionally, it is clear that researchers who focus on collaborative learning (e.g., Johnson et al., 1994) consider this type of assessment essential for the success of group work. In L2 education, further support for formative assessment is found in the *NCSSFL-ACTFL Can-Do Statements*, in the parameters and descriptors in *ACTFL Performance Descriptors for Language Learners* and *World-Readiness Standards for Foreign Language Learning*, and in L2-performance assessment frameworks such as Integrated Performance Assessment (IPA; Adair-Hauck et al., 2006, 2013).[4] For example, in IPA, assessment is implemented in a recurring learning-assessment cycle that involves modeling, practice, performance (assessment), and comprehensive and effective feedback. Feedback can be deemed effective when learners can clearly determine how their performance compares to expected outcomes (i.e., what they have accomplished and what they need to work on), and they can set goals to get closer to the learning expectations. Chan et al. (2014, p. 97) believe that to "enhance the effectiveness of [their] feedback, [instructors] should focus on success ... rather than deficits, and [offer comments that are] immediate, specific, and actionable." The information resulting from assessment will shape teachers' feedback, and will also be incorporated into their practice, becoming part of the modeling for the next learning cycle (Adair-Hauck et al., 2013).

Besides formative assessment, Kalantzis and Cope (2012; Kalantzis et al., 2005, 2016, 2019) recommend the implementation of two other kinds of assessment, *diagnostic* and *summative,* for the adoption of *L-by-D*'s reflexive pedagogy and the achievement of the goals of a transformative curriculum. *Diagnostic assessment* is carried out before the implementation of instructional moves, and it is useful for determining what learners know (in terms of L2 performance and/or discipline-specific knowledge). Based on the data gathered, instructors can then establish new learning outcomes, or modify existing ones, and create content and activities that will specifically answer their students' needs. Furthermore, teachers can combine this type of assessment with tasks like the one presented on page 47 of this chapter to get a comprehensive view of who their students are (both at the personal and academic level). The second form of assessment, *summative*, can offer information about the overall results of students' learning process not only to educators and parents, but also to other stakeholders (e.g., school districts, curriculum developers), which could lead to changes in curricula or the allotment of new resources to improve learners' educational experiences.

Kalantzis et al. (2016) believe these three types of assessment—diagnostic, formative, and summative—need to be part of instruction based on *L-by-D* to:

- Support student learning by providing useful "before, during, and after" information to learners;
- Inform parents and friends of what students have been learning at school, and report on their progress;
- Inform teachers about what has been successfully taught and what they still need to teach; [and]
- Provide differentiated information about individual students so their learning programs can be customized to meet every learner's particular needs. (pp. 502–503)

Regardless of the kind of assessment that is undertaken at a particular point in the learning process, when integrating *L-by-D* into L2 teaching and learning, it is also important to consider that the framework "takes a holistic and integrated approach to assessment" (Kalantzis et al., 2005, p. 94). Kalantzis and her colleagues offer key principles for instructors to bear in mind while developing assessment tools based on *L-by-D*. These principles, which I have adapted to L2 education, include:

- The idea that "it's not (just) the test at the end."
- Measuring learners' multiliteracies and L2 active use in interpersonal, interpretive, and presentational tasks, as well as collaboration skills, problem solving, creativity-imagination-innovation.

- The assessment of L2 performance and L2 learners' work over a whole instructional sequence, or a special assessment task, which tests the full range of knowledge processes required to complete the work assigned.
- The inclusion of more holistic assessment techniques such as project-based tasks (see Chapter 4) and ePortfolios.
- The assessment of personal knowledge and performance: Linguistic and multimodal, as well as experiential, conceptual, analytical, and applied.
- The assessment of students in a group context, with a focus on the ability to make productive social connections through the L2 (to texts and people, and collaboratively constructed knowledge).
- The incorporation of peer assessment (e.g., open, one-way blind, two-way blind, moderated).
- The utilization of qualitative judgments to justify quantitative ratings. (Adapted from Kalantzis et al., 2005, p. 94.)

These principles can be materialized in the L2 classroom by combining assessment criteria directly related to the *L-by-D* (Table 3.1) with those for collaborative learning (Tables 3.4 and 3.6), the *NCSSFL-ACTFL Can-Do Statements* (ACTFL- NCSSFL, 2017), and others created by practitioners based on L2 performance standards and descriptors for expected outcomes tied to performance level and/or provided by scholars working with assessment frameworks (e.g., IPA).[5]

Summary

In the first section of this chapter, I introduced the final dimension of *L-by-D*: Its notion of reflexive pedagogy. I discussed the classroom practices associated with it, which I adapted to reflect the needs of L2 instructors and learners, and I tied them to the other components of the framework, namely, the principles of *belonging* and *transformation*, the eight knowledge processes, the five metafunctions, and the goals of a transformative curriculum. In addition, I showed how UDL, an important current framework for equity education, is compatible with both reflexive pedagogy and the vision of L2 teaching and learning presented in Chapter 2. I proposed that UDL's guidance for instructional planning and teaching can be integrated with *L-by-D*'s reflexive pedagogy and specific L2 performance-related outcomes to maximize diverse and equitable learning opportunities for L2 students.

In the second part of the chapter, I described four pedagogical practices that I consider essential for the success of L2 teaching and learning grounded in *L-by-D*. Specifically, I focused on the need for L2 instructors to explicitly introduce *L-by-D* and its knowledge processes to their students and to provide clear instructional objectives for units, lessons, and tasks. Additionally, I discussed the importance of collaborative learning in *L-by-D*'s reflexive pedagogy, and I made reference to the five evidence-based components that need to be considered for this type of learning to be successful. To facilitate L2 teachers' work, I provided resources that could be adapted for use in different educational settings. In the final part of the section, I examined assessment in connection to reflexive pedagogy and L2 performance-based instruction, and I offered information about the principles that instructors should consider when developing assessment tools grounded in *L-by-D*. In the next two chapters, I transfer the theoretical content I have presented in this chapter and the previous two to the realm of L2 practice. In the chapter that follows, I describe two current teaching approaches that can be grounded in *L-by-D* and can facilitate L2 use in the three modes of communication. In the last chapter of the book, I provide detailed examples of multimodal tasks for L2 students of diverse ages.

Notes

1 Educators can use digital tools such as *Flipgrid* (Appendix B) to facilitate students' completion of the proposed task. Another possible alternative in lieu of solely a written assignment would be for students to prepare a multimodal digital poster or infographic with *Canva* (Appendix B) or a similar resource. See Chapter 5 for ideas.
2 L2 instructors who want to learn more about these practices can consult the two excellent volumes written by Glisan and Donato (2017, 2021) on the topic.
3 Teaching centers in institutions of higher education usually offer open resources that can be adapted for a variety of educational environments (e.g., see the document *Teamwork Skills: Being an Effective Group Member* by the Centre for Teaching Excellence at the University of Waterloo; https://bit.ly/3kwPLUe).
4 For detailed information on IPA, I recommend the comprehensive implementation guide developed by Adair-Hauck et al. (2013).
5 Another useful resource for L2 teachers is Race et al.'s (2005) book *{500 Tips} on Assessment*, which offers a myriad of practical guidelines for formative and summative assessment, as well as for students' group and self-assessment.

References

Works Cited

Adair-Hauck, B., Glisan, E. W., Koda, K., Swender, E. B., & Sandrock, P. (2006). The Integrated Performance Assessment (IPA): Connecting assessment to instruction and learning. *Foreign Language Annals*, 39(3), 359–382. https://doi.org/10.1111/j.1944-9720.2006.tb02894.x

Adair-Hauck, B., Glisan, E. W., &Troyan, F. J. (2013). *Implementing integrated performance assessment*. ACTFL.

Agarwal, S. (2019, October 11). *What is social reading? The 5 best social reading apps*. MUO. https://www.makeuseof.com/tag/best-social-reading-apps/

Allen, H. W., & Paesani, K. (2010). Exploring the feasibility of a pedagogy of multiliteracies in introductory foreign language courses. *L2 Journal*, 2(1), 119–142. https://doi.org/10.5070/L2219064

American Council on the Teaching of Foreign Languages (ACTFL). (2012). *ACTFL performance descriptors for language learners*. ACTFL.

American Council on the Teaching of Foreign Languages (ACTFL), & National Council of State Supervisors for Languages (NCSSFL). (2017). *NCSSFL-ACTFL can-do statements*. https://www.actfl.org/resources/ncssfl-actfl-can-do-statements

Anstey, M., & Bull, G. (2006). *Teaching and learning multiliteracies: Changing times, changing literacies*. Australian Literacy Educators' Association and International Reading Association.

Anstey, M., & Bull, G. (2018). *Foundations of multiliteracies: Reading, writing and talking in the 21st century*. Routledge.

Ball, D. L., & Forzani, F. M. (2009). The work of teaching and the challenge for teacher education. *Journal of Teacher Education*, 60(5), 497–511. https://doi.org/10.1177/0022487109348479

Barron, B. (2000a). Achieving coordination in collaborative problem-solving groups. *Journal of the Learning Sciences*, 9(4), 403–436. https://doi.org/10.1207/S15327809JLS0904_2

Barron, B. (2000b). Problem solving in video-based microworlds: Collaborative and individual outcomes of high-achieving sixth-grade students. *Journal of Educational Psychology*, 92(2), 391–398. https://doi.org/10.1037/0022-0663.92.2.391

Barron, B. (2003). When smart groups fail. *Journal of the Learning Sciences*, 12(3), 307–359. https://doi.org/10.1207/S15327809JLS1203_1

Bosworth, K. (1994). Developing collaborative skills in college students. *New Directions for Teaching and Learning*, 59, 25–31. https://doi.org/10.1002/tl.37219945905

Center for Open Educational Resources and Language Learning. (n.d.) *eComma* [Computer software]. University of Texas at Austin. https://ecomma.coerll.utexas.edu/

Chan, P. E., Konrad, M., Gonzalez, V., Peters, M. T., & Ressa, V. A. (2014). The critical role of feedback in formative instructional practices. *Intervention in School and Clinic*, 50(2), 96–104. https://doi.org/10.1177/1053451214536044

Cope, B., & Kalantzis, M. (2015). The things you do to know: An introduction to the pedagogy of multiliteracies. In B. Cope & M. Kalantzis (Eds.), *A pedagogy of multiliteracies: Learning by Design* (pp. 1–36). Palgrave Macmillan.

Cope, B., & Kalantzis, M. (2020). *Making sense: Reference, agency, and structure in a grammar of multimodal meaning*. Cambridge University Press.

Cope, B., Kalantzis, M., & Tzirides, A. O. (Forthcoming). Meaning without borders: From translanguaging to transposition in the era of digitally-mediated multimodal meaning. In K. K. Grohmann (Ed.), *Multifaceted multilingualism* (pp. 1–33). John Benjamins.

Darling-Hammond, L., Barron, B., Pearson, P. D., Schoenfeld, A. H., Stage, E. K., Zimmerman, T. D., Cervetti, G. N., & Tilson, J. L. (2008). *Powerful learning: What we know about teaching for understanding*. Jossey-Bass.

Douglas Fir Group. (2016). A transdisciplinary framework for SLA in a multilingual world. *Modern Language Journal*, 100(S1), 19–47. https://doi.org/10.1111/modl.12301

Dyjur, P., Ferreira, C., & Clancy, T. (2021). Increasing accessibility and diversity by using a UDL framework in an infographics assignment. *Currents in Teaching & Learning*, 12(2), 71–83.

Fovet, F. (2021). UDL in higher education: A global overview of the landscape and its challenges. In F. Fovet (Ed.), *Handbook of research on applying universal design for learning across disciplines: Concepts, case studies, and practical implementation* (pp. 1–23). IGI Global. http://doi:10.4018/978-1-7998-7106-4.ch001

García, O., & Wei, L. (2018). Translanguaging. In C. A. Chapelle (Ed.), *The encyclopedia of applied linguistics* (pp. 1–7). John Wiley & Sons.

Glisan, E. W., & Donato, R. (2017). *Enacting the work of language instruction: High-leverage teaching practices.* ACTFL.

Glisan, E. W., & Donato, R. (2021). *Enacting the work of language instruction: High-leverage teaching practices* (Vol. 2). ACTFL.

Hanauer, D. I. (2012). Meaningful literacy: Writing poetry in the language classroom. *Language Teaching, 45*(1), 105–115. https://doi.org/10.1017/S0261444810000522

Jewell, T. (2021). *This book is anti-racist journal.* Quarto Publishing.

Johnson, D. W., & Johnson, R. T. (1981). Effects of cooperative and individualistic learning experiences on interethnic interaction. *Journal of Educational Psychology, 73*(3), 444–449. https://doi.org/10.1037/0022-0663.73.3.444

Johnson, D. W., & Johnson, R. T. (1999). Making cooperative learning work. *Theory into Practice, 38*(2), 67–73. https://doi.org/10.1080/00405849909543834

Johnson, D. W., Johnson, R. T., & Holubec, E. J. (1994). *Cooperative learning in the classroom.* Association for Supervision and Curriculum Development.

Kalantzis, M., & Cope, B. (2012). *New learning: Elements of a science of education.* Cambridge University Press.

Kalantzis, M., & Cope, B. (2022). After language: A grammar of multiform transposition. In C. Lütge (Ed.), *Foreign language learning in the digital age: Theory and pedagogy for developing literacies* (pp. 34–64). Routledge.

Kalantzis, M., Cope, B., Chan, E., & Dalley-Trim, L. (2016). *Literacies* (2nd ed.). Cambridge University Press.

Kalantzis, M., Cope, B., & the Learning by Design Project Group. (2005). *Learning by Design.* Victorian Schools Innovation Commission and Common Ground Publishing.

Kalantzis, M., Cope, B., & Zapata, G. C. (2019). *Las alfabetizaciones múltiples: Teoría y práctica.* Octaedro.

Kern, R. (2000). *Literacy and language teaching.* Oxford University Press.

Kyndt, E., Raes, E., Lismont, B., Timmers, F., Cascallar, E., & Dochy, F. (2013). A meta-analysis of the effects of face-to-face cooperative learning. Do recent studies falsify or verify earlier findings? *Educational Research Review, 10,* 133–149. https://doi.org/10.1016/j.edurev.2013.02.002

Loh, R. C. Y., & Ang, C. S. (2020). Unravelling cooperative learning in higher education: A review of research. *Research in Social Sciences and Technology, 5*(2), 22–39. https://files.eric.ed.gov/fulltext/EJ1265259.pdf

Moll, L. C., Amanti, C., Neff, D., & Gonzalez, N. (1992). Funds of knowledge for teaching: Using a qualitative approach to connect homes and classrooms. *Theory into Practice, 31*(2), 132–141. https://www.jstor.org/stable/1476399

National Academies of Sciences, Engineering, and Medicine. (2018). *How people learn II: Learners, contexts, and cultures.* The National Academies Press. https://doi.org/10.17226/24783

National Education Association (NEA). (2011). *Preparing 21st century students for a global society: An educator's guide to the "Four Cs".* https://dl.icdst.org/pdfs/files3/0d3e72e9b873e0ef2ed780bf53a347b4.pdf

National Research Council. (2000). *How people learn: Brain, mind, experience, and school* (Expanded ed.). The National Academies Press. https://doi.org/10.17226/9853

National Standards in Foreign Language Education Project. (2015). *World-readiness standards for foreign language learning.* ACTFL.

Nelson, L. L., & Basham, J. D. (2014). *A blueprint for UDL: Considering the design of implementation*. UDL-IRN.

New London Group. (1996). A pedagogy of multiliteracies: Designing social futures. *Harvard Educational Review*, 66, 60–92. https://doi.org/10.17763/haer.66.1.17370n67v22j160u

Osborn, T. A. (2006). *Teaching world languages for social justice: A sourcebook of principles and practices*. Routledge.

Partnership for 21st Century Skills (P21). (2011). *21st century skills map*. https://www.actfl.org/sites/default/files/resources/21st%20Century%20Skills%20Map-World%20Languages.pdf

Pittaway, D. S. (2004). Investment and second language acquisition. *Critical Inquiry in Language Studies: An International Journal*, 1(4), 203–218. https://www.tandfonline.com/doi/pdf/10.1207/s15427595cils0104_2

Race, P., Brown, S., & Smith, B. (2005). *{500 tips} on assessment* (2nd ed.). Routledge.

Richards, J. C. (2013). Curriculum approaches in language teaching: Forward, central, and backward design. *RELC Journal*, 44(1), 5–33. https://doi.org/10.1177/0033688212473293

Rohrbeck, C. A., Ginsburg-Block, M. D., Fantuzzo, J. W., & Miller, T. R. (2003). Peer-assisted learning interventions with elementary school students: A meta-analytic review. *Journal of Educational Psychology*, 95(2), 240–257. https://doi.org/10.1037/0022-0663.95.2.240

Rose, D. H., & Meyer, A. (2002). *Teaching every student in the digital age: Universal design for learning*. Association for Supervision and Curriculum Design.

Scott, V. M., & Huntington, J. A. (2007). Literature, the interpretive mode, and novice learners. *The Modern Language Journal*, 91(1), 3–14. https://doi.org/10.1111/j.1540-4781.2007.00506.x

Smith Budhai, S., & Brown Skipwith, K. (2022). *Best practices in engaging online learners through active and experiential learning strategies* (2nd ed.). Routledge.

Teaching Tolerance. (2018). *Social justice standards: The Teaching Tolerance anti-bias framework*. https://www.learningforjustice.org/sites/default/files/2020-09/TT-Social-Justice-Standards-Anti-bias-framework-2020.pdf

Tobin, T. J., & Behling, K. T. (2018). *Reach everyone, teach everyone*. West Virginia University Press.

UDL-IRN. (2011). *UDL in the instructional process* (version 1.0.). UDL-IRN. https://www.learningdesigned.org/sites/default/files/UDL%20Instructional%20Planning%20Process.pdf

Vygotsky, L. S. (1978). *Mind in society: The development of higher psychological processes*. Harvard University Press.

Watson, W. E., & Michaelsen, L. K. (1988). Group interaction behaviors that affect performance on an intellective task. *Group and Organizational Studies*, 13(4), 495–516.

Wiggins, G., & McTighe, J. (1998). *Understanding by design* (1st ed.). Merrill Prentice Hall.

Zapata, G. C., & Mesa-Morales, M. (2018). The beneficial effects of technology-based social reading in L2 classes. *Lenguas en Contexto*, 9(Suplemento 2018–2019), 40–50. http://www.facultaddelenguas.com/lencontexto/?idrevista=25#25.40

Instructional Resources Cited

Cutts, S. (2012, December 21). *Man* [Video]. https://www.youtube.com/watch?time_continue=7&v=WfGMYdalClU

Ramos Aranda, G. (2013). *Bosque...jas.* https://www.concienciaeco.com/2014/06/11/el-poeta-defensor-del-medio-ambiente/

4 Genre- and Project-Based Instruction Grounded in Learning by Design

In the first two chapters of this volume, I introduced *Learning by Design* (*L-by-D*) (Cope & Kalantzis, 2015, 2020; Cope et al., Forthcoming; Kalantzis & Cope, 2012, 2022; Kalantzis et al., 2005, 2016, 2019), and I examined its theoretical and pedagogical connections with current L2 frameworks, perspectives, and foci (in terms of thematic content and L2 use). In the previous chapter, I focused on the practical aspects of the incorporation of *L-by-D* in L2 classes, describing the elements and principles that constitute its *reflexive pedagogy*, and the instructional moves that I deem essential for the success of the framework in L2 education (e.g., collaborative learning and formative assessment). Additionally, I discussed how the principles of *Universal Design for Learning* (UDL-IRN, 2011) are compatible with *L-by-D* and can be integrated with the framework when planning and enacting teachers' practice to answer the needs of diverse groups of students.

In this chapter, my objective is to describe two instructional models that are theoretically and pedagogically compatible with *L-by-D*—*genre-based instruction* and *project-based learning*. I believe *L-by-D* can ground L2 instructors' practice and students' work and L2 use when these two forms of instruction are incorporated into the L2 classroom. In the sections that follow, I will discuss both pedagogies in depth based on existing literature, and I will show how *L-by-D* can be weaved with their instructional moves.

Genre-Based Instruction

Since both *L-by-D* and genre-based instruction are grounded in Systemic Functional Linguistics (Halliday, 1985; Halliday & Hassan, 1985), they view language from a functional perspective. Language (and, of course, other modes of communication) is used for meaning-making, to *do* things in specific social situations, guided by meaning-makers' purposes and motivations. When it comes to pedagogy, both, *L-by-D* and genre-based instruction, as expected, promote a functional orientation to learning as well. What does this kind of orientation entail in classes with a focus on L2 development? Derewianka (1990) characterizes a functional approach to language teaching as follows:

DOI: 10.4324/9781003106258-4

- It is interested above all in **meaning**, not in empty conventions.
- Because meaning is found within a text as a **whole**, [it] ... describes how language [and other semiotic resources] operate at the text level, not at the level of individual [elements] in isolation.
- [It] stresses how meanings are made **in conjunction with other people**. This strongly supports [collaborative learning] practices.
- It is concerned with **real** language [or other meaning-making modalities] used by real people—not schoolbook exercises contrived purely to teach some point of grammar, or reading texts devised to teach some aspect of reading.
- It is not interested in simply teaching language for the sake of teaching language. Rather, it demonstrates how language [and other semiotic resources] operate.
- [Students] are encouraged to [use language and other semiotic resources] with a particular **audience** in mind. A functional model describes how texts will vary according to whom you are addressing and how distant the audience is.
- If [learners] have an explicit knowledge of what language [and multimodal] resources are available [for meaning-making], they are in a better position to make **informed choices** when developing texts of their own. (pp. 4–5; emphasis in original)

This kind of pedagogical approach is clearly connected to the objectives and foci of *L-by-D*'s reflexive pedagogy, students' work within the eight knowledge processes, and the analysis and creation of multimodal meaning. That is, like *L-by-D*, functional models provide students with the tools to discover how meaning is structured and organized in texts to convey specific social messages, depending on purpose, topic, audience, and context, and the available semiotic resources (including language) to which a person can resort to do so.

The most important current pedagogical model with this instructional focus in both L1 and L2 learning and teaching is *genre-based instruction* (GBI; Hyland, 2014; Troyan, 2021b). Like *L-by-D*, GBI originated in Australia, as an evidence-based practice that, through the incorporation of explicit instruction, allowed practitioners to guide students in the understanding and production of the types of texts that they needed to master to succeed in academic settings. The impetus behind the research that gave birth to GBI (e.g., see Callaghan & Rothery, 1988; Martin, 1986, 1997, 2013) was the need to create an equitable "'visible pedagogy' to improve the educational outcomes of students marginalized by mainstream schooling" (Kalantzis et al., 2016, p. 158).

The fundamental basis of GBI is the concept of *genre*. In GBI, genre makes reference to the relatively stable structure of texts (written, oral, or multimodal) that share the same rhetorical patterns and are used to achieve specific social purposes. That is, different kinds of texts belong to different genres because they exhibit unique structures, organization, and linguistic (or multimodal) elements that are tied to the kind of meaning they convey, their purpose, and the audience toward which they are geared. For example, narratives and information reports can be said to belong to different genres because they have different social purposes, thematic foci, structure, organization, linguistic (or multimodal) elements, and audience. Because of this strong connection between texts and what they are used for in society, Hyland (2014, p. 15) posits that genres can also be considered

> social processes, [as] members of a culture interact to achieve them; they are goal-oriented, [as] they have evolved to achieve things; and they are staged, [as] meanings are made in steps, and it usually takes [meaning-makers] more than one step to reach their goals.

The objectives of GBI are, therefore, two-fold. The first goal is to provide learners with the pedagogical tools to understand the social connections between meaning and the social purpose of texts belonging to specific genres, and the way in which those texts are rhetorically created for meaning-making. The second objective is to guide students in the oral, written, or multimodal production of texts belonging to specific genres.

These pedagogical objectives make GBI ideal for the implementation of the vision of L2 teaching and learning I introduced in Chapter 2. Indeed, in their recent work, L2 scholars like Hyland (2014) and Troyan (2021a) have emphasized the benefits that genre-based pedagogies, like GBI, can bring to current L2 classrooms, and they have offered evidence for their effectiveness (e.g., see the studies in Troyan's [2021b] edited volume). Based on his work on GBI and L2 writing, Hyland identifies seven pedagogical advantages that can result from the incorporation of GBI into L2 teaching, namely:

1. **GBI is explicit**: It "offers [meaning-makers] an explicit understanding of how target texts are structured and why they are [created] in the ways they are ... This explicitness gives teachers and learners something to shoot for, a 'visible pedagogy' that makes clear what is to be learned" (p. 11).
2. **GBI is systematic**: It "provides a coherent framework for focusing on both language" and other semiotic resources, and the social contexts in which they are used. This "means that teaching materials are based on the ways language [and other modes of meaning-making] are actually used in particular contexts rather than on general impressions of what happens." Also linguistic and other meaning-making patterns "are seen as pointing to contexts beyond the [text], implying a range of social constraints and choices" (pp. 10 and 12).
3. **GBI is needs-based**: It "ensures that [instructional] objectives and content are derived from student needs" (p. 11). In other words, the genres of focus will be determined based on specific learner needs.
4. **GBI is supportive**: It "gives teachers a central role in scaffolding student learning and creativity ... This scaffolding is most evident at the early stages of learning a genre ... [and] is gradually reduced until the learner has the knowledge and skills to perform independently" (pp. 11 and 14).
5. **GBI is empowering**: It is "committed to a redistribution of literacy resources to help learners to gain admission to particular discourse communities; to operate successfully in them; and, in the long run, to develop an informed creativity in using these discourses ... It provides the means to reveal

[meaning-making] as relative to particular groups and contexts and help students unpack the requirements of their target communities" (p. 14).
6. **GBI is critical**: It "has the potential for aiding students to reflect on and critique the ways that knowledge and information are organized and constructed in [specific] texts. Genre perspectives stress the view that a text is constructed in response to context and therefore [is] only comprehensible because of its relationship to a context … Understanding how texts are socially constructed and ideologically shaped … reveals the ways that they work to represent some interests and perspectives and suppress others" (p. 15).
7. **GBI is consciousness-raising**: It "not only address[es] the needs of [L2 students as meaning-makers] but also draw[s] teachers into considering how texts actually work as communication. Knowledge of genres has an important consciousness-raising potential for teachers, with significant implications for both their understanding of writing and their professional development" (p. 15).

Undoubtedly, the integration of GBI into L2 teaching and learning can facilitate instructors' and students' work with L2 oral, written, and multimodal authentic texts, even in classes for novice students (as we will see in Chapter 5). Troyan (2021) offers support for this view by positing that,

> because of their focus on how language functions to make meaning in … texts within a particular cultural context, genre-based pedagogies [such as GBI] provide a powerful tool for realizing the goals of world language instruction articulated in the W-RSFLL [*World-Readiness Standards for Foreign Language Learning*]. (p. 14)

L2 instruction based on GBI is organized around five pedagogical moves: *Setting the Context, Modelling and Deconstructing the Text, Joint Construction of the Text, Independent Construction of the Text*, and *Text Comparison* (Feez, 1998; Hyland, 2014). Before integrating these moves into their practice, however, L2 instructors need to choose model texts that exhibit the features of the genre on which they want to focus with their students. The ensembles chosen need to exemplify authentic oral, written, and/or multimodal manifestations of the genre, and be related to curricular outcomes as well as students' personal and academic needs and level of L2 performance. The work that is planned around the model text(s) also needs to be meaningful and purposeful (Glisan & Donato, 2021). Ideally, practitioners (and/or curriculum developers) will resort to texts originating in the target cultures and/or in L2 local discourse communities with connections to students' lifeworld. And this is the moment when the open resources we made reference to in Chapter 2 might play an important role. For example, before creating their own materials, teachers can consult repositories housed in resource centers such as the *Center for Open Educational Resources and Language Learning* or the *Open Language Resource Center*, and adopt and/or adapt existing OERs.[1] The important aspect to remember, regardless of how materials are developed, is that GBI always entails work with *full*, authentic texts, and *not* just isolated sentences or semiotic elements.

In the first step of the GBI pedagogical sequence, *setting the context*, the L2 teacher and students collaborate in the initial examination of the model text(s). L2 practitioners first situate learners in the social and thematic context of the genre of focus by activating their schemata and by establishing connections with students' identities, lived experiences, and previous knowledge (including funds of knowledge [Moll et al., 1992] and informal learning). After that, learners work collaboratively to discover what the text is about (comprehension), and how it might be related meaning-wise with their lifeworld/lived experiences (interpretation). Learners also determine what message the author wants to convey, and to whom (audience), as well as why the text has been created (communicative objective of the text; i.e., in what type of social activity we could find the text and similar ones, where it has been published, and why its meaning-maker has chosen that particular medium).

Once students have tackled the meaning behind the text in terms of message, audience, and meaning-maker, they can start deconstructing it to discover its rhetorical structure and the semiotic resources used to convey specific ideas tied to the meaning-making goal. This is the second stage of the pedagogical process—*Modelling and Deconstructing the Text*. Learners first explore how the text is organized by analyzing what kind of meaning is expressed in each of its parts; i.e., students unveil what meaning and social purposes each component of the ensemble serves. Based on the results of this analysis, learners can arrive at generalizations about the structure of texts belonging to the genre of focus (e.g., if working with a narrative, they determine what kinds of ideas are expressed in the orientation, complication, and resolution). The next step entails the discovery of the connections between the meaning expressed in each part of the text, and the linguistic elements (or other semiotic resources) that are used by the meaning-maker. Here the focus is on the microstructures that are characteristically part of texts belonging to the genre with which students are working. For example, in a narrative, students will consider the use of past tenses and connectors of time. I provide activity suggestions for this step in Table 4.1.

The next step in the GBI pedagogical sequence, *Joint Construction of the Text*, entails students' collaborative construction of a text belonging to the same genre as the model text(s) they have deconstructed. Students' work can take different forms (see Table 4.1), and it does not necessarily imply that learners are required to work just in pairs. Instructors will need to consider their students' specific needs (including their level of L2 performance), and decide how the joint construction will be organized. Once learners have had the opportunity to delve into the production of texts in the genre of focus with their classmates, they undertake text creation on their own, in the *Independent Construction of the Text* stage. Even though in this move students work individually, it still needs to be scaffolded by the L2 instructor, who provides clear and detailed instructions, discusses expectations and outcomes, and organizes collaborative activities such as structured peer reviews. For example, the foci of peer activities could be the organization of ideas (in connection to the genre), the expression of meaning (in relation to genre, topic, and audience), and the use of specific linguistic elements or other semiotic resources.

Table 4.1 Genre-Based Instruction Activities Grounded in *Learning by Design*

Genre-Based Instruction and **Learning by Design**	Activities
Setting the Context *Experiencing the Known* *Experiencing the New* *Analyzing Critically* Meaning-Making Metafunctions: Reference (what) Agency (who) Context (where/when) Interest (why/for whom)	• Brainstorming (predictions, personal connections with topic) • Class survey (personal experiences and knowledge) • Show-and-tell (personal experiences with topic) • Knowledge journey (related to what is known about the topic) • Questions for analysis of model text(s) (Think-Pair-Share): 　• What is this text about? 　• What purposes does it serve? 　• Who produced the text, and who for (intended audience)? 　• What are the meaning-maker's qualifications for creating the text? 　• In what social situations and/or activities could we find a text like this one? 　• Where was this text published (e.g., on a website, an academic book, etc.)? 　• Why has the meaning-maker chosen this medium to publish the text? 　• If the medium is open source (i.e., people do not have to pay to access the text), what can we hypothesize about the meaning-maker? 　• What social voices are present in the text and which ones are absent? What does this say about the meaning-maker?
Modeling and Deconstructing the Text *Conceptualizing by Naming* *Conceptualizing with Theory* *Analyzing Functionally* *Analyzing Critically* Meaning-Making Metafunctions: Reference (what) Agency (who) Context (where/when) Structure (how) Interest (why/for whom)	**Foci of these activities:** • Parts of the text and what role each of them plays in the text • How each part contributes to the social purpose of the text as a whole • The linguistic elements (and other semiotic resources) that contribute to the expression of meaning in each of the text parts • How we discover what the text refers to • How the meaning-maker establishes their relationship to the intended audience • What rhetorical aspects (e.g., purpose, meaning-making resources, and structure) distinguish the genre of focus

(*Continued*)

Table 4.1 Continued

Genre-Based Instruction and **Learning by Design**	Activities

	• **Focus on meaning:**
	• Jigsaw activity:
	  • Students work in groups. Each group focuses on the identification of one part of the text and what meaning purpose it serves
	  • A member of each group shares their information with members of the other groups
	  • Groups define genre in terms of its social purposes (in what social situations we find texts belonging to it, and for what purpose)
	• Sequencing, rearranging, matching, and labeling text parts
	• Comparing texts with omissions, changes, or different structure
	Focus on form (linguistic elements and/or other rhetorical devices):
	• Creating a Venn diagram to connect meaning and forms (what micro elements are used to convey specific types of ideas)
	• Reorganizing or recreating scrambled or unfinished parts of a text
	• Disappearing story: The teacher removes focus feature/stage from a text and students refer to it (e.g., read it) as if it were still there
	• Learners collect examples of a text feature (e.g., tense samples, a list of connectors, sample images) and summarize how they are used to convey specific meaning
	• Students create a comparison matrix by comparing texts where features have been altered to discover meaning and social purpose changes

Joint Construction of the Text *Applying Appropriately* *Applying Creatively* Meaning-Making Metafunctions: Reference (what) Agency (who) Context (where/when) Structure (how) Interest (why/for whom)	• Teacher leads whole-class construction on blackboard or using digital documents in a collaborative environment (e.g., Google Docs) • Small groups construct texts for presentation to the whole class. Options: Digital construction in collaborative environments [e.g., Google Docs] or performance-based (oral or multimodal) • Students complete unfinished or skeletal texts • Students listen to a text in groups and act on it • Students experiment with the genre by creating a parallel text (meaning- and genre-wise) using other semiotic resources (e.g., images, gestures, etc.) • Storyboarding the model text • Editing a completed text for meaning, structure, and form • Negotiating an information/opinion gap to construct a text

(*Continued*)

82 Genre- and Project-Based Instruction

Table 4.1 Continued

Genre-Based Instruction and **Learning by Design**	Activities
Independent Construction of the Text *Applying Appropriately* *Applying Creatively* Meaning-Making Metafunctions: Reference (what) Agency (who) Context (where/when) Structure (how) Interest (why/for whom)	• Pre-writing activities (brainstorming, freewriting, etc.) • Think-Pair-Share: Collaborative planification of individual task • Students organize ideas and develop the first version of the text. Use of graphic organizers, storyboards, and spider maps • Students modify the joint and/or model text for another purpose (e.g., they experiment with another genre) • Students modify the joint and/or model text resorting to other meaning-making modalities (e.g., visual, gestural, oral) • Students use the genre-based tools learned to dissect a new text and discover ideologies. Students provide suggestions to make the text more inclusive and equitable
Text Comparison *Experiencing the New* *Conceptualizing by Naming* *Conceptualizing with Theory* *Analyzing Functionally* *Analyzing Critically* Meaning-Making Metafunctions: Reference (what) Agency (who) Context (where/when) Structure (how) Interest (why/for whom)	• Comparing the use of the genre across different disciplines, institutions, cultures, and/or communities • Investigating what other genres can be found in similar situations to those analyzed, and discovering how the new genres relate to the one studied • Students modify their joint or individual texts to serve a different purpose • Students transform their joint or individual texts to convey their message in a different modality (e.g., visual, oral, gestural) • Researching how a key feature (e.g., linguistic) is used in other genres • Simulating the impact of using the genre in another social context • Interviewing expert text users on their impressions of text meanings and genre practices

Adapted from Feez, 1998, pp. 126–128; Hyland, 2014, pp. 130–138; and Kalantzis et al., 2005, pp. 120–121; 2019, pp. 82–85.

The final GBI instructional move, *Text Comparison*, offers the L2 teacher and students the opportunity to explore the relationship, in terms of meaning-making and structure, between the model text(s) and those produced by the learners, or other texts within the same genre and/or texts belonging to other genres that could be found in the same social contexts as the ensembles analyzed. Additionally, in this stage, it is important for practitioners to establish connections with learners' lifeworlds and/or L2 discourse communities (and others) of which they are part.

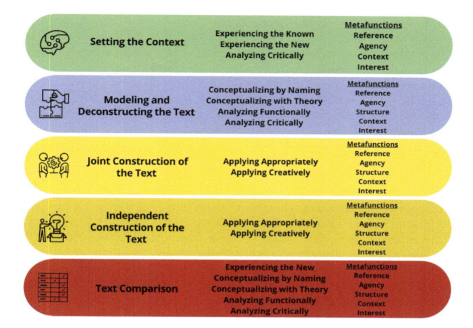

Figure 4.1 Relationship between genre-based instruction's instructional sequence and *Learning by Design*'s knowledge processes and metafunctions.

So how can *L-by-D* contribute to the implementation of GBI in L2 classes? As previously stated, Kalantzis and Cope's framework shares the same theoretical base as GBI, and many of GBI pedagogical moves are compatible with the kind of work learners do within *L-by-D*'s knowledge processes, as well as through the analysis of the five meaning-making metafunctions. This means that *L-by-D* can provide L2 instructors with a blueprint for activities that can facilitate L2 learners' work in each of GBI's stages. In Figure 4.1, I offer a summary of the relationship between GBI's moves and *L-by-D*'s epistemic moves and metafunctions. In Table 4.1, I present instructional suggestions that I have adapted from the work carried out by Kalantzis et al. (2005, 2019), Hyland (2014), and Feez (1998). Some of the activities I make reference to could be applied to the development of written texts, and others to oral or multimodal ensembles.

In Chapter 5, I will provide examples of GBI L2 tasks grounded in *L-by-D* that can be adapted for use in a variety of L2 instructional contexts.

Project-Based Learning

The second pedagogical approach that can be supported by *L-by-D* in L2 classes is *project-based learning* (PBL), which can be defined as "a teaching method in which students gain knowledge and skills by working for an extended period of time to investigate and respond to an authentic, engaging, and complex question, problem, or challenge, and make their work public" (PBLWorks, 2021, p. 9). In this definition, we can clearly see the instructional connections between PBL and *L-by-D*, and also the vision of L2 learning and teaching I described in Chapter 2 and the classroom practices presented in Chapter 3 (including UDL [UDL-IRN, 2011]). When PBL grounded in *L-by-D* is incorporated into L2 classes, learners in diverse educational settings work collaboratively, using the L2 in the three modes of communication (interpersonal, interpretive, and presentational). Together, students carry out a series of tasks within the knowledge processes that will result in the creation of a product connected both to their academic and diverse personal needs, and that will extend language use *beyond* the classroom. PBL can take three different forms: A short project that lasts between three and five days; an average project, lasting between three and five weeks; or a long project, extending for six or more weeks (PBLWorks).

Regardless of what length a project exhibits, like any other instructional intervention, it requires planning and the implementation of a specific pedagogical sequence. The scholars in the Buck Institute of Education (PBLWorks, 2021, pp. 12–13) identify seven key elements that educators need to consider when planning and developing PBL, namely:

1. **A challenging problem or question**: The project is framed by a meaningful problem to solve, or a question to answer, at the appropriate level of challenge.
2. **Sustained inquiry**: Students engage in a rigorous, extended process of asking questions, finding resources, and applying information.
3. **Authenticity**: The project features real-world context, tasks and tools, quality standards, or impact—or speaks to students' personal concerns, interests, and issues in their lives.
4. **Student voice and choice**: Students make some decisions about the project, including how they work and what they create, and express their own ideas in their voice.
5. **Reflection**: Students and teachers reflect on the effectiveness of their inquiry and project activities, the quality of student work, obstacles, and how to overcome them.
6. **Critique and revision**: Students give, receive, and use feedback to improve their process and products.
7. **Public product**: Students make their project work public by sharing it with and explaining or presenting it to people beyond the classroom.

These seven elements mirror the practices I discussed in Chapters 2 and 3. For example, PBL relies on collaborative learning, and some of the resources I offered in Chapter 3 could be used to plan for students' cooperative work, reflection, and assessment. Additionally, the meaningfulness and purposefulness that Glisan and Donato (2021) make reference to in connection with current L2 teaching practices are embedded in PBL's authenticity, the need for socially significant project outcomes, and the implicit opportunity for L2 use with audiences beyond the classroom. When planning authentic and relevant projects for their specific student population, L2 instructors can incorporate aspects of learners' lifeworlds and communities as well as issues connected to Osborne's (2006) four critical inquiry thematic pillars (see page 26) and local realities. L2 teachers also need to be mindful of active L2 use in the three modes of communication and create tasks to achieve this goal. Other important aspects of L2 instruction that need to be part of PBL are the development of learners' Four Cs (see page 22; NEA, 2011; P21, 2011) and their multiliteracies in terms of meaning-making, the use of new media and digital tools, and the production of multimodal ensembles in which the L2 contributes to the totality of the message with other contemporary modalities (e.g., visual, audio, etc.). Also significant is PBL's emphasis on students' active roles, agency, and unique voices when it comes not only to the organization and completion of the project but also, within the parameters set by the instructor, the shape of their work. This is clearly connected to the principles and goals of UDL (see page 43; UDL-IRN, 2011). A final crucial pedagogical aspect for L2 educators to bear in mind is level of L2 performance: Projects have to reflect the seven PBL elements and the instructional demands I have just discussed; however, they also need to be appropriate for students' L2 needs.

Scholars in PBLWorks (2021, p. 61) recommend these four instructional phases for PBL implementation:

- **Phase 1.** Launch project: Entry event and driving question.
- **Phase 2.** Build knowledge, understanding, and skills to answer driving question.
- **Phase 3.** Develop and critique products and answers to driving question.
- **Phase 4.** Present products and answers to the driving question.

When PBL is integrated into L2 classes, work in these phases can be weaved with *L-by-D*'s eight knowledge processes and five metafunctions. For example, the *experiencing* processes can facilitate the launching of the project, first situating learners thematically through the activation of schemata and the establishment of personal connections with the chosen topic (*experiencing the known*). This step gives way to the introduction of the project's driving question(s), its expected length, and the goals and outcomes to be achieved in terms of results (e.g., what form the answer to driving question[s] will have; who the audience will be; what kind of message is to be conveyed). In this phase, students also learn how they will be assessed, how their group (or pair) work will be structured, and what milestones they will need to reach to show their progress. This information is part of *experiencing the new* and embedded in it, we can also find the five metafunctions because students need to consider topic (*reference*), their own *agency*, and the *structure* of their work (and expected result[s]). Additionally, learners need to take into account the sociocultural *context* tied to the creative process and final product, and their social purpose (*interest*—i.e., in terms of motivation as meaning-makers and intended audience).

In the second PBL phase, students develop their thematic, linguistic, and multimodal knowledge. Work takes place within the *experiencing the new, conceptualizing,* and *analyzing* epistemic moves, and it involves the analysis of the five meaning-making metafunctions. For example, learners "dissect" authentic texts in terms of the information they offer about the theme of focus, and their structure, semiotic resources used (including, of course, the L2), and sociocultural meaning-making (motivation, audience, and message). Students gather data for their own work and start categorizing new knowledge, arriving at generalizations and patterns (linguistic and multimodal) that can be transferred to their own work. Learners participate in collaborative tasks, using the L2 in the interpersonal and interpretive modes of communication. However, depending on the level of L2 performance, the L1 can also play a role in the facilitation of task completion (see Chapter 3, page 43). In the next phase, students apply their new knowledge in the creation of the products to answer the guiding question(s), and they participate in peer assessment and critique. Based on the feedback received, learners undertake revisions, perhaps going back to Phase 2 to gather more data and/or to revisit concepts for a more in-depth understanding. The final phase involves the presentation of the resulting, revised ensembles (and embedded answers to the driving question[s]) to audiences beyond the classroom. These two phases involve all the knowledge processes and five metafunctions. In Figure 4.2, I offer a visual representation of the connections between each PBL phase and *L-by-D*'s epistemic moves and metafunctions.

To illustrate what PBL grounded in *L-by-D* might look like in the L2 classroom, I present a practical example in Table 4.2. The project described is included in the PBL manual developed by PBLWorks (2021, p. 63) for elementary school teachers. I have adapted it for L2 instruction.

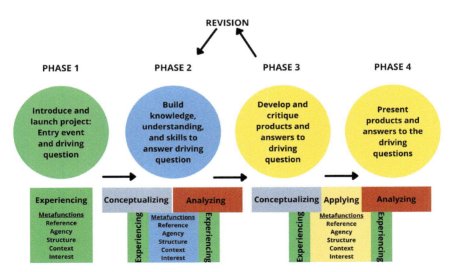

Figure 4.2 Relationship between project-based learning's instructional phases and *Learning by Design*'s knowledge processes and metafunctions.

Table 4.2 Sample Project Grounded in *Learning by Design*

Driving question	What makes someone a community hero?
Community and target cultural focus	Local (or state) Latinx community; project related to Hispanic Heritage Month
Target language	Spanish
Educational setting	Linguistic foci: Terminology related to professions, present tense, adjectives Dual language program for grades 4–6 in the state of Texas
Project summary	Students work with multimodal texts in the L1 and L2 about well-known figures who have worked in different ways to make their communities better (e.g., Emma Tenayuca, Tomás Rivera, Pat Mora, José de la Luz Sáenz, etc.). Sample texts: • Children's books (e.g., *Soldier for Equality* by Duncan Tonatiuh; *Tomás y la señora de la biblioteca* by Pat Mora; *That's not Fair!/¡No es justo! Emma Tenayuca's Struggle for Justice/La lucha de Emma Tenayuca por la justicia* by Carmen Tafolla and Sharyll Tenayuca) • Videos • Art pieces Students also talk about people in their own lives and local communities that they have seen working to improve conditions locally. These people might be their family members, teachers, neighbors, or others. Students work together, as a class and in groups, to create a shared set of characteristics for a community hero. Then each student chooses (with support from the teacher) one community (local or state-wise) Latinx hero on which to focus. Each student produces a multimodal poster or collage to create a portrait of the hero. Learners also write a paragraph in the L2 to explain who the hero is and how this person contributes to their community. The multimodal products and accompanying paragraph are exhibited in a school display titled "Gallery of Local Heroes/Galería de héroes locales"

(*Continued*)

Table 4.2 Continued

Phase	Activities

Phase #1. Launch project: Entry event and driving question
Experiencing the Known
Experiencing the New
 	
Modes of Communication:
• Interpersonal
• Presentational
• Interpretive
	1. **Thematic and personal connections: Brainstorming, show-and-tell, Think-Pair-Share**
	• Students present their favorite super heroes or people they consider heroes to the class. This presentation can include:
	  • A photograph or image of the hero
	  • A short oral explanation (in the L2 or both, the L1 and L2) in which students explain who the person is and why they are their heroes
	• After the presentations, students begin to establish an initial definition of a hero. This can be done as a whole class (brainstorming) or in pairs or groups (Think-Pair-Share)
	2. **L2 teacher introduces project and driving question**
	Students are provided with information about work expectations, expected outcomes and results, project length, milestones, etc., as well as with detailed instructions

Phase #2. Build knowledge, understanding, and skills to answer driving question
Experiencing the New
Conceptualizing by Naming
Conceptualizing with Theory
Analyzing Functionally
Analyzing Critically
 	
Modes of Communication:
• Interpretive
• Interpersonal
	1. Students work with a variety of multimodal texts chosen by the instructor. They focus on content, but they also gather information about the individuals' actions and personal characteristics. Through activities such as concept organizers, cross-classification, mind maps, comparison charts, Venn diagrams, etc., they discover:
	• How heroes are defined based on the analysis of portrayals in multimodal ensembles:
	• What semiotic resources are used to provide evidence of heroic actions
	• What qualities are highlighted and how it is done
	  • L2 linguistic features (adjectives; descriptive and action verbs in the present tense)
	  • Visual and gestural modes (color, foregrounding, gestures, etc.)
	2. Based on their work, students revise their original characterization of heroes, and they develop a list of resources they can use to describe heroes. They also identify and discuss examples of people in their lives and communities who strive to improve conditions at the local (or state) level

Genre- and Project-Based Instruction 89

Phase #3. Develop and critique products and answers to the driving question

Applying Appropriately
Applying Creatively
Experiencing the New
Conceptualizing
Analyzing

Modes of Communication:
- Presentational
- Interpersonal
- Interpretive

1. Students develop the first drafts of their products and participate in peer reviews with the members of their groups. Instructors also assess learners' work in terms of products and group work (formative assessment). Students might also assess their work as a group (individual accountability and/or group processing; see page 63 in Chapter 3)
2. Students incorporate the feedback received from their peers and instructor and revise their products. If needed, they review the conceptualizations and analysis from work in **Phase #2**
3. Students present their revised products to their peers and prepare for public presentations, taking into account project expectations and intended audience; they also focus on pose, gestures, clothes, register. Students prepare for possible questions from the audience.
4. Students undertake further revisions (products and presentation) based on peer and instructor feedback

Phase #4. Present products and answers to the driving question

Experiencing
Conceptualizing
Analyzing
Applying Appropriately
Applying Creatively

Modes of Communication:
- Interpretive
- Presentational
- Interpersonal

1. Conceptualization and analysis of exhibits:
   - Based on multimodal examples, instructor and students explore the characteristics of exhibits and define them:
     - Purpose
     - Type of organization and reasons behind specific organizational patterns
   - Instructor and students decide how their exhibit ("*Gallery of Local Heroes/Galería de héroes locales*") will be organized, and they develop a rationale for their choice
2. Instructor and students set up the display in the school halls
3. Students present their work to parents and other guests (e.g., school administrators, community leaders, etc.): They stand by their products and answer questions from their audience in the L2 and L1
4. After the exhibit, the instructor and students reflect on their work in the project and the presentation of their products and group work

Adapted from "Project Based Learning Handbook for Elementary School" by PBLWorks, 2021, p. 63.

Summary

In this chapter, I introduced two pedagogical models, *genre-based instruction* and *project-based learning*, that are connected both theoretically and pedagogically with *L-by-D*. I described both approaches, and I offered information about their implementation grounded in *L-by-D* in L2 classes. In the next chapter, I will introduce examples of L2 tasks for diverse educational settings. All the sample activities will be guided by *L-by-D*.

Note

1 Web addresses: Center for Open Educational Resources and Language Learning: https://www.coerll.utexas.edu/coerll/; Open Language Resource Center: http://olrc.ku.edu/.

References

Callaghan, M., & Rothery, J. (1988). *Teaching factual writing: A genre based approach.* NSW Department of Education.

Cope, B., & Kalantzis, M. (2015). The things you do to know: An introduction to the pedagogy of multiliteracies. In B. Cope & M. Kalantzis (Eds.), *A pedagogy of multiliteracies: Learning by Design* (pp. 1–36). Palgrave Macmillan.

Cope, B., & Kalantzis, M. (2020). *Making sense: Reference, agency, and structure in a grammar of multimodal meaning.* Cambridge University Press.

Cope, B., Kalantzis, M., & Tzirides, A. O. (Forthcoming). Meaning without borders: From translanguaging to transposition in the era of digitally-mediated multimodal meaning. In K. K. Grohmann (Ed.), *Multifaceted multilingualism* (pp. 1–33). John Benjamins.

Derewianka, B. (1990). *Exploring how texts work.* Primary English Teaching Association.

Feez, S. (1998). *Text-based syllabus design.* McQuarie University/AMES.

Glisan, E. W., & Donato, R. (2021). *Enacting the work of language instruction: High-leverage teaching practices* (Vol. 2). ACTFL.

Halliday, M. A. K. (1985). *An introduction to functional grammar.* Edward Arnold.

Halliday, M. A. K., & Hasan, R. (1985). *Language, context, and text: Aspects of language in a social-semiotic perspective.* Oxford University Press.

Hyland, K. (2014). *Genre and second language writing.* The University of Michigan Press.

Kalantzis, M., & Cope, B. (2012). *New learning: Elements of a science of education.* Cambridge University Press.

Kalantzis, M., & Cope, B. (2022). After language: A grammar of multiform transposition. In C. Lütge (Ed.), *Foreign language learning in the digital age: Theory and pedagogy for developing literacies* (pp. 34–64). Routledge.

Kalantzis, M., Cope, B., Chan, E., & Dalley-Trim, L. (2016). *Literacies* (2nd ed.). Cambridge University Press.

Kalantzis, M., Cope, B., & the Learning by Design Project Group. (2005). *Learning by Design.* Victorian Schools Innovation Commission and Common Ground Publishing.

Kalantzis, M., Cope, B., & Zapata, G. C. (2019). *Las alfabetizaciones múltiples: Teoría y práctica.* Octaedro.

Martin, J. R. (1986). *Writing to mean: Teaching genres across the curriculum.* Applied Linguistics Association of Australia.

Martin, J. R. (1997). Analyzing genre: Functional parameters. In F. Christie & J. R. Martin (Eds.), *Genres and institutions: Social processes in the workplace and school* (pp. 3–39). Cassell Academic.

Martin, J. R. (2013). Systemic functional linguistics. In M. R. Hawkins (Ed.), *Framing languages and literacies: Socially situated views and perspectives* (pp. 24–50). Routledge.

Moll, L. C., Amanti, C., Neff, D., & Gonzalez, N. (1992). Funds of knowledge for teaching: Using a qualitative approach to connect homes and classrooms. *Theory into Practice, 31*(2), 132–141. https://www.jstor.org/stable/1476399

National Education Association (NEA). (2011). *Preparing 21st century students for a global society: An educator's guide to the "Four Cs"*. https://dl.icdst.org/pdfs/files3/0d3e72e9b873e0ef2ed780bf53a347b4.pdf

Osborn, T. A. (2006). *Teaching world languages for social justice: A sourcebook of principles and practices*. Routledge.

Partnership for 21st Century Skills (P21). (2011). *21st century skills map*. https://www.actfl.org/sites/default/files/resources/21st%20Century%20Skills%20Map-World%20Languages.pdf

PBLWorks. (2021). *Project based learning handbook for elementary schools*. Buck Institute for Education.

Troyan, F. J. (2021a). Genres in contextualized world language assessment and learning. In F. J. Troyan (Ed.), *Genre in world education: Contextualized assessment and learning* (pp. 2–31). Routledge.

Troyan, F. J. (Ed.) (2021b). *Genre in world education: Contextualized assessment and learning*. Routledge.

UDL-IRN. (2011). *UDL in the instructional process (version 1.0.)*. UDL-IRN. https://www.learningdesigned.org/sites/default/files/UDL%20Instructional%20Planning%20Process.pdf

5 Sample Second Language Tasks Grounded in Learning by Design

This chapter offers examples of L2 tasks that can be adapted for use in different educational contexts. All activities originate in evidence-based practices. Some were presented in studies carried out by scholars in the fields of L2 learning and L1 literacy education, while others have been proposed by organizations such as the National Education Association and Learning for Justice. The samples are described in general terms. Therefore, before incorporating them into their practice, teachers will need to adapt them according to their school's/institution's discipline-specific and L2 standards (e.g., ACTFL's *World-Readiness Standards for Foreign Language Learning* [National Standards in Foreign Language Education Project, 2015]), curricular outcomes, and learners' academic and personal needs. Additionally, it is essential that L2 instructors enact the pedagogical moves discussed in Chapters 3 and 4 (see pages 39 and 75).

My main objective in this chapter is to provide L2 practitioners with ideas that they can adopt to facilitate their students' meaningful and purposeful L2 use (Glisan & Donato, 2021), as well as their growth as multiliterate people (the activities below engage learners in the critical analysis and production of multimodal L2 artifacts). Embedded in all tasks are the tenets of *Learning by Design*'s (*L-by-D*) reflexive pedagogy and transformative curriculum (Kalantzis & Cope, 2012; Kalantzis et al. 2005, 2016, 2019), *Universal Design for Learning*'s principles and recommended practices (Tobin & Behling, 2018; UDL-IRN, 2011), and the vision of L2 teaching and learning I discussed in Chapter 2 (also, see Chapters 1 and 3). In a word, it is my hope that the incorporation of the suggested pedagogical interventions will allow students to

- Understand the influence of increasing social, cultural, and linguistic diversity on literacy and literate practices;
- Investigate how literacy and literate practices operate in a variety of contexts;
- Develop understandings about and application of critical literacy;
- Use literacy and literate practices in socially, culturally, and linguistically diverse contexts;
- Develop understandings about how literate practices relate to social, cultural, political, economic, and ideological aspects of society;

DOI: 10.4324/9781003106258-5

- [Work with and create] texts that use individual and combined semiotic systems [including the L2]; [and]
- [Be] able to use a range of texts and technologies.

(Anstey & Bull, 2006, p. 57)

Before I present the instructional samples, in Table 5.1, I offer a summary of recommended activity types for each of *L-by-D*'s knowledge processes. The activities can be combined with the questions and multimodal analysis foci in Appendix A.

Additionally, in Appendix C, I provide questions and categories for the assessment of the multimodal artifacts (i.e., combining the L2 with other semiotic resources) that could result from learners' work with the tasks in this chapter. My suggestions make reference to the depth of *content* development, as well as the possible semiotic systems students could resort to and the level of *cohesion* that could be achieved through their combination. Both *content* and *cohesion* were chosen as the main assessment features based on existing literature (e.g., Hung et al., 2013; Levy & Kimber, 2009). *Content* indicates the depth and "quality of information contained within the text—its relevance, potency, accuracy, and organization," while *cohesion* describes "the way in which the various elements of the text are drawn together to achieve unity ... The degree of success or effectiveness ... is linked to the user's cognitive ability, technological facility, and aesthetic sense" (Levy & Kimber, p. 493). L2 instructors can modify the proposed questions and categories to address their students' needs and to render them compatible with product content, and they can combine them with some of the rubrics introduced in Chapter 3 (e.g., see pages 51, 59, and 63–66).

1. Community Development: Talk to an Expert

This task allows L2 teachers to integrate socially relevant issues into the L2 classroom, and to involve students with interdisciplinary projects, which makes it ideal for learning across the curriculum or for teaching the L2 for specific purposes. L2 instructors can choose a topic in one of the areas within Osborn's (2006) four critical inquiry pillars (i.e., identity, social architecture, language choices, and activism; see page 26), and they can collaborate with colleagues in other disciplines (e.g., history, economics, education) who might contribute with specialized knowledge on the area of focus. In the first part of the project, learners are expected to use the target language to communicate with an expert (who also speaks the L2) to gather information about issues connected to the chosen topic in relation to international or local (L2) communities. The information gathered is then summarized and used for the proposal of possible solutions.

Instructional Information and Guidance (Task Idea Inspired by NEA, 2011, p. 15)

Educational context: Appropriate for all ages (topics will be chosen according to learners' age).

94 Sample Second Language Tasks

Table 5.1 Activities for *Learning by Design*'s Knowledge Processes

Knowledge Processes	Activities
Experiencing *Recall, describe,* *discuss, explore,* *identify,* *investigate,* *listen to,* *read, record,* *research, view*	• Brainstorming • Class survey • Data charts • Graffiti board (http://bit.ly/GraffitiBoardsAct) • Guided comprehension and interpretation (through questions) • Hot potato (ideas/experiences/previous knowledge in connection to topic) (http://bit.ly/HotPotatoAct) • Inner/outer circles (http://bit.ly/InnerOurterCircles) • Jigsaw (http://bit.ly/JigsawAct) • Mix-pair-share (http://bit.ly/MixPairShare) • People/concept bingo • Picture-associated ideas • Show-and-tell • Think-pair-share (http://bit.ly/ThinkPairShareAct) • Word association • Word splash (http://bit.ly/WordSplashAct)
Conceptualizing *Categorize,* *compare,* *contrast,* *define, describe,* *generalize,* *hypothesize,* *identify,* *understand*	• Attribute listing organizer • Bundling • Concept map • Diorama • Double bubble map • Fishbone • Graphic outline • Jigsaw • Mix-pair-share • Semantic web • Think board • Venn diagram
Analyzing *Analyze, assess,* *compare,* *contrast,* *deduce, discuss,* *interpret, judge,* *rate, synthesize*	• Concept map • Cross-impact matrix • Debates • Effect wheel • Flow chart • Guided inference (through questions) • Inner/outer circles • Reflection sheets • Six thinking hats (http://bit.ly/SixThinkingHatsAct) • SWOT analysis (http://bit.ly/SWOTAnalysisAct) • Team stand-n-share • Venn diagram

(*Continued*)

Table 5.1 Continued

Knowledge Processes	Activities
Applying *Apply, assess, compile, construct, demonstrate, design, illustrate, investigate, plan, synthesize*	• Peer reviews • Peer assessment • Advertising campaign • Autobiographies (e.g., identity texts, personal narratives, etc.) • Brochure • Comics • Digital poster • Digital story • Documentary • Drama/play/visual representation • Exhibit • Infographics • Multimedia presentation • Movie • Oral presentation • PowerPoint presentation • Poetry • Photo journal • Song lyrics • Text combining different genres • Website • Written text belonging to a specific genre See examples in this chapter.

Adapted from "Learning by Design," by Lanyon Cluster of Schools (n.d.), available at https://newlearningonline.com/_uploads/lanyon_toolkit.pdf.

L2 performance level: Intermediate or advanced. The task could be used with novice (beginning) students, but it would have to be simplified (e.g., the interaction with the expert would be in the L1).

Modes of communication: Interpersonal, interpretive, and presentational (written, oral, and/or multimodal).

Project length: Average (three to five weeks). This task can be structured as an instructional unit.

Possible topics:
- The environment (e.g., climate change, displacement caused by environmental problems, renewable sources of energy, etc.)
- Health care (e.g., linguistic barriers, lack of services, effects of COVID, etc.)
- Education (inclusion and equity, first-generation students, etc.)
- Migrant workers
- Immigration
- Inclusive language

L2 focus: Terminology related to specific topic; present tense; commands/modals; impersonal or passive constructions (to propose solutions).

Student organization: Groups.
Pedagogical sequence:
- **Phase 1. Launch project**
  Experiencing the known
  Meaning-making metafunctions of focus: Reference (what), agency (who), structure (how), context (when/where—sociocultural/sociohistorical), and interest (why/for whom)
  - The L2 instructor introduces the topic of focus, eliciting students' previous knowledge and personal experiences. For example, the instructor can use newspaper headlines, word clouds, or photos to trigger ideas and activate schemata.
  - Once learners are situated within the topic, the teacher provides information about the expert with whom students will be interacting.
  - The instructor also presents the driving question, project calendar, division of labor, outcomes, and expected results.
  - Students are divided into groups, and they are asked to create five or six questions for the expert. Possible foci:
    - Aspects of the issue to be discussed
    - Population it affects: Location, age, race/ethnicity, gender
    - Causes
    - Consequences
    - Socioeconomic, sociocultural, and/or political effects
    - Need for change
  - Each group presents their questions, and the class votes on the ones to ask the expert. However, each group should have the opportunity to contribute with at least one question.
  - Learners prepare for the interaction with the expert with their instructor's guidance (e.g., focus on format, register, non-verbal language, etc.).
  - Depending on learners' level of L2 performance and identities (i.e., bilingual/multilingual bicultural/multicultural), instructors can allow the use of both the L1 and L2.
- **Phase 2. Build knowledge, understanding, and skills**
  Experiencing the new, conceptualizing, analyzing
  Meaning-making metafunctions of focus: Reference (what), agency (who), context (when/where—sociocultural/sociohistorical), and interest (why/for whom)
  - Students interact with the expert face-to-face or virtually. Representatives from each group ask the questions resulting from work in **Phase 1**. All learners take down notes.
  - Students work in their groups, and they summarize the information provided by the expert (each member contributes with their notes). For example, they categorize the information, and make connections among different aspects of the issue discussed by the expert (e.g., in terms of meaning, community, the expert's own work and positionality). Summaries for each question should not be longer than three

sentences, or they can be formatted as charts, tables, or graphs (e.g., spider map, fishbone).
- Each group posts their summaries in the discussion board of the class's Learning Management System (LMS; e.g., Canvas, Blackboard, etc.) or collaborative canvas (e.g., Milanote, Jamboard, or Padlet; Appendix B).

- **Phase 3. Develop and critique products**
  Applying appropriately
  Meaning-making metafunctions of focus: Reference (what), agency (who), structure (how), context (when/where—sociocultural/sociohistorical), and interest (why/for whom)
  - Students use the class's summaries on the information provided by the expert to develop their project.
    - Option #1:
      - If the expert has focused on international L2 communities, students will explore how the issues discussed affect their local community(ies). The expected outcome will be a multimodal summary (e.g., a digital presentation) comparing the international and local communities in connection with the issues addressed by the expert. The presentation will also include a proposal for possible solutions. To complete this task, learners will be expected to provide more data and make reference to existing organizations/groups (e.g., how they could contribute to the enactment of the proposed actions).
    - Option #2:
      - If the expert has focused on local (L2) communities, learners will develop a multimodal proposal (e.g., a digital presentation) with possible solutions to the issues discussed. The solutions will have to be comprehensive, and based on existing organizations and/or possible changes to policies. This option might require more research on students' part.
  - Important: For either option, teachers will need to provide students with clear guidelines for the development of their artifacts, including:
    - Data sources (e.g., websites to which learners can resort to carry out the needed research).
    - Specific instructions and guidance on the tools to be used for the development of their texts (e.g., PowerPoint or web-based platforms such as Prezi or Google Slides; Appendix B) and the expected structure and content.
  - Once each group completes the first draft of their work (e.g., presentation's written parts + links to possible visual and multimodal resources), they share it with another group. This first draft can also be shared in the class's LMS or collaborative canvas.
  - Groups offer and receive feedback. Instructors can also provide suggestions.
  - Based on the feedback received, groups revise their work. If needed, they revisit concepts summarized in **Phase 2**.

- **Phase 4. Present products**
Applying appropriately and creatively
Meaning-making metafunctions of focus: Reference (what), agency (who), structure (how), context (when/where—sociocultural/sociohistorical), and interest (why/for whom)
  - Students combine all semiotic elements and make their texts public.
  - All projects are unveiled in a public symposium. The expert is invited, as well as parents, members of the L2 community in their school/institution, and/or representatives from local (L2) communities, etc. For example, a panel of experts can be invited to comment on the presentations, and engage in discussions with students and audience.
  - Groups present their projects. Each member should have a role in the presentation.
  - The presentations are previously discussed and rehearsed with the instructor and classmates. Learners receive feedback, and they revise their work before the public event.
  - Also, students can share their proposed solutions with local authorities, and/or community members and organizations.

2. Endangered, Threatened, or Vulnerable Flora and Fauna: Expository Texts and Infographics

The National Education Association (NEA, 2011) proposes this task as the possible basis for a telecollaboration initiative in which L2 students in the United States work with learners who speak the target language in another country. However, the project can also be implemented in L2 classes independent of the international pedagogical component. The thematic focus is endangered, threatened, or vulnerable flora and/or fauna in local and/or target-language geographical regions. Learners use the L2 and other semiotic resources to create an expository infographic on an endangered, threatened, or vulnerable animal or plant in their local area or state.[1] As with the project presented in #1 "Community Development: Talk to an Expert," this instructional example could involve the interdisciplinary collaboration of L2 instructors with colleagues in animal, agricultural, botanical, and/or environmental sciences, and, thus, it is ideal for learning across the curriculum or L2 teaching for specific purposes. Additionally, it allows for a focus on a socially relevant issue, and the products that result from students' work could become open materials to be used for further educational purposes (e.g., as L2 instructional materials and/or information sources for the general public).[2]

Learners' work in this task can be grounded in genre-based instruction (GBI; see Chapter 4). Since students use the L2 to develop expository infographics, the model texts belong to the same genres. Krum (2014, p. 6) defines infographics as multimodal texts "that combine data visualizations, illustrations, text, and images together into a format" that conveys a comprehensive and cohesive message. Because of their communicative versatility, these types of ensembles can reflect the characteristics of a variety of genres. In this example, the focus is on the provision of information on endangered, threatened, or vulnerable species, and, therefore, the genre of interest is exposition. At the same time, the creation of infographics also entails students' engagement with another genre, the infographics themselves; i.e., the communicatively appropriate, in terms of rhetorical organization and meaning-making elements, and socially relevant melding of at least three semiotic systems: Linguistic, visual, and spatial (Dunlap & Lowenthal, 2016; Krishnan et al., 2020).

Infographics are ideal ensembles for L2 classes for a variety of reasons. First, they can be used to incorporate a variety of topics into instruction, and they can be easily connected to learners' lifeworlds, communities, and personal and academic needs (e.g., see Dyjur et al., 2021; Krishnan et al., 2020; Maamuujav et al., 2020). Second, they allow students to analyze how different modalities contribute to the meaning of a text, as well as what role each semiotic element plays in meaning-making, which promotes their growth as multiliterate persons (see the introduction to this chapter). Third, since the use of linguistic resources can vary, infographics can cater to learners with diverse levels of L2 performance. Finally, students' interaction with and cooperative creation of these types of texts can result in the development of their Four Cs—critical thinking and problem solving, communication, collaboration, and creativity and innovation (Matrix & Hodson, 2014; NEA, 2011; P21, 2011).

Instructional Information and Guidance (Task Idea Inspired by NEA, 2011, p. 20)

Educational context: Appropriate for all ages; however, the topic is ideal for elementary- and middle-school students. It could also work in high school and university classes with a more in-depth scientific/interdisciplinary focus (e.g., L2 for specific purposes).
L2 performance level: Novice (beginning), intermediate, or advanced.
Modes of communication: Interpersonal, interpretive, and presentational (multimodal).
Project length: Average (three to five weeks). This task can be structured as an instructional unit.
L2 focus: Terminology related to animals (e.g., characteristics, habitats, etc.) and environmental issues connected to endangered species; descriptive vocabulary; present tense; passive voice; descriptive verbs.
Student organization: Pairs and groups.
Pedagogical sequence:
- **Setting the context**
  Experiencing, analyzing critically
  Meaning-making metafunctions of focus: Reference (what), agency (who), context (when/where—sociocultural/sociohistorical), and interest (why/for whom)

- Students prepare a short multimodal (including the L2), video presentation (e.g., in Flipgrid; see Appendix B) on their favorite animal/plant. Elements to be included:
  - At least a photo or image of the animal/plant of focus
  - A short description:
    - Type of animal/plant
    - Habitat/area of growth
    - Feeding habits/growth needs
    - How it contributes to the environment
- Teachers can provide learners with guidance on information sources (i.e., where data and images can be found).
- Learners watch their peers' presentations: Students are organized in groups, and are assigned the presentations prepared by their group mates. Also, learners investigate what it means for an animal/plant to be *endangered*, *threatened*, or *vulnerable*.
- In class, students work in their groups, and they compare their definitions of *endangered*, *threatened*, and *vulnerable*. They also discuss whether any of the group's animals/plants can be classified in that way and why this is the case.
- Each group shares their ideas with the rest of the class, and the class as a whole develops common definitions for the three terms in the L2.

Experiencing the new, analyzing critically

Meaning-making metafunctions of focus: Reference (what), agency (who), context (when/where—sociocultural/sociohistorical), and interest (why/for whom)

- Teachers choose infographics related to animals in the L1 and L2. The complexity of the texts chosen will depend on students' age and level of L2 performance.[3]
- The analysis work is structured as a jigsaw activity. Each group is assigned an L1 and an L2 infographic. Students analyze their texts for meaning and to discover the meaning-maker's motivation and purpose. The teacher provides questions for analysis (for sample questions, see Table 4.1 on page 80, and Appendix A).
- Once all groups have finished their work, members of each group form new groups, and share the results of their work. The new groups start generalizing their ideas in connection to the message conveyed in the texts, intended audience, and semiotic resources used. These generalizations are shared with other groups in the class's LMS or collaborative digital canvas (e.g., Milanote, Jamboard, or Padlet; Appendix B).

- **Modeling and deconstructing the text**

  Conceptualizing

  Meaning-making metafunctions of focus: Reference (what), agency (who), and structure (how)
  - Based on the ideas posted in the *setting the context* stage, the class as a whole develops definitions for both expository texts and infographics,

including the type of information they communicate, objectives, rhetorical organization, and semiotic elements that are used for meaning-making.

Analyzing

Meaning-making metafunctions of focus: Reference (what), agency (who), structure (how), context (when/where—sociocultural/sociohistorical), and interest (why/for whom)

- The initial groups get together once more, and students work with the L2 infographic example they analyzed for meaning and structure.
- Learners identify the relationship among:
  - Semiotic elements (linguistic, visual, spatial; see Appendix A for possible foci).
  - Message conveyed.
  - Purpose of the text (including meaning-maker's motivation).
  - Social context in which it is used (including intended audience).
- **Joint construction of the text**

  Applying appropriately

  Meaning-making metafunctions of focus: Reference (what), agency (who), structure (how), context (when/where—sociocultural/sociohistorical), and interest (why/for whom)
  - Learners work in pairs within their group. Each pair has to rewrite the model text (or a novel, but similar one) to improve it or to add other information that they deem relevant.
  - Once students have modified their infographics, they participate in oral peer reviews within their group:
    - They show the reviewers their work, explaining what changes they have made to the original text. Each pair justifies their creative choices.
    - Peers provide feedback, and the meaning-makers take down notes.
    - Based on the feedback received, each pair revises their work.
  - The pairs then collaborate once more, and they apply their separate visions in the development of a new version of the infographic.
  - Each group's new infographic(s) is(are) displayed in the class's LMS or collaborative canvas for later use in the *text comparison* stage.
- **Independent construction of the text**

  Applying appropriately and creatively

  Meaning-making metafunctions of focus: Reference (what), agency (who), structure (how), context (when/where—sociocultural/sociohistorical), and interest (why/for whom)
  - Students develop individual infographics on the topic of the project. Information to be included:
  - At least a photo or image of the animal/plant of focus.
  - A short description:
    - Name (popular and scientific).
    - Habitat/area of growth (if possible, a map should be provided).

- Status: Endangered, threatened, or vulnerable.
- Reasons that contribute to its status.
- Possible actions to protect the animal/plant.
- The complexity and length of the infographic will depend on students' age and level of L2 performance.
- Important: Instructors must offer guidance in connection to:
    - Sources of information (i.e., where students can find evidence-based data on the chosen animal/plant).
    - Possible digital tools (e.g., Canva, Snappa, Venngage, or Visme; Appendix B), and how to use them.
    - Sources for multimodal elements such as icons and images (e.g., Creative Commons Search, Flaticon, Noun Project, Unsplash; Appendix B). In order for their work to be shared for future use, students will need to use **open resources**, and provide their work with **an open license**. To learn more about this topic, instructors and students are encouraged to consult the information offered by **Creative Commons** on **licenses and attributions for open resources**.[4]
- Learners develop their first drafts: Text + collection of other semiotic elements to be used (e.g., links to the resources and/or small versions of them). Once they have finished, students participate in the following collaborative activities:
    1. They post their work in the same collaborative canvas (or LMS) used in previous stages.
    2. They provide and receive feedback, working with partners they have not worked with before. Instructors also offer comments.
    3. Based on the feedback received, learners revise their work, and develop the multimodal version of the infographic, sharing it with their teacher.
- Instructors disseminate their students' work. For example, they can publish their learners' artifacts on a website with a Creative Commons license or in an OER repository (for a list of possible options, see the open appendix in Blyth and Thoms, 2021 [a link to this document is provided in the reference section of this chapter]). Also, the infographics can be shared with interest groups in L2 teachers' organizations such as ACTFL or with other interested parties.
- **Text comparison**
  Experiencing the new, conceptualizing, analyzing
  Meaning-making metafunctions of focus: Reference (what), agency (who), structure (how), context (when/where—sociocultural/sociohistorical), and interest (why/for whom)
    - Possible options (for other activities, see Table 4.1 on page 80):
        - Students compare the original model infographics with the new versions created by the groups (see *joint construction* stage) in terms of meaning and structure. Learners study the class's info-

graphics, and they make a list of observed changes. Then, as a class, students reflect on how the new designs convey similar or different messages in comparison with the originals, and what that says about multimodal meaning-making and meaning-makers' motivations. Learners also consider intended audience (e.g., has it changed? If so, how? Why?).
- Learners transduce their infographics. *Transduction* is defined by Kress (2010, p. 125) as "the process of moving meaning-material from one mode to another—[e.g.,] from speech to image; from writing to film … [and it] entails a re-articulation of meaning from the entities of one mode into the entities of the new mode." For example, students can transduce their infographics into written (linguistic) expository texts, or into oral presentations for different audiences (e.g., in terms of age). Once learners have completed the task, the class can reflect on what the transduction process entails and on the effectiveness of different semiotic systems for meaning-making. Also, the reflection can focus on the L2 (e.g., changes in register and/or dialect that are needed to create artifacts for different audiences).

3. Fan Fiction

Fan fiction (or *fanfic*) can be characterized as a social practice that results in "original works of fiction based on forms of popular media such as television, movies, books, music, and video games" (Black, 2005, p. 118). Fanfic meaning-makers usually belong to a digital community of fans of a particular fictional story (e.g., *Harry Potter*), and publish their stories in online repositories such as Wattpad or FanFiction.net (Appendix B). To create their work, authors can focus on specific characters belonging to the known narrative, and can create new versions by "remix[ing] media, combin[ing] … genre conventions and us[ing] multiple languages and cultural themes" (Thorne, 2013, p. 203). In L2 learning, existing research (e.g., Black, 2005, 2006; Sauro & Sundmark, 2016) has shown that participation in this type of meaning-making activity can offer students the opportunity to use the L2 authentically and creatively, and can result in the development of their writing (and sometimes multimodal) skills. Additionally, if students are part of online fanfic communities, they can use the L2 to interact with other community members (interpersonal mode of communication), they can feel legitimized as L2 users, and they can receive authentic feedback from fellow fanfic participants, all of which can contribute to their linguistic as well as intercultural growth (Black, 2008).

I believe the most effective way of incorporating fanfiction tasks in L2 classrooms is GBI (see Chapter 4). For example, L2 instructors can create a fanfic community within their class (or, if possible, with other classes in their language program), and they can introduce students to the genre (and the one embedded in it, narrative) enacting GBI's pedagogical moves. In order to do so, the first step is to find sample model texts in the target language. Three excellent sources are Archive of Our Own, FanFiction.net, and Wattpad (see Appendix B). I recommend choosing texts connected to popular stories that the particular student population might know (e.g., *The Lord of the Rings*, *Bleach* [anime], *Naruto* [manga], etc.). Text choice should be guided by learners' age, identities, and lifeworlds, and not by instructors' preference. Once students have worked with GBI, and they have produced their fanfic texts, they can publish them on a fan fiction platform, and a new journey of L2 use begins.

Instructional Information and Guidance (Task Idea Inspired by Sauro & Sundmark, 2016)

Educational context: High school and university.

L2 performance level: Can be adapted to all levels—novice (beginning), intermediate, or advanced.

Modes of communication: Interpersonal, interpretive, and presentational (written and/or multimodal).

Project length: Average (three to five weeks). The fanfic task can be structured as an instructional unit.

L2 focus: Present or past tenses (depending on level of L2 performance); action verbs; verbs and terms to express verbal and mental processes; time connectors; dialogues (tense changes, conventions); descriptive verbs; adjectives; nouns.

Student organization: Groups.

Pedagogical sequence:

- **Setting the context**

  Experiencing, analyzing critically

  Meaning-making metafunctions of focus: Reference (what), agency (who), context (when/where—sociocultural/sociohistorical), and interest (why/for whom)

  - Before the start of the pedagogical sequence, students are asked to prepare a short oral (or multimodal) presentation on their favorite book, movie, or videogame. Options for presentation:
    - A pre-recorded video (e.g., Flipgrid, Animoto, YouTube; Appendix B) that can be posted in the class's LMS.
    - An oral in-class presentation (e.g., PowerPoint, Prezi, or Google Slides; Appendix B) with multimodal features (e.g., images, excerpts from scenes, etc.).
  - Information to include:
    - Title of original story source and media classification (e.g., movie, videogame).
    - Summary of the plot and intended audience.
    - Data about favorite character(s) (no more than two): Who they are, what they are like, what role they play in the story, what is special about them. Students need to explain their character choices.

- Learners also explain why the piece chosen is their favorite book, movie, or videogame.
- After the presentations, the instructor guides students in the discussion of fanfiction. With instructor's guidance, students talk about what they know about fanfic sites. If some learners already participate in this social practice, they can collaborate with the teacher to guide the class discussion.
- Students write ideas about possible characteristics of fanfictions (e.g., objective, audience, where it is published, meaning-makers' motivation).
- Depending on learners' level of L2 performance and identities (i.e., bilingual/multilingual bicultural/multicultural), instructors can allow the use of both the L1 and L2.

Experiencing the new, analyzing critically

Meaning-making metafunctions of focus: Reference (what), agency (who), context (when/where—sociocultural/sociohistorical), and interest (why/for whom)

- Students analyze the model fanfic text(s) for meaning and to discover the meaning-maker's motivation and purpose. The teacher provides questions for analysis (for sample questions, see Table 4.1 on page 80 and Appendix A).

- **Modeling and deconstructing the text**

Meaning-making metafunctions of focus: Reference (what), agency (who), structure (how), context (when/where—sociocultural/sociohistorical), and interest (why/for whom)

Conceptualizing

- Students continue working with the model text(s), but they now focus on text structure. They explore what role each part of the text plays, and how each part contributes to the social purpose of the ensemble as a whole.
- Based on this analysis and their work in the *setting the context* stage, learners develop a definition of the fanfic genre (and its embedded narrative nature), including the type of information texts communicate, objectives, semiotic elements that are used for meaning-making, and rhetorical organization.

Analyzing

- Students identify the relationship among:
  - Semiotic elements (e.g., L2 forms used).
  - Message conveyed.
  - Purpose of the text (including meaning-maker's motivation).
  - Social context in which it is used (including intended audience).

- **Joint construction of the text**

Applying appropriately

Meaning-making metafunctions of focus: Reference (what), agency (who), structure (how), context (when/where—sociocultural/sociohistorical), and interest (why/for whom)

- Students work in pairs within their group. Each pair has to rewrite the model text (or a novel, but similar one) to improve it and make it more appealing to fans of the story to which it is connected. Instructors need to ensure that learners know the original story on which the model is based.
- Once learners have finished their work, they participate in peer reviews within their group. To mirror online practices, students can write reviews similar to the ones found in fanfic sites. If teachers decide to incorporate this option, they will need to prepare students to write this type of text (i.e., the reviews will become another curricular element within the pedagogical sequence). Unless this activity is used in an intermediate high/advanced L2 class, I recommend that instructors allow learners to use their L1 when providing feedback, as it will facilitate the successful and expedited completion of the task and the reviews' comprehensiveness.
- Based on the feedback received, each pair revises their work.
- The revised versions are published in the class's LMS, and, anonymously, the class votes to choose the most effective piece.

- **Independent construction of the text**
  Applying appropriately and creatively
  Meaning-making metafunctions of focus: Reference (what), agency (who), structure (how), context (when/where—sociocultural/sociohistorical), and interest (why/for whom)
  - Students develop their written (or multimodal) texts, narrating a story of which their favorite character(s) is(are) part. The length and complexity of the text will depend on the level of L2 performance and educational context.
  - Option #1:
    - Learners publish their stories in the class's LMS, and they receive feedback from two other classmates and the instructor.
  - Option #2:
    - After they have finished their drafts, learners participate in peer reviews within their groups, but with different classmates (i.e., not with their joint construction partners).
  - Based on the feedback received, students revise their work.
  - Learners publish their texts on fanfic sites or on other online platforms (e.g., a class website or a digital anthology in magazine/book form on a publication platform such as issuu or Flipsnack; Appendix B).
  - Also, L2 teachers can organize a public, multimodal display (e.g., written texts + images + QR codes with links to video excerpts of the original story and/or extra information on fanfic) or presentation for other students, L2 community within the school/university, and/or parents.
  - If learners become part of a fan fiction community, they can talk about their experience and/or share any reviews of their work within their group or with the rest of the class.

- **Text comparison**
  Experiencing the new, conceptualizing, analyzing
  Meaning-making metafunctions of focus: Reference (what), agency (who), structure (how), context (when/where—sociocultural/sociohistorical), and interest (why/for whom)
  - Possible options (for other activities, see Table 4.1 on page 80):
    - Within their groups, students compare their joint and individual texts with the model text(s) in terms of meaning and structure. They create a comparison matrix or a Venn diagram, and present it to the rest of the class, highlighting similarities and differences in terms of meaning-making, structure, and semiotic resources.
    - Learners choose one of the stories in their groups, and they create a script for a performance. They perform the script (or parts of it) for the rest of the class.
    - Students assume the identity of their character/one of their characters, and they orally recount their joint or individual story from the character's perspective. Learners then reflect on the differences between writing the story and "living" it through the character's recount.
    - Students storyboard (e.g., with tools such as Canva, Storyboarder, or makeStoryboard; Appendix B) their joint or individual stories to narrate them in visual form, and they reflect on the similarities and differences between the linguistic and visual/gestural modes (e.g., what is gained or lost in the transduction [see page 103]; which modality is more effective and why this is the case).

4. Identity Texts

Identity texts are learner-created artifacts "which can be written, spoken, visual, musical, dramatic, or multimodal combinations, [and] are positive statements that students make about themselves" (Cummins et al., 2005, p. 40). That is, these ensembles are directly related to students' personal experiences and lifeworlds, and therefore, they naturally foster a sense of belonging. Additionally, since the texts are expected to be shared with different audiences (e.g., instructors, family, L2 community), they can have empowering effects "through the positive feedback [they can bring about] and affirmation of [the] self in interaction with these audiences" (Cummins & Early, 2011, p. 3). When developing their work, learners not only use the target language, but they also incorporate other modes of meaning-making into their products (e.g., images, audio, etc.), which can result in their growth as multiliterate meaning-makers. Identity texts are also ideal for cooperative learning, and their "identity-affirming [nature is] likely to increase students' … engagement" in the learning process (Cummins et al., 2015, p. 557).

These instructional benefits have been highlighted in existing studies in Canada (e.g., Cummins, 2006; Cummins et al., 2005, 2015), and, more recently, in the United States. For example, Alessandra Ribota and I (Zapata & Ribota, 2021a) investigated the use of identity texts in required L2 Spanish university classes. Our findings showed that these types of projects can foster belonging and investment, and can also result in the development of students' multiliteracies as well as the Four Cs (NEA, 2011; P21, 2011)—critical thinking and problem solving, communication, collaboration, and creativity and innovation. Additionally, the participants in our study reported beneficial effects for their L2 use in the presentational (writing) and interpretive modes of communication, which made them feel more confident as L2 meaning-makers.

Instructional Information and Guidance (Based on Zapata & Ribota, 2021a)

Educational context: Appropriate for all ages.
L2 performance level: Can be adapted to all levels—novice (beginning), intermediate, or advanced.
Modes of communication: Interpersonal, interpretive, and presentational (written, oral, and/or multimodal).
Project length: Average (three to five weeks) or long (six weeks +), depending on content.
Possible topics:
- Student life: Classes, daily/weekend routines, curricular and extracurricular activities
- Family
- Neighborhood and community
- Favorite celebrations (music, food, activities, etc.)
- Favorite places in the world
- Personal heroes
- Favorite organizations and causes (activism)
- Dream jobs

L2 focus: Terminology related to specific topics; present and past tenses.
Student organization: Groups or pairs.
Pedagogical sequence:
- **Phase 1. Launch project**
  Presentation of driving question, project calendar, division of labor, outcomes, and expected results
  Experiencing the known, conceptualizing, analyzing critically
  Meaning-making metafunctions of focus: Reference (what), agency (who), structure (how), context (when/where—sociocultural/sociohistorical), and interest (why/for whom)
  - Students are divided into groups.

- With instructor's guidance, learners discuss what they know about texts that feature personal profiles (e.g., social media profiles, biographies), focusing on their existing knowledge of the structure of these kinds of texts, information provided in them, and semiotic resources used (e.g., linguistic, visual, spatial). Also, students can talk about the information in their own profiles, considering what elements appear in them and why this is the case (motivation, purpose, and intended audience).
- Depending on learners' level of L2 performance and identities (i.e., bilingual/multilingual bicultural/multicultural), instructors can allow the use of both the L1 and L2.

- **Phase 2. Build knowledge, understanding, and skills to create identity texts**

  Meaning-making metafunctions of focus: Reference (what), agency (who), structure (how), context (when/where—sociocultural/sociohistorical), and interest (why/for whom)

  Experiencing the new, analyzing critically
  - Students are introduced to multimodal digital identity texts in their native and target languages, and they collaboratively compare the semiotic features in these texts to the ideas expressed in *experiencing the known* (**Phase 1**). Even though novice students might not be able to fully understand the L2 texts, they can still focus on visual and spatial semiotic elements, discovering any potential differences in the way in which ideas might be presented in texts produced in different cultures.
  - Focus of discussion (adapted from Anstey & Bull, 2006, pp. 25 and 27; also, see Appendix A):
    - Type of text (paper, electronic, live).
    - Purpose of the text (message it conveys and intended audience) and context in which it is being used (e.g., where it has been published).
    - Semiotic resources employed:
      - Linguistic (oral and written language).
      - Visual (still and/or moving images; use of colors, salience of different images [e.g., size, color, location], viewpoint).
      - Auditory (music and sound effects; use of volume, pitch, and rhythm [e.g., pauses]).
      - Gestural (facial expression and body language; clothing; use of movement and stillness).
      - Spatial (layout and organization of objects and space; use of proximity, direction, and position).
      - Types of information conveyed by each semiotic system.

  Conceptualizing, analyzing
  - Students examine how ideas are organized in the texts and identify patterns (connections between text structure and meaning; i.e., what type of information is conveyed in each part).

- Based on this discussion and work in the previous stage, learners create a definition of identity texts, including the type of information they communicate, objective, semiotic elements that are used for meaning-making, and structure (genre).
- Students identify the relationship among semiotic elements (e.g., L2 forms used), message conveyed, purpose of the text, and social context (including intended audience) in which it is used.
- Learners critically analyze the meaning-makers' motivation and purpose, and how effectively they are conveyed by the chosen semiotic elements. (Adapted from Anstey & Bull, 2006, p. 27.)

- **Phase 3. Develop and critique products**
  Applying appropriately
  Meaning-making metafunctions of focus: Reference (what), agency (who), structure (how), context (when/where—sociocultural/sociohistorical), and interest (why/for whom)
  Different parts of the identity texts can be developed progressively. The stages below can be implemented throughout the project.
  - Students use the L2 to create the written/oral sections of their identity texts. They write the first draft of their texts or scripts (if text is oral). They also compile the multimodal elements (e.g., visual, auditory, gestural, etc.) that will be part of the final version of their artifacts.
  - Learners work collaboratively within their groups in structured peer reviews (see Chapter 3, page 62), and they offer feedback to their group mates. Instructors can also provide suggestions.
  - Based on the feedback received, students revise their work. If needed, they revisit concepts discussed in **Phase 2**.

- **Phase 4. Present products**
  Applying appropriately and creatively
  Meaning-making metafunctions of focus: Reference (what), agency (who), structure (how), context (when/where—sociocultural/sociohistorical), and interest (why/for whom)
  - Students combine all semiotic elements and make their texts public:
    - If the L2 is used orally, the linguistic part and other semiotic resources can result in a Flipgrid, Animoto, or YouTube video (Appendix B). Also, all identity texts in a class can be compiled in a video, and uploaded onto a platform such as YouTube or the class's LMS.
    - If the L2 is written, the textual parts and other multimodal resources (e.g., images, videos, links) can be published as webpages (e.g., in Adobe Spark or Google Sites; Appendix B). Also, all identity texts can be combined, and published as a class digital magazine (e.g., in issuu or Flipsnack; Appendix B).
  - All projects are unveiled in a public presentation (e.g., parents, members of the L2 community in their school/institution, etc.).

- Students prepare a short, oral presentation to introduce their projects. The presentations are previously discussed and rehearsed in class, before the public event. Learners receive feedback from their peers and instructor, and they revise their work.

Other Formats

Graphic Novels/Comics (Based on Danzak, 2011)

A possible variation for identity texts consists of the development of short graphic stories or comics in which students narrate significant personal or family events that have shaped who they are. This type of project is based on the conceptualization of identity as *narrative*; i.e., identity is seen as "comprised of narratives that people create for themselves and others, actively construct[ing] and co-construct[ing] the stories that define them, [which] highlights human agency and the dynamic nature of identity" (Danzak, 2011, p.188). An example of this kind of work is described by Danzak (2011) in her study of 32 English learners in grades 6 and 8 in the United States, who created a graphic novel to tell their or their families' stories of immigration to that country. Working collaboratively in the production of their multimodal artifacts allowed students in Danzak's study to use their L2 (sometimes combined with their L1) meaningfully and purposefully in the interpersonal, interpretive, and presentational modes of communication. Additionally, learners' manipulation and use of diverse semiotic resources (e.g., linguistic, visual, spatial) and digital tools contributed to their growth as multiliterate meaning-makers. Also, the active participation of the learners' families both in the production and presentation of the ensembles resulted in the celebration of students' unique bicultural/bilingual lifeworlds and communities, which fostered belonging and classroom engagement.

The steps described in the previous section can be adapted for the adoption of graphic novels/comics as identity texts in novice, intermediate, and advanced L2 classes. For example, if the focus is immigration, students can work with classic and more recent L1 and L2 model texts such as *Almost American Girl* (Ha, 2020), *American Born Chinese* (Yang, 2006), *The Arrival* (Tan, 2007), or *Travesía: A Migrant Girl's Cross-Border Journey/El viaje de una joven migrante* (Gerster & Dunnett, 2021). As in Danzak's (2011) study, learners first connect to the texts at a personal level, identifying similarities and differences with their own lived experiences (*experiencing*). In the next step, within the *conceptualizing* and *analyzing* knowledge processes, students collaborate to understand graphic novels/comics as genre, focusing on rhetorical structure, semiotic elements (including, of course, the L1 and L2), and meaning-makers' motivation and purpose. Finally, in the *applying* epistemic moves, learners create their stories (e.g., in Storyboarder, makeStoryboard, Comic Life, Pixton, or Make Beliefs Comix; Appendix B), and they participate in peer review activities. Students' artifacts are then presented to parents and/or communities (school and beyond). Danzak believes these types of tasks are powerful because they allow L2 learners to use their "narrative voice, [which] can empower [them] to simultaneously express their identities and advance confidently in their [linguistic and multiliterate] abilities" (p. 196).[5]

Identity Blogs (Based on Mills & Levido, 2011)

Mills and Levido (2011) describe several tasks in which 75 elementary-school students between the ages of 8 and 9 in Australia critically analyzed and developed multimodal texts. One of them was personal blogs. This could be another form that identity texts could take. To guide learners' activities, the teachers who participated in the study created questions for a focus on "issues of audience, purpose, interests, and Internet safety" (p. 83), which children had to consider while working on their texts. For example, students had to bear in mind the following:

- Why am I creating this blog?
- What text features (e.g., words, images, audio) will best suit my purpose?
- Who is my intended audience?
- Who else potentially has access to my blog?
- What information about myself should I share or hide?
- How does my blog build on the contributions of my peers [e.g., through peer reviews or the collaborative analysis carried out in **Phase 2** [see page 109]?
- How do my blog entries show respect for my teacher and others in my class (e.g., manners, language use)?
- What do my blog entries say about people of different ages, occupations, and cultures?
- Whose views have I included or left out? Why?
- Who benefits from my blog? Why?

(Mills & Levido, p. 84)

In their multimodal blogs, the participants in Mills and Levido's (2011) work made reference to topics related to their personal interests (e.g., movies) and aspects of their academic and personal lives, as well as their communities (e.g., some of the children were aboriginal, while others belonged to various racial/ethnic and sociocultural groups). The learners' artifacts were multimodal, and the pedagogical sequence was similar to the one I proposed in the first paragraphs of this section. L2 teachers who might choose to incorporate this identity text format in their classes will need to find personal blogs that they can use as models appropriate for their students' age and L2 needs, and connected to their lifeworlds. Learners can resort to tools such as Canva, Blogger, or Wix (Appendix B) to create their blogs. If working with children, instructors will need to find a secured server where they can post the products created by the class. This, of course, applies to all the instructional options presented in this chapter.

Drama-Based Identity Texts (Based on Yaman Ntelioglou, 2011)

In this modified version of the identity texts task, L2 learners develop scripts to portray significant personal experiences for themselves or their families. This format is ideal for intermediate and advanced learners, in high school or university classrooms or in adult L2 classes (e.g., ESL). For example, like the participants in Yaman Ntelioglou's (2011) and Danzak's (2011) study, students can explore their or their family's immigration stories, and/or aspects of their lives in their new communities. Other possible topics might be those focusing on new events in learners' lives (e.g., first day of classes in a new school/institution). Students develop their scripts, and they read or perform them for their peers and other audiences. Learners also interact with their audience (e.g., peers, teachers, family, members of the L2 community, etc.), and they answer questions from them. Additionally, students can then be asked to reflect on how they felt writing and performing their scripts, either multimodally (e.g., recording a short video in the L1 and/or L2, and using photos from the drama performance to guide their reflections) or in writing. Once the presentations have been finalized, the class can discuss all students' lifeworlds, finding similarities among lived experiences.

Yaman Ntelioglou's (2011) work examined the use of drama-based identity texts in L2 English classes in Canada. Based on the positive results of her study, this researcher advocates the use of this type of pedagogical move in L2 classes, stating that

> through these performed identity texts, using their new language … students [can] express their understandings of their lives in [a] new … context, [and they can bring their] immediate, often urgent experiences of newcomers … (e.g., their first harrowing journeys on public transit, the crushing disappointment of realizing that their qualifications are not recognized) [to] the foreground … These performed identity-texts provide a space for multimodal representations of meaning, [and] th[e] process of creating [them] engage[s] students creatively, emotionally, physically and cognitively.
>
> (pp. 603 and 611)

To implement this kind of practice, L2 instructors can resort to genre-based instruction (see Chapter 4, pages 75–83) to introduce students to script-writing as a genre, creating opportunities for them to analyze model texts and develop scripts jointly, before moving to independent construction.[6]

Related Topics

My Nepantla

This short task (one to two weeks long) introduces students to Latina writer and activist Gloria Anzaldúa's (1987) concept of *nepantla*, a Nahuatl word that means "land in-between." Anzaldúa takes the original conception, and appropriates it to characterize her experiences as a bicultural/bilingual person living in Texas, on the border between Mexico and the United States. For this scholar, *nepantla* is a liminal, [personal] space where transformations [can] occur … It is unstable [and] unpredictable because of its constant state of transition … It is … the space where one is able to reflect and analyze the contradictions encountered in our daily lives … *Nepantla* also offers the essential space to explore and find a language to express the ambivalence and uncertainty [that a particular moment of our life] is provoking on the self … It is in *Nepantla* that we [find] a new attitude that can be channeled toward the promise and hope for [relief] and resolution.

(Espinosa-Dulanto et al., 2020, pp. 18–19)

The activity I am proposing offers learners the opportunity to use their L2 (and other semiotic resources) to explore and describe their own *nepantlas*. I have successfully enacted this pedagogical move in my L2 intermediate-mid Spanish university classes, and my students have applied Anzaldúa's notion to reflect on their identities and intersectionality, the uncertainties brought about by COVID-19, and/or personal changes/transitions. To implement this type of identity text, I organize students' work as follows:

Experiencing, conceptualizing, analyzing
Meaning-making metafunctions of focus: Reference (what), agency (who), structure (how), context (when/where—sociocultural/sociohistorical), and interest (why/for whom)
- I ask learners whether they write a personal diary and/or they reflect on their everyday experiences. As a class, we discuss how we make sense of what happens to us, and what we do to deal with changes or transitions.
- After that, I introduce students to Gloria Anzaldúa and her concept of *nepantla*:
  - Students work in groups. Each group is provided with a copy of Anzaldúa's (1987) poem *To Live in the Borderlands* and two examples of *nepantla* representations created by artists, poets, and/or L2 students.[7]
  - Each group discovers how Anzaldúa defines *nepantla* (i.e., what it means to her in terms of identities, experiences, personal transitions), and how the concept is represented by others multimodally. For example, learners focus on the use of visual elements (I use the template questions and foci in Appendix A) and aspects of the concept that they convey, intended audience, and sociocultural setting. I also encourage students to reflect on the significance of *nepantla* for minoritized populations and social groups.
  - Also, based on what they know about Anzaldúa, learners need to establish connections between her life experiences and the concept.
- Groups present their ideas, and, as a class, we develop our understanding of Anzaldúa's notion; i.e., what *nepantla* means to the whole group, how we can relate to it, and how we can apply it to reflect on our personal experiences. This discussion is in the L2, but the L1 is allowed when students want to express complex ideas.

Applying

Meaning-making metafunctions of focus: Reference (what), agency (who), structure (how), context (when/where—sociocultural/sociohistorical), and interest (why/for whom)

- Learners develop their personal *nepantla*. The options I offer them are the following:
  - A visual representation with text.
  - A video with images and oral narrative and/or written text.
  - A text-based representation (e.g., a word cloud in a specific shape [also considered a semiotic element]).
  - A linguistic and visual conceptual map.
  - A bilingual poem (L1 and L2) with an image.

  Possible digital tools: Canva, Google Slides, Padlet, Prezi, etc. For word clouds, I recommend Word Art, WordClouds, or WordItOut, and for conceptual maps, I suggest tools such as Lucidchart, MindMeister, or Popplet (see Appendix B).

  Possible instructions:
  - Develop your *nepantla*. Express any contradictory emotions you might be feeling, any transitions that are happening in your life, or personally defining moments/events. You can also use this project to give voice to your different social identities, focusing on those that place you in *nepantla* (e.g., bicultural/biracial/bilingual identities).
  - Get ready to present your work in class. You will explain your representation (you can be as personal as you want) and the reasons why you have chosen the semiotic resources you have used. Do you share some of the feelings expressed by Anzaldúa and the *nepantla* representations you analyzed with your group?

- After students have created their *nepantlas*, they present them in class, explaining their meaning and choice of semiotic resources. This happens in the L2, but learners are also allowed to use the L1 if needed.
- Since students communicate very personal experiences through their artifacts (e.g., some of my students have used their *nepantlas* to convey painful transitions/changes in their lives, their coming out stories, mental health issues related to the COVID pandemic, etc.), it is imperative to create a safe space (indeed, a *nepantla*) in the L2 classroom. Learners need to feel free to disclose personal feelings without fear of judgment or dissemination of information. Thus, it is crucial for instructors to establish clear community and confidentiality rules before the presentations.

My People, My Histories, My Future (Based on Jewell, 2021)

In this rendering of the identity texts task, learners explore their family's roots and history, and they reflect on significant events and experiences (present, past, and future). Possible foci and information that could be included:

- Ancestors
    - Who they were (e.g., race/ethnicity, place of birth, professions, other relevant information).
    - Important events in their lives.
    - Why they inspire the student.
    - What the learner would like to know more about.
    - Images and photos of the ancestors or artifacts related to them. For inspiration, students can explore initiatives such as *Your Story, Our Story*.[8]
- Histories
    - Students create a multimodal outline of one of their family's significant stories they have always been told (multimodal narrative; e.g., text [oral and/or written] + other semiotic elements [images, music, animation]). Useful digital tools: Sutori (Appendix B).
    - Learners interview one of their family members about the story.
    - Students compare their version of the story with that of their family member. Learners point out the similarities and differences, and they reflect on them: Are similarities/differences related to their age? What role do their identities play in the conceptualization of the story?
    - Based on their reflections, students modify the original multimodal outline they created, adding more multimodal resources.
    - Finally, learners write a short paragraph explaining how their story has changed, and what they have learned, in general terms, about their family.

Students can also create multimodal identity texts in the shape of multimodal timelines focusing on aspects of their own personal histories (*"I" Histories*; see options below), using digital tools such as Office Timeline, Preceden, Sutori, or Timetoast (see Appendix B). Prompt examples:

- Prompt #1: What is your ["I"] history beyond your family?
    - [How] is it related to the land around you?
    - What moments in our collective [sociocultural] history have had a large impact on you?
    - How did those moments contribute to who you are now?

    (Jewell, 2021, p. 53)

- Prompt #2: Your history is important. Reflect on and create a multimodal timeline of your own history (*"I" History*). Use text, images (e.g., photos, illustrations, etc.), hyperlinks, and music to portray it. Use these questions for guidance:
    - Where are you going to start?
        - Does your "I" history begin before you were born?
        - Does it start with your name? Or with the place where you took your first breath?
    - What people in your life will be part of your timeline?
    - Will you add stories from your community and beyond?

- What significant events and experiences will you include? What makes them significant?

(Adapted from Jewel, 2021, p. 49)

Another option is for students to write letters to their future selves to reflect on their present life. For example, learners can

> share who [they] are [e.g., identities, family, present educational experiences, hobbies, etc.], what [their] dreams are, what [they] are learning [e.g., at the personal and academic level], and [think about] how [they] are growing as [members of society who celebrate diversity and work towards equity and inclusion].
>
> (Jewell, 2021, p. 43)

The letters can be multimodal: The L2 text (oral and/or written) can be accompanied by visual and/or auditory elements. L2 teachers can employ the suggestions given in this whole section to provide learners with support in the exploration of the proposed topics.

5. Media Collection (Critical Analysis)

This task is inspired by work by the organization Learning for Justice (see Chapter 2, page 28), and it fosters both students' L2 use as well as their critical multiliteracies. The objective of the activities presented below is to offer learners the opportunity to analyze how different kinds of popular media (e.g., advertisements/commercials, social media posts) "influence the development of self in young people … and [might dictate some of] their life choices" (Cameron, n.d.) in both the L1 and L2. Also, students focus on issues of representation and inclusion (i.e., what "voices" are highlighted and which ones are hidden) in the target cultures and their own. L2 teachers need to choose media samples according to their students' age and level of L2 performance. I suggest a focus on locally produced media (e.g., school/university social media posts, infographics [see example #2 in this chapter, "Endangered, Threatened, or Vulnerable Flora and Fauna: Expository Texts and Infographics"], multimodal advertisements or commercials) in the L1 (or L2 if available) and related pieces in the L2. Learners can create their own collection of media (e.g., an ePortfolio), or they can collect two or three samples, and use the L2 to reflect on the pieces chosen and/or propose changes to improve the messages conveyed.

Instructional Information and Guidance (Task Idea Inspired by Cameron, n.d.)

Educational context: Appropriate for middle- and high-school learners and university students.

L2 performance level: Intermediate or advanced. It could be adapted for novice students, but the critical reflections will need to be in the L1.

Modes of communication: Interpersonal, interpretive, and presentational (written and/or oral).
Project length: Average (three to five weeks). This task can be structured as an instructional unit.
Possible topics:
- Representation (e.g., race, ethnicity, body type, sexual orientation)
- Gender equity
- Gender identity
- Socioeconomic status
- Commercially promoted lifestyles

L2 focus: Descriptive vocabulary; present tense; modals; passive voice/impersonal constructions.
Student organization: Pairs and groups.
Pedagogical sequence:
Experiencing the known, conceptualizing, analyzing
Meaning-making metafunctions of focus: Reference (what), agency (who), structure (how), context (when/where—sociocultural/sociohistorical), and interest (why/for whom)
- Students are asked to find one public artifact (e.g., one advertisement/commercial and/or one social media post) that they like, and bring it to class. L2 instructors provide specific guidelines (i.e., what is allowed in terms of topic, length, ideology, etc.), and, based on their learners' age, they also offer possible sources (i.e., where students can find artifacts).
- Students work in pairs, and they share their artifact with their classmate. Partners discuss the following in the L2, and, also possibly in the L1, depending on the level of L2 performance and identities:
  - What the artifact is about and where it appeared (where students found it).
  - What makes it attractive to them (e.g., use of images, colors, font, slogan, music, animation—see Appendix A).
  - How the information is organized:
    - What comes first/last (in the case of videos or animation).
    - What elements are more prominent: Images vs. text; music vs. images.
  - Who it is for (intended audience; e.g., children, teenagers, people in their 20s, etc.) and why they think this is the case (focus on semiotic elements used).
  - What the purpose of the artifact is (message the meaning-maker wants to convey).
- Learners compare their artifacts, and provide a definition for "media" based on their examples. That is, each pair needs to explain what they see as "media."

Experiencing the new, analyzing, conceptualizing

Meaning-making metafunctions of focus: Reference (what), agency (who), structure (how), context (when/where—sociocultural/sociohistorical), and interest (why/for whom)
- Each pair shares their definition of "media," and the class as a whole develops a collective definition.
- The L2 instructor organizes students in groups. She provides learners with L2 media samples.
- Each group analyzes their sample, using similar questions to those used in the pair interaction. They reflect on the following:
    - What the artifact is about and where it appeared (students hypothesize where it might have been published). Learners justify their ideas.
    - What they find attractive about it (e.g., use of images, colors, font, slogan) and what they don't. Learners justify their ideas.
    - How the information is organized:
        - What comes first/last (in the case of videos or animation).
        - What elements are more prominent: Images vs. text; music vs. images, etc.
    - Who it is for (intended audience; e.g., children, teenagers, people in their 20s, etc.) and why they think this is the case (focus on semiotic elements used).
    - What the purpose of the artifact is (message the meaning-maker wants to convey).
- Students compare the artifact to their own (i.e., those discussed in pairs in *experiencing the known*), and create a Venn diagram finding similarities and differences in general terms.
- Groups present their diagrams to the rest of the class. The instructor takes the presentations as the point of departure for the critical analysis of the media artifacts. The class reflects on the messages conveyed by their own artifacts and those in the L2. For the discussion, teachers might choose the richest (in terms of semiosis) L2 artifact. Also, practitioners might want to include some of the foci included in Appendix A as part of the analysis.
- The instructor and students collaborate in the development of a critical report on the chosen artifact, incorporating the information presented by the groups, and also considering the following:
    - Is the artifact fair to the people pictured in it?
    - Are they depicted as real-looking, or are they too skinny or muscular?
    - Are they posed in natural ways or in strange positions?
    - Are the images positive or negative? Why?
    - Is the artifact representative of the population of the place/social group for which it is intended/where it has been published?
    - To what extent can the information offered by the meaning-maker be trusted? Explain. (Adapted from Cameron, n.d.)
- After the discussion, learners revise their conceptualizations of "media," focusing on ideological dimensions and social effects.

- Also, the teacher shares the collaborative report with all the students. This will become the model for learners' work in the *Applying* knowledge processes.

  Applying, analyzing

  Meaning-making metafunctions of focus: Reference (what), agency (who), structure (how), context (when/where—sociocultural/sociohistorical), and interest (why/for whom)

  - Students choose a new artifact in the L2. Teachers will need to provide possible sources (e.g., Twitter/Facebook/Instagram accounts; websites of L2 companies/organizations; digital publications).
  - Learners create an analysis report based on similar questions to the ones used in previous discussions. Instructors can adapt the following options (and they can complement them with the templates/analysis foci offered in Appendix A).

Artifact theme/topic:
  Artifact source:
  Elements that make it attractive (briefly describe each element):

1. Images:
2. Colors:
3. Font:
4. Music:
5. Animation:
6. Slogan:
7. Other elements:

Organization of information (briefly describe how the information is organized):
Intended audience (provide a brief justification):
Message conveyed by the artifact:
Critical analysis: Based on the following questions, offer a critical view of the artifact, focusing on its weaknesses and strengths.
  Consider whether:

- The artifact is fair to the people pictured in it.
- The people depicted in it are real-looking, or too skinny or muscular.
- The people are posed in natural ways or in strange positions.
- The images chosen convey positive or negative messages about a particular group of people.
- The artifact is representative of the population of the social group for which it is intended/place where it has been published.

> - You can or cannot trust the information offered by the meaning-maker and the reasons why this is the case.
>
> Offer your analysis in paragraph form.
>   Reflection (this can be done in the L1): Reflect on the reasons why you have chosen your artifact. Also, provide suggestions for its improvement. What would you do to make it more inclusive and to eliminate elements that might have a harmful effect on people?

- Students participate in peer reviews and offer and receive feedback.
- Learners use the feedback received to revisit their analysis, and they might choose to revise it.

Applying appropriately and creatively
Meaning-making metafunctions of focus: Reference (what), agency (who), structure (how), context (when/where—sociocultural/sociohistorical), and interest (why/for whom)
- Option #1:
  - Students choose a new artifact in the L2. Teachers will need to provide possible sources (see section above).
  - Learners modify the artifact using different multimodal resources to make it more inclusive, and to eliminate elements that might negatively influence the intended audience. Also, students write a short paragraph explaining why they chose the artifact, and why they have decided to modify it in such a way (i.e., they justify the changes made).
  - Learners participate in peer reviews within their groups, and provide and receive feedback. Based on the feedback received, they reflect on their analysis and, if desired, modify their work.
- Option #2 (ideal for novice or intermediate-low students):
  - Students gather four or five samples of the ways in which media depict people in advertising in the L2. They may focus on one type of person (based on gender, body depiction, or race/ethnicity) or gather a variety of samples. Teachers offer suggestions for sources where the sample might be found (e.g., digital publications, companies' websites, etc.).
  - Students create a collection of their samples. They develop a decorative cover, and for each example, they include the title, the source, and the date it was made public. Learners describe each artifact using the L2 and L1:
    - L2:
      - What the artifact is about and where it appeared.
      - Who it is for (intended audience; e.g., children, teenagers, people in their 20s, etc.).

- What the purpose of the artifact is (message the meaning-maker wants to convey).
- L1:
  - Does it depict gender/race/ethnicity in positive or negative ways? Why?
  - Who might see it?
  - Who might be influenced?
  - To what extent can the information offered by the meaning-maker be trusted? Explain.
  - What would you do to improve the artifact?
- The class creates a list of recommendations for young people to follow when exposed to media to detect negative or harmful messages.

Memes (Based on Beucher et al., 2020 and Domínguez Romero & Bobkina, 2021)

Another popular media form that teachers can incorporate into their L2 curricula are memes, which Goriunova (2016, p. 55) defines as "digital images, often superimposed with text ... separate pieces of text, formulaic behaviors, animations and sometimes memetic videos ... which emerge in a grass-roots manner through [social] network[s], acquire a viral character, and [also exhibit an] ability to mutate" (e.g., they can be reused and remixed to be used in a different social context than the original). Because of their sociocultural nature, popularity, ease of adaptation and dissemination, and specific format, Wiggins (2019) believes memes can be considered a genre. That is, when "viewed as a genre, [memes] represent a complex system of social motivations and cultural activity that is both a result of communication and impetus for that communication" (Wiggins, p. 40). Also, although memes are complex in terms of meaning-making, they can be linguistically simple, which can allow for their use with students of all levels of L2 performance.

In Beucher et al.'s (2020) study, memes were used with students in grades 6 to 8 in a charter school in the United States to critically explore a socially relevant issue connected to some of the learners' lifeworld. The focus was the 2016 protests carried out by Native Americans to prevent the construction of the Dakota Access Pipeline across the Standing Rock Sioux people's land in North Dakota. First, students critically analyzed photos from the protest, considering the message conveyed (in terms of power and positioning), intended audience, and meaning-makers' motivation and affect (the questions created by the teachers were very similar to those in the first section of Appendix A). In the next step, learners developed memes based on the images they had worked with, "applying critical thinking when composing and discussing their reasoning when designing [their] multimodal texts" (Beucher et al., p. 48). Also, students reflected on stereotypes and biased views, and how memes can contribute to their dissemination. The researchers in charge of the investigation reported that, "overall, students composed humanizing messages around a polarizing topic, [and they] demonstrated nuanced understandings of rhetoric, argumentation, and multimodal redesign" (p. 41). Clearly, this project resulted in both personal and academic growth.

Memes have also been integrated into L2 university classes. For example, in their 2021 work, Domínguez Romero and Bobkina described how 52 L2 English students in Spain developed their critical multimodal interpretive skills and intercultural understanding through the analysis of memes related to the Trump presidency that also included references to the history of the United States. The meme task incorporated questions that allowed learners to work within three analytical dimensions based on Serafini's (2010) model for the interpretation of multimodal texts. The students analyzed the political memes "noticing the visual [elements] [perceptual dimension]; [focusing on] visual grammar and design [structural dimension], [and] exploring images from a socio-semiotic perspective [ideological dimension]" (p. 3). The results of the scholars' work pointed to the need to emphasize the critical and in-depth interpretation of memes in order to guide students beyond superficial understandings of the message(s) conveyed. Students' work in Domínguez Romero and Bobkina's article entailed the activities listed below, which were also utilized for assessment. In the proposed instructional sequence, learners:

- Examine the text describing the foregrounded elements, the dominant colors and the position of the image in relation to the text.
- Examine the text in relation to the image: contents, position, font and size.
- Discuss the background knowledge necessary to understand the text.
- Interpret the cultural meaning and possible readings that can be constructed for the text.
- Discuss the social and cultural functions of the text and the way in which these functions shape the structural organization of the text.
- Evaluate the influence of the text on the reader, including the description of the overall impression, the way humor is created, and the sociocultural phenomenon represented in the text as much as their personal attitudes towards this phenomenon.
- Discuss the possible identity of the author, reflecting upon their interests and values.
- Analyze the possible characteristics of the target audience, reflecting upon their interests and values.

(p. 6)

These pedagogical interventions are compatible with *L-by-D*'s knowledge processes and metafunctions, and could be organized around the steps discussed in the first part of this section, and through the incorporation of the template questions and foci presented in Appendix A. Also, students' analysis could be extended to application in two different ways: (1) Learners could find new images that would be compatible with the message(s) communicated in the original memes, or (2) they could create new text to change the meaning of the

124 *Sample Second Language Tasks*

memes (e.g., to express a view opposite to that of the original meaning-maker). In both cases, students would also critically consider their changes to the original artifacts and the effects on meaning, intended audience, and themselves as meaning-makers.

6. Multimodal Stories

Multimodal stories (e.g., picture books combining linguistic, visual, gestural, and spatial semiotic elements) are one of the most widely used media types in L1 and L2 classrooms, and they are ideal for a focus on the narrative genre. Also, they can be adapted for classes with students of different ages and levels of L2 performance. Indeed, Nathanson (2006, p. 5) posits that narratives

> are easier to comprehend [than other genres] because they provide signals or cues of sequence, use repetition of familiar names and phrases and vocabulary words, and generate interests in a main character or characters. Such redundancies facilitate the reader's organization of information and active processing ... [and] significantly speed up reading time, compensating for elements such as grammatical complexity, vocabulary load, and topic familiarity.

Another advantage of the genre lies in the closeness that we, human beings, feel toward stories, as they are an intrinsic part of our social nature and lifeworlds, and many times they become the way in which we pass on our beliefs and cultural heritage (Blyler & Perkins, 1999; Kelly & Zak, 1999). This closeness and the inevitable personal connections between a story and our lived experiences make this genre attractive to both learners and practitioners (see Galda et al., 2000 and Martínez & McGee, 2000).

Existing literature has offered us a myriad of pedagogical sequences that can be enacted when working with stories in L2 classes.[9] In this section, I will present an example that combines my work with L2 intermediate-mid Spanish students with that of Jewitt (2012), Mills and Unsworth (2018), and Zammit (2016). In this type of task, learners analyze different versions, in terms of modality, of the same story (e.g., video/audio vs. textual/visual narratives). The activities below were built around students' exploration of Argentinean writer Julio Cortázar's (2008 [1953]) short story *La noche boca arriba* (*The Night Face Up*) and its video version (Zumbastico Studios, 2020).

Instructional Information and Guidance

Educational context: All ages. Stories will be chosen according to students' age. However, I have used illustrated children's books in my university classes with much success.

L2 performance level: Can be adapted to all levels—novice (beginning), intermediate, or advanced.

Modes of communication: Interpersonal, interpretive, and presentational (written and/or multimodal).
Project length: Short (one to two weeks) or average (three to five weeks). The task could be part of an instructional unit with a focus on the narrative genre.
L2 focus: Present or past tenses (depending on level of L2 performance); action verbs; verbs and terms to express emotions; time connectors; descriptive verbs; adjectives; nouns.
Student organization: Pairs and groups.
Pedagogical sequence:
- Step #1: Video version of the story
  Experiencing
  Meaning-making metafunctions of focus: Reference (what), agency (who), context (when/where—sociocultural/sociohistorical), and interest (why/for whom)
  - The story of focus could be classified as an example of magical realism, a 20th-century literary movement in which reality is mixed with elements of fantasy. Thus, situating students in the topic could involve these possible activities:
    - Learners need to think of their favorite fantastic story (e.g., *Harry Potter*), and make a list of the reasons why it is classified as such.
    - Students need to find an image or photo that depicts a fantastic scene or set of elements, and they need to explain their choices (i.e., why they believe the image/photo could be characterized as fantasy).
  - In class, learners present their ideas/photos/images. Based on students' presentations, the class as a whole creates a spider map summarizing the characteristics of fantastic stories, focusing on common plot elements, types of characters, settings, etc.
  - In the next step, the instructor organizes students in groups. Then, based on the title of the story of focus (i.e., *La noche boca arriba*), learners hypothesize what it might be about, providing ideas about possible plot, setting (in terms of time and location), characters, etc.
  - Also, since the chosen narrative incorporates a historical event (*la guerra florida/flower war*), students also investigate when it happened and what it was about. Based on the new information, learners revise their original, hypothetical ideas about the story.
  - Depending on learners' level of L2 performance and identities (i.e., bilingual/multilingual bicultural/multicultural), instructors can allow the use of both the L1 and L2 in this first part of the task.

  Experiencing the new, analyzing critically
  Meaning-making metafunctions of focus: Reference (what), agency (who), context (when/where—sociocultural/sociohistorical), and interest (why/for whom)
  - Students watch the video version of the story with the members of their group, and they check whether there exist similarities between their hypothetical ideas about the story and its plot.

- Learners collaborate in the analysis of the video story with a focus on meaning. Instructors can resort to the questions in Table 4.1 (page 80) and/or Appendix A to guide students' work.
- Students also consider the meaning-maker's motivation and purpose.

Conceptualizing, analyzing

Meaning-making metafunctions of focus: Reference (what), agency (who), structure (how), context (when/where—sociocultural/sociohistorical), and interest (why/for whom)

- Students continue working with the video story, but they now focus on its structure and the semiotic elements used by the director to convey meaning. For example, learners explore what role each part of the video plays, and how they contribute to the meaning of the ensemble as a whole. The emphasis is on timeline and parts of the plot (i.e., orientation, complication, and resolution).
- Learners also analyze how each of the present semiotic systems—linguistic (oral and written text), visual, gestural, auditory, and spatial—contributes to the narrative. They also consider their effectiveness both as separate elements and in the construction of the artifact as a whole (e.g., is it easy to understand the story? Does the combination of all the modalities make sense? Which modality is the most effective?). Instructors can resort to Appendix A to guide learners' work.

- Step #2: Textual version of the story

Experiencing the new, analyzing critically

Meaning-making metafunctions of focus: Reference (what), agency (who), structure (how), context (when/where—sociocultural/sociohistorical), and interest (why/for whom)

- After working with the video version, students read the printed story in their groups. Group members collaborate in the analysis of the story with a focus on meaning. Instructors can adapt the questions in Table 4.1 (page 80) and/or Appendix A to guide learners' work.
- Learners compare the video and text versions in terms of meaning:
  - Do both versions include the same events? If not, what are the plot differences?
  - Are the texts structured in similar ways (i.e., is the story organized along the same timeline?)?
  - Which of the two versions is richer (in terms of meaning)?
  - What aspects of the ensemble make it richer?
  - What affordances does each meaning-maker (director and writer) have that give them an advantage over the other meaning-maker?
  - Which of the two versions is easier to understand? Why?
- Learners also compare the two versions in terms of the meaning-makers' motivation and purpose (e.g., does the director of the video have the same audience in mind as the writer? Do both meaning-makers have the same purpose?).

- Each group develops a comparison matrix to show the similarities and differences between the two versions of the story in terms of meaning.

Conceptualizing, analyzing

Meaning-making metafunctions of focus: Reference (what), agency (who), structure (how), context (when/where—sociocultural/sociohistorical), and interest (why/for whom)

- Groups analyze the structure of the textual version. They investigate whether the narrative is organized in the same way as the video (i.e., orientation, complication, and resolution).
- Learners also explore what role each part of the text plays, and explain their contribution to its meaning as a whole.
- Students also analyze what linguistic elements are used to convey meaning in the orientation, complication, and resolution. For example, learners work with past tenses and time connectors, focusing on what ideas each tense communicates, and how the writer has weaved his narrative to guide the reader.

- Step #3:
- Option #1: Use of semiotic elements to express emotions (task idea inspired by Mills & Unsworth, 2018)

  This pedagogical sequence focuses on the multimodal expression of emotions. Mills and Unsworth (2018, p. 610) believe it is important for learners to understand how meaning-makers convey emotive meaning resorting to different modalities because "the widespread production and increased circulation of multimodal texts in online communication environments requires the capability to interpret and represent emotion multimodally." This implies that activities like the ones that will be presented in this section can foster learners' growth as multiliterate L2 users.

  Analyzing, applying

  Meaning-making metafunctions of focus: Reference (what), agency (who), context (when/where—sociocultural/sociohistorical), and interest (why/for whom)

  - Instructors capture a series of screenshots from the video version of the story which feature characters expressing emotions (e.g., pain, confusion, empathy, fear, etc.), and they compile a list of L2 words that could be used to describe the depicted feelings.
  - Learners work in pairs. Each pair is in charge of one or two images. The pairs match words to images, and they also consider how emotions are expressed by other semiotic elements. For example, the pairs can find the images in the video, and they can analyze the character's gestures (facial expressions and body movements), as well as the sounds and color used to convey feelings.
  - Students present their work, and the class discusses the effectiveness of each mode for the communication of emotive meaning.

- In the next step, the L2 instructor organizes the pairs into groups. Learners work with students they have not worked with before.
- The teacher provides each group with an excerpt of the textual version of the story in which emotions are expressed by the protagonist or other characters.
- Students create an animation or picture series of the character, visually portraying the emotions conveyed linguistically. If learners have access to iPads or tablets, they can develop their animations with apps such as Animation Creator HD (Apple), Animation Desk Draw & Animate, PicsArt Animator, or FlipaClip (these three apps are compatible with Apple and Android). Other useful digital web-based tools are Renderforest or Moovly (Appendix B).[10] Another alternative can be for students to draw various versions of the character to express the progression or detailed expression (e.g., through different facial/body movements) of the emotion of focus.
- When groups have finished their work, they present it in class, using the L2 (and, if needed, the L1) to discuss their choices. Other groups can ask questions. Also, the class reflects on the ease or difficulty of transducing (see page 103) an emotion from one semiotic system to a different one.

- Option #2: Use of multimodal semiotic elements to convey comprehension and interpretation (task idea inspired by Zammit, 2016)

The task I propose in this section is inspired by Zammit's (2016) work with two elementary-school classes (grades 5 and 6) in Australia. However, it can be adapted for use with high school and university students. The focus of the investigation was learners' work with a printed novel. The scholar examined the ways in which students transformed the written description of a storm in the novel of focus into a multimodal artifact reflecting their interpretation of the linguistically depicted scene. The activity was similar to the social-reading task presented in Chapters 2 and 3, and it could also be adapted for use with Cortázar's story (or any other narrative) in the following way:

Analyzing, applying

Meaning-making metafunctions of focus: Reference (what), agency (who), structure (how), context (when/where—sociocultural/sociohistorical), and interest (why/for whom)

- Instructors choose a vivid scene from the story with which their students are working.
- Learners work in groups. Each group analyzes and interprets the written scene, developing a multimodal digital text including the following elements:
  - Images: A collage of digital images collected from the Internet or of photos taken by the group members. To create their work, learners can resort to Adobe Spark, Canva, Google Slides, or PowerPoint (Appendix B).

- Sounds: Students add sounds to create a soundscape for their visual interpretation, using open tools such as Audacity or WavePad (Appendix B).
- Text: Learners write and/or record a paragraph in the L2 describing the character's feelings from a first-person perspective while experiencing the scene portrayed multimodally.

- Each group posts their work (either uploaded or via a link) in the class's LMS or collaborative canvas (e.g., Milanote, Jamboard, or Padlet; Appendix B).
- Each group provides and receives feedback (e.g., two groups can work together). Based on the comments received, each group revises their artifact.
- The revised versions are published in the class's LMS/canvas, and the class votes anonymously to choose the most effective artifact in terms of meaning.
- Learners can also reflect on their creative process as a class:
  - How easy or difficult was it for the group to transform the scene?
  - What semiotic elements were easier to manipulate? Why was that the case?
  - What meaning-making affordances does each modality offer meaning-makers?
  - What was gained and lost in the transduction?

7. Podcasts and Vodcasts

Two of the most popular current media in and outside various educational settings are podcasts and vodcasts (i.e., podcasts with a video or visual component [e.g., animations or images]; Brown & Green, 2007). For example, the last two years have seen an increase in people's interest in podcasts, and according to Winn (2021a), currently, 50% of all homes in the United States can be characterized as "podcast fans." When considering listeners' age, 48% are within the 12-to-34-year-old age group, which implies that this type of media might be part of our students' lifeworlds, and thus, it might be an attractive and effective pedagogical tool in our L2 classes. This statement is supported by an extensive body of research on the use of podcasts and vodcasts in education, including for L2 learning, that has highlighted their academic and personal benefits for learners. For instance, L2 existing literature has reported beneficial effects for the development of the interpretive mode of communication, in terms of both overall listening skills (e.g., Cross, 2014; Gonulal, 2020; Şendağ et al., 2018) and vocabulary learning (e.g., Bueno-Alastuey & Nemeth, 2020; Faramarzi et al., 2019; Kargozari & Zarinkamar, 2014; Saeedakhtar et al., 2021), as well as for student motivation (e.g., Indahsari, 2020; Phillips, 2017).

In this section, I propose a podcast project inspired by recent work with L2 Spanish university students.[11] The example is guided by Moyna's (2019) work, in which learners with an intermediate-mid level of L2 performance created podcasts to explore local L2 communities from a sociocultural perspective. In order to do so, students interviewed community members.

Instructional Information and Guidance (Based on Moyna, 2019)

Educational context: Middle, high school, and university classes.[12]
L2 performance level: Intermediate or advanced.
Modes of communication: Interpersonal (interviews, project development), interpretive (audio), and presentational (written and oral).
Project length: Long (six weeks +).
Possible topics: Topics related to L2 local communities (e.g., music, art, non-profit organizations, festivals, activism, etc.).
L2 focus: Terminology related to specific topics; present and past tenses; registers/local dialects.
Student organization: Groups.
Pedagogical sequence:
- **Phase 1. Launch project**
  Presentation of driving question, project calendar, division of labor, outcomes, and expected results.[13]
  Experiencing the known, conceptualizing, analyzing critically
  Meaning-making metafunctions of focus: Reference (what), agency (who), structure (how), context (when/where—sociocultural/sociohistorical), and interest (why/for whom)
    - Learners are asked to develop short oral L2 presentations about their favorite L1 podcasts, including the following information:
        - Podcast title and series to which it belongs (if it is an episode of a particular show)
        - Length
        - Where it can be found
        - What the podcast (and show) is about
        - Why the student likes it
    - If students don't listen to podcasts, the instructor can provide L1 suggestions. Learners develop their presentations on one of the suggested options.
    - Students are divided into groups. Each group member presents their information to their group mates. Based on their presentations, learners create a list of podcast characteristics, focusing on:
        - Topics
        - Length
        - Sources (where the podcasts have been published)
        - Semiotic elements
        - Organization of information
        - What makes podcasts attractive

- Each group presents the results of their discussion, posting their ideas on the class's LMS or collaborative canvas (e.g., Milanote, Jamboard, or Padlet; Appendix B).
- Based on all the contributions, the class develops a list of podcast/vodcast characteristics.
- Depending on learners' level of L2 performance and identities (i.e., bilingual/multilingual bicultural/multicultural), instructors can allow the use of both the L1 and L2 in this section's discussions.

- **Phase 2. Build knowledge, understanding, and skills to create podcast**
  Experiencing the new, analyzing critically
  Meaning-making metafunctions of focus: Reference (what), agency (who), structure (how), context (when/where—sociocultural/sociohistorical), and interest (why/for whom)
  - Students are introduced to L2 podcasts. Each group works with a different one. Learners collaboratively explore the message conveyed, and they analyze the podcast's semiotic features, resorting to the ideas developed in *experiencing the known* (**Phase 1**). For example, students discuss:
    - Title, topic, and source
    - Message conveyed (summary of main points)
    - Intended audience
    - Oral and auditory semiotic resources (for possible foci, see Appendix A)
    - Types of information communicated by each semiotic element
    - Similarities and differences between L1 and L2 podcasts

  Conceptualizing, analyzing
  Meaning-making metafunctions of focus: Structure (how), context (when/where—sociocultural/sociohistorical), and interest (why/for whom)
  - Students examine how ideas are organized in their L2 podcast, identifying connections between text structure and meaning; i.e., what type of information is communicated in each part.
  - Learners identify the relationship among semiotic elements (e.g., register, intonation, use of music, etc.), message conveyed, purpose of the text, intended audience, and source (where the podcast was published).
  - Learners critically analyze the meaning-makers' motivation and purpose, and how effectively they are conveyed by the semiotic elements in the L2 podcast.
  - Each group offers an oral summary of their discussion, and the class compares the groups' information, finding similarities to develop a common vision of the structure of L2 podcasts.

- **Phase 3. Develop and critique products**
  Applying appropriately
  Meaning-making metafunctions of focus: Reference (what), agency (who), structure (how), context (when/where—sociocultural/sociohistorical), and interest (why/for whom)

Learners start working on their collaborative podcasts. Instructors can choose to maintain the Phase 1 and 2 groups, or they can create new ones. Different parts of the podcasts are developed progressively. The stages below are implemented throughout the project.

- Groups find a topic and a representative of the L2 local community they can interview. For example, Moyna's (2019) students focused on music and the experiences of bicultural students. Other topics could be immigration stories, labor experiences, artistic manifestations, educational experiences, local organizations, etc. Depending on learners' age, instructors can assist with information and contacts with the community.
- Once students have identified a story and interviewee, they contact the person to organize the interview. Also, with teacher guidance, each group will develop their set of questions.
- Groups carry out and record their interviews, and then they choose the excerpts to be used in their podcasts.
- Each group develops their podcast script, including all expected elements:
  - Teaser
  - Intro music
  - Welcome
  - Ad spot
  - Interview
  - Call to action ("Review us on iTunes!")
  - Outro music (Winn, 2021b)

For example, students can storyboard their podcast (e.g., with tools such as Canva, Storyboarder, or makeStoryboard; Appendix B). To find open music, learners can consult sources that offer free tracks such as Incompetech, Silverman Sound Studios, or Free Music Archive (Appendix B).

- Also, learners need to choose a title, create/find an image to serve as cover, and determine what role each group member will play.
- The script draft should also include links to the chosen music and samples of the visual elements.
- Each group works with another one in peer reviews, providing and receiving feedback.
- Based on the feedback received, students revise their scripts. If needed, they revisit concepts discussed in **Phase 2**.
- The instructor offers comments on the revised script, and the students incorporate them in a second revision.

- **Phase 4. Present products**
  Applying appropriately and creatively
  Meaning-making metafunctions of focus: Reference (what), agency (who), structure (how), context (when/where—sociocultural/sociohistorical), and interest (why/for whom)

- Each group records their podcast, combining all required elements. To do so, learners can resort to free audio recording tools such as Audacity or WavePad (Appendix B).
- Once students have finished their podcasts, instructors can publish them in free platforms such as Anchor, Buzzsprout, PodBean, or Spreaker (Appendix B).
- Also, all projects can be unveiled in a public presentation (e.g., parents, members of the L2 community interviewed, etc.).
- Groups prepare a short, oral presentation to introduce their podcasts, discussing, for example, how they chose their topic, their creative process, and overall experience. Each member of the group actively participates in the presentation.
- The presentations are previously discussed and rehearsed in class, before the public event. Learners receive feedback from their peers and instructor, and they revise their work.

8. Recipes and Other Procedural Texts

The tasks in this section are grounded in genre-based instruction (GBI; see Chapter 4), and they provide students with the opportunity to work with and produce procedural texts. The activities I propose are based on my work with L2 Spanish intermediate university students, unpublished data I have collected in my classes, and Lewis's (2015) work with historical menus.

An extensive body of multidisciplinary literature has explored diverse socio-historical and sociocultural aspects of food preparation and consumption (e.g., see studies in Albala, 2013), and the relationship that exists among language, identity, and food (e.g., Karrebæk et al., 2018; Riley & Paugh, 2019; Rodney et al., 2017). Because of food's cultural, social, and personal relevance, scholars (e.g., Bender et al., 2011; Durá et al., 2015; Swift & Wilk, 2015) have also emphasized the pedagogical role that it can play in educational contexts, highlighting the possibilities it offers to "engage students with forms of knowledge from a wide variety of disciplines [and through] a multisensorial, [authentic] … learning [experience]" (Trubek & Belliveau, 2009, p. 16). Indeed, recent studies have shown how food-related content can be successfully integrated into different academic areas. For example, Lewis (2015) has described the benefits of a project in which high school instructors learned how to teach American history using food as a teaching tool by uncovering associations between historical events and culinary traditions. Anderson and Rose (2016) have revealed how L2 Spanish university learners in content language classes in Australia achieved a more in-depth understanding of Spain's Civil War by connecting political events with the socioeconomic undercurrents embedded in cookbooks and recipes published at that time. Cognard-Black and Goldthwaite (2008) have integrated cookbooks as part of university English classes, and, based on their experience, have posited that to teach food ... is to teach a part of what it means to be human. Through the record of food traditions, culture and history are transmitted as well as transformed—practices of sharing, preparing, and eating recipes both create and convey human interactions. Moreover, like humanity, food is both elastic and contradictory ... Food texts are multifaceted in terms of their content, and yet they're also complex in terms of genre, tone, and approach ... [Through a culinary focus,] students [can] connect their writing and learning to the multiplicities of their own personal food literacies.

(p. 422)

These works inspired my work with recipes in L2 Spanish university classes. I have adopted recipes as model procedural texts based on the literature I have discussed, and as an effort to establish connections between content and students' lifeworld.

Instructional Information and Guidance

Educational context: Appropriate for all ages.
L2 performance level: Novice (beginning), intermediate or advanced.
Modes of communication: Interpersonal, interpretive, and presentational (written, oral, and/or multimodal).
Project length: Average (three to five weeks). This task can be structured as an instructional unit.
L2 focus: Terminology related to food (e.g., ingredients, measurements, verbs related to cooking); infinitive (novice students); present tense; passive voice; commands; connectors to show sequence (first, then, etc.).
Student organization: Pairs and groups.
Pedagogical sequence:
- **Setting the context**
  Experiencing, analyzing critically
  Meaning-making metafunctions of focus: Reference (what), agency (who), context (when/where—sociocultural/sociohistorical), and interest (why/for whom)
  - Learners prepare a short (no more than five minutes) multimodal (including the L2) video presentation (e.g., on Flipgrid; Appendix B) on their favorite dish, and they upload it to the class's LMS. Elements to be included:
    - At least a photo or image of the dish
    - A short description:
    - Name of the dish and when they eat it
    - Ingredients
    - Description of its flavor
    - Why they like it
  - Students watch their peers' presentations: Learners can be organized in groups, and can be assigned to watch the presentations prepared by their

group mates. Students are asked to classify their peers' dishes in terms of origin (e.g., whether the dish could be classified as Indian, Italian, Mexican, etc.).
- In class, students work in their groups, and they compare their dishes. What do they all have in common? What kinds of food do most members of the group like? What do the dishes say about group members' lifeworlds, diversity, and heritage?
- Each group shares their ideas with the rest of the class, and the class as a whole, with the teacher's guidance, compiles statistical data (e.g., in graphs and/or tables) about students' preferences, heritage, and the most common ingredients found in the dishes.
- The class reflects on the data, and what they say about the members of the class and their communities.

Experiencing the new, analyzing critically
Meaning-making metafunctions of focus: Reference (what), agency (who), context (when/where—sociocultural/sociohistorical), and interest (why/for whom)
- Teachers choose three or four recipes in the L2. I usually expose my students to video and text-based recipes featuring different levels of formality and grammatical structures. All the ensembles I use are open, and some of them have been produced by my students.[14]
- Learners analyze the recipes. The analysis work is structured as a jigsaw activity. Each group is assigned a video or text-based recipe. Students analyze their texts to discover:
    - The dish's name and possible source
    - Ingredients
    - Its origin (or culinary tradition) based on ingredients and other semiotic elements in the recipe (e.g., use of colors, music, vocabulary [dialectal differences])
    - L2 structures that are used to convey instructions (guided by choices and examples provided by the instructor)
    - Register (level of formality) and intended audience

- **Modeling and deconstructing the text**

Conceptualizing, analyzing critically
Meaning-making metafunctions of focus: Reference (what), agency (who), structure (how), context (when/where—sociocultural/sociohistorical), and interest (why/for whom)

Once all groups have finished their analysis, members of each group form new groups, and share the results of their work.
- The new groups start generalizing their ideas in connection to the characteristics that all recipes have in common (e.g., what semiotic elements are present in each artifact, what information they convey, how they are organized). Learners also focus on the similarities and differences between the recipes in terms of audience and meaning-makers' motivation/objective.

- Each group shares their generalizations with other groups in the class's LMS or collaborative digital canvas (e.g., Milanote, Jamboard, or Padlet; Appendix B).
- Based on the ideas posted, the class as a whole develops definitions for procedural texts as represented by the recipes analyzed, including type of information they communicate, objectives, rhetorical organization, and semiotic elements that are used for meaning-making.

Analyzing

Meaning-making metafunctions of focus: Reference (what), agency (who), structure (how), context (when/where—sociocultural/sociohistorical), and interest (why/for whom)

- Students continue working with their new groups, and they focus on the L2 structures used in each recipe. The instructor guides this work by providing students with resources (e.g., grammatical information from open resources). Learners use this information, and they explore what linguistic resource each meaning-maker has chosen. They provide the following information:
  - Names of the structures used.
  - Information that each structure gives the audience.
  - Connection between the structure and the recipe's level of formality.
  - Students also determine how the structure is related to the intended audience (e.g., in terms of age), the meaning-maker's motivation, and the other semiotic elements in the text.
- Each group posts a summary of their work in the class's LMS or collaborative canvas, and, based on everyone's contribution, the class makes generalizations about the social use of the L2 in the procedural texts analyzed.

- **Joint construction of the text**

Applying appropriately

Meaning-making metafunctions of focus: Reference (what), agency (who), structure (how), context (when/where—sociocultural/sociohistorical), and interest (why/for whom)

- Learners work in pairs within their group. Each pair has to recreate one of the model texts for a different audience. For example, the video recipes are transduced (see page 103) to become written and visual (e.g., with only images) ensembles. Also, the informal recipes become formal, and vice versa. Each pair in the group is assigned a different recipe. The change of register also implies a change of L2 structure.
- When pairs have finished their work, they participate in oral peer reviews within their group. Based on the feedback received, students revise their work.
- The instructor provides comments on the revised versions. Learners incorporate the new feedback, and revise their work once more.
- Final versions are posted on the class's LMS. Students compare their texts with that of pairs that have worked on the same ensemble, and

they reflect on similarities and differences in terms of meaning and semiotic resources used by each pair.
- **Independent construction of the text**
  Applying creatively
  Meaning-making metafunctions of focus: Reference (what), agency (who), structure (how), context (when/where—sociocultural/sociohistorical), and interest (why/for whom)
  - Students develop their own recipes[15] or other procedural texts (e.g., how-to topics related to their hobbies/majors). I ask learners to choose a recipe that is not too complex, and encourage them to cook it.
  - The texts are developed as digital posters. My favorite tool is Canva (Appendix B) because it offers free templates for students, and it is user-friendly. Learners need to include the following elements in their work:
    - Title of the recipe/procedure to be explained
    - Ingredients with measurements/materials needed
    - Instructions including at least five different steps
    - Photos to illustrate at least four major procedural steps
    - Photo of the dish/object resulting from procedure
  - The ensembles developed by the students need to have a Creative Commons license (e.g., CC BY-SA). This is the reason why learners are required to use their own photos or images with a Creative Commons license. In order to facilitate this step, I offer training on licenses and ways in which to find open materials. I recommend instructors familiarize themselves with the following:
    - Resources for image search (e.g., Creative Commons Search, Unsplash; Appendix B).
    - Creative Commons licenses and attributions for open resources (see note #4).
  - Students work on the first drafts of their procedural texts: Text (e.g., ingredients and procedure) + images to be used (e.g., small versions or links to each image). Once learners have developed their drafts, they participate in the following collaborative activities:
    1. They post their work in the same collaborative canvas (or LMS) used in previous stages.
    2. They provide and receive feedback, working with partners they have not worked with before. Teachers also provide comments.
    3. Learners revise their work taking into account peer and instructor feedback.
  - Students create their multimodal recipes/procedural texts, and they share them with their instructors.[16]
  - Teachers can combine students work into a digital cookbook (e.g., in platforms such as issuu or Flipsnack; Appendix B), and they can unveil the publication in a social event (e.g., for parents, L2 community members, etc.). Also, for the unveiling event, learners can be encouraged to cook their dishes, and share them with their classmates and audience.

- Another alternative is for instructors to share their students' work with their professional community. For example, they can upload products to an OER repository (for a list of possible options, see Appendix in Blyth & Thoms, 2021 [the link to this open resource is included in the reference section of this chapter]), and/or share them with interest groups in L2 teachers' organizations.
- **Text comparison**
  Experiencing the new, conceptualizing, analyzing
  Meaning-making metafunctions of focus: Reference (what), agency (who), structure (how), context (when/where—sociocultural/sociohistorical), and interest (why/for whom)
  - Possible activities (for other options, see Table 4.1 on page 80):
    - Learners analyze the class's recipes, and they collect information about the kinds of dishes chosen, their ingredients, and semiotic resources. What do the artifacts say about the class community? Students reflect on aspects of the class members' lifeworld and experiences embedded in the recipes, and celebrate the diverse identities reflected in the ensembles (e.g., through the creation of a word cloud with tools such as Word Art, WordClouds, or WordItOut; Appendix B).
    - Students transduce their recipes (see page 103), creating scripts to convert their recipes into video ensembles.
      - Learners storyboard their texts (e.g., with tools such as Canva, Storyboarder, or makeStoryboard; Appendix B), planning how each part will be presented in the new format. Also, they offer ideas for music and setting (i.e., where the video will be recorded).
      - Once learners have finished their work, they share it with a partner with whom they have not worked. Each student explains their semiotic choices.
      - Both students reflect on what the transduction process has entailed and on the effectiveness of different semiotic systems for meaning-making, and they summarize their main points.
      - Each pair's summary is posted in the class's LMS or collaborative canvas.
      - The class uses the summaries to reflect on the different forms procedural texts might take, and on which of them appears to be the most effective.

9. School Brochures[17]

In the activities presented in this section, inspired by Zammit's (2019) work with elementary-school children, learners make use of the L2 to develop digital brochures to promote their school or academic institution to attract new students.

The intended audience are local parents who speak the L2, or individuals in regions where the L2 is spoken. Because the goal of the artifacts is to encourage prospective parents/students, they can be classified as persuasive texts. Thus, the instructional sequence could be organized around genre-based instruction (see Chapter 4). The steps presented below could also guide the development of other persuasive texts.[18]

Instructional Information and Guidance (Task Idea Inspired by Zammit, 2019)

Educational context: Appropriate for all ages.
L2 performance level: Can be adapted to all levels—novice (beginning), intermediate, or advanced.
Modes of communication: Interpersonal, interpretive, and presentational (multimodal [including L2 written text]).
Project length: Average (three to five weeks). This task can be structured as an instructional unit.
L2 focus: Terminology related to academic aspects, extracurricular activities, numbers, percentages; present tense; passive voice; impersonal constructions; descriptive vocabulary (adjective, verbs); connectors to express reasoning (e.g., thus, because of, therefore, furthermore, etc.).
Student organization: Pairs and groups.
Pedagogical sequence:
- **Setting the context**
  Experiencing, analyzing critically
  Meaning-making metafunctions of focus: Reference (what), agency (who), context (when/where—sociocultural/sociohistorical), and interest (why/for whom)
  - The instructor surveys students about the reasons why they have chosen to study at the institution or what they like the most about their school.
  - The class summarizes the ideas presented by each student, creating a list of aspects that make the institution unique. The summary is posted in the class's LMS or collaborative canvas (e.g., Milanote, Jamboard, or Padlet; Appendix B).
  - Learners are organized in groups. Each group works with an official institutional brochure in the L1, focusing on the information provided, semiotic resources used, and intended audience. Group members also assess the brochure as a whole in terms of effectiveness and the institutional image reflected in the content:
    - Does the brochure represent the diversity of the student body?
    - Does it focus on certain aspects of the institution more than on others? Why might that be the case?
    - What are the strengths and weaknesses of the brochure in terms of meaning and design (e.g., font, color, etc.)?

- In the next step, each group joins another one, and they present their ideas to the other group's members. The two groups summarize their combined findings, and present them to the rest of the class.
- With the teacher's guidance, the class as a whole determines what makes the brochure an effective artifact or not, and to what meaning-making elements the institution resorts to "sell" itself to parents/students.

Experiencing the new, analyzing critically

Meaning-making metafunctions of focus: Reference (what), agency (who), context (when/where—sociocultural/sociohistorical), and interest (why/for whom)

- Learners work with L2 brochures. Ideally, the texts are connected to academic institutions in L2 communities. However, if this type of material is difficult to find, students could work with artifacts developed by commercial companies or non-profit organizations.
- Students collaborate with the members of their original groups, and they analyze a sample brochure. Each group has a different text. Learners focus on the following:
  - Institution or company promoted
  - Semiotic elements (e.g., L2, images) and the information conveyed by each semiotic system (e.g., linguistic, visual, gestural, etc.)
  - Intended audience
- To organize this work, instructors can resort to the questions in Table 4.1 (see page 80 and Appendix A).
- Groups summarize their findings in the class's LMS or collaborative canvas. For example, the instructor can post each brochure and learners' upload their ideas next to or below it, in a table format. This could also be done through a collaborative document such as a Google document.

- **Modeling and deconstructing the text**

Conceptualizing, analyzing

Meaning-making metafunctions of focus: Reference (what), agency (who), structure (how), context (when/where—sociocultural/sociohistorical), and interest (why/for whom)

- In the next step, each group focuses on the organization of ideas and each semiotic element in their artifact. They analyze the following:
  - Layout (position of each element) and organization of the content.
  - Characteristics of each semiotic element (based on foci in Appendix A).
  - Contributions of each semiotic element to the overall meaning of the artifact and to its persuasive nature.

  Also, students pay specific attention to the use of the L2, highlighting the expressions and structures that have been chosen by the meaning-maker to persuade the audience.
- Based on their work, each group attempts to define what a persuasive text is.

- All groups share their definitions with the rest of the class. The instructor guides the class discussion, directing students toward the understanding of the artifact's *hook* (what attracts the audience's attention to the brochure); *sell* (the elements that convince the audience that choosing the institution/company would be a good decision); and *call to action* (how the audience is encouraged to act [i.e., by applying to the institution/buying the company's products]).
- The class discussion results in a common definition for persuasive texts, including their objective, the kind of information they convey, the organization of ideas, and the meaning-making resources that can be used to convince the audience.

- **Joint construction of the text**
  Applying appropriately
  Meaning-making metafunctions of focus: Reference (what), agency (who), structure (how), context (when/where—sociocultural/sociohistorical), and interest (why/for whom)
  - Students are organized in pairs, working with classmates not belonging to their group.
  - Each pair works with a new text from the bank of model ensembles (i.e., an artifact different from the one analyzed in the two students' groups).
  - Pairs improve their model text. For example, they rewrite the existing L2 text to make it more persuasive, and they suggest changes to other semiotic elements (e.g., new colors, different fonts, new images, etc.).
  - After pairs have finished their work, they participate in peer reviews. Each pair presents their changes to the members of another pair using the L2 (and L1), and they receive feedback.
  - Based on their peers' comments, learners incorporate (or not) the proposed changes to their artifacts. If students decide not to accept their classmates' suggestions, they need to justify their decision, making reference to meaning and the persuasive objective of the text.
  - Each pair submits their new versions of the model texts to the instructor, including explanations for the rejection of peers' suggestions if needed. Students' justifications can be written in the L1.

- **Independent construction of the text**
  Applying creatively
  Meaning-making metafunctions of focus: Reference (what), agency (who), structure (how), context (when/where—sociocultural/sociohistorical), and interest (why/for whom)
  - The pairs are joined with other pairs to form groups.
  - The new groups develop a digital brochure to promote their school/college/institution. Possible general instructions:
    - The school/college/university needs your help to boost enrollment numbers, and to diversify the student body. The principal/dean/provost is hiring you and your group members to design a digital

brochure that can be distributed to parents/prospective students who speak [target language]. The objective is to persuade them to enroll [their child] at our school/institution.

The brochures should provide information about the following:
- The city where the school/university is located (e.g., population data, attractions)
- The student body (gender percentages, origin, ethnicity)
- Education programs
- Facilities

Meaning-making elements to be included:
- Different colors and font types/sizes
- L2 text [instructors should provide detailed information on L2 structures to be used]
- A small map
- Five to six photos [students can be encouraged to take their own, or to use the institution's photo bank—if available]
- Hyperlinks
- Citations/attributions

(Adapted from Zammit, 2019, pp. 54–55)

- To develop their digital brochures, learners can use word processing tools such as Microsoft Word or Google Docs, or more comprehensive platforms (in terms of templates and creative elements) such as Canva, Lucidpress, or Venngage (Appendix B).
- Depending on the school/institution, the brochures developed by each group could be used as promotional materials (this was the case in Zammit's [2019] work).
- Alternatively, learners' artifacts could become instructional materials for future L2 classes. In that case, the texts would need to carry a Creative Commons license (e.g., CC BY-SA), and all the semiotic elements in them would need to be open. For more information about this possibility, see page 102 in the example "Endangered, Threatened, or Vulnerable Flora and Fauna: Expository Texts and Infographics", and page 137 in the example "Recipes and Other Procedural Texts".
- Groups work on the first drafts of their brochures, with a fair division of labor. For example, each group member can be assigned a section of the brochure. The initial versions of the artifacts need to include the L2 text, information on colors, sample fonts to be used, and small versions of the photos chosen (or links to them).
- Once groups have completed their drafts, they participate in peer reviews with members of another group. Each group member can review a section of the other group's ensemble. Again, it is important that groups monitor the fair assignment of tasks (see page 62) in Chapter 3 for detailed information on cooperative learning).
- After the peer reviews, groups revise their drafts, incorporating their peers' suggestions. Instructors can also offer comments.

- Once revisions are complete, the groups create their digital, multimodal brochures, and they submit them to their instructor.
- Teachers can choose to share their students' work with the school/institution, or with their peers (for suggestions, see page 102 in this chapter).
- **Text comparison**
  Experiencing the new, conceptualizing, analyzing
  Meaning-making metafunctions of focus: Reference (what), agency (who), structure (how), context (when/where—sociocultural/sociohistorical), and interest (why/for whom)
  - Students work in groups, and compare their L2 brochure to the original L1 institutional artifact they analyzed at the beginning of the pedagogical sequence. They explore similarities and differences in terms of meaning (e.g., what makes the two brochures effective?), semiotic resources used (e.g., which modes/mode combination works better in persuasive texts?), and meaning-makers' motivation (e.g., what biases do they detect in the two artifacts? How are they connected to the authors' lifeworld/lived experiences/ideologies?). Groups report their findings to the rest of the class. Have groups reached similar conclusions?
  - Learners go back to the list the class created in *setting the context*. In groups, they add to its contents, incorporating the information about their school/college/institution that they have gathered through their work on the brochure. What positive aspects have they discovered? What do they think needs to change? What kind of persuasive text could they create for the school/institution administrators to encourage action for change?
  - Instructors choose samples of persuasive digital posters or infographics (an example is presented in Figure 5.1). Learners can be organized in groups. Each group works with one artifact, and analyzes its objective, intended audience, semiotic resources used, and meaning-maker's motivation. Based on their analysis, students suggest changes to make it a more effective/less biased persuasive text.

Final Recommendations

As stated in this chapter's introductory paragraphs, the enactment of the examples presented in the previous sections in L2 classes presupposes the incorporation of L-by-D's reflexive pedagogy and knowledge processes and a focus on its metafunctions, as well as the L2 practice recommendations delineated in Chapters 2, 3, and 4. Before I close the chapter, I would like to complement this information with practical tips based on my more than 20 years of experience as an L2 practitioner, teacher trainer, language program director, and materials developer.

As you have seen, none of the samples I presented are based on the use of commercial textbooks. Instead, all of them rely on the adoption of authentic, multimodal materials and instructors and learners' collaboration with members of local L2 communities. Why is this the case? Well, no mass-produced materials could ever offer the multimodal semiotic and sociocultural richness of artifacts

144 Sample Second Language Tasks

Figure 5.1 Example of a persuasive infographic. Note: Infographic: which kind of activist are you? By developmenteducation.ie and Dóchas as part of the European Year for Development, licensed under CC BY-SA 4.0. https://bit.ly/3Cyaluk.

created by target-language meaning-makers and/or communities of L2 students who might share lifeworlds and lived experiences with other learners. That is, "when student works are openly [shared with others], each work becomes the beginning of an ongoing conversation in which other learners participate as they contextualize and extend the work in support of their own learning" (Wiley & Hilton, 2018, p. 136). Other drawbacks of commercial textbooks are the limitations brought about by their one-size-fits-all pedagogical approach, which cannot answer all students' needs, and content that is subject to publisher-imposed ideological limitations (see Apple & Christian-Smith, 1991). As is clearly evident from this and previous chapters, I strongly believe that open education is the path we need to follow in L2 learning and teaching.

Nevertheless, I also understand (based on my experience and research; e.g., Zapata, 2020) that materials development can be overwhelming for L2 teachers. Therefore, I have tried to simplify the projects in this chapter as much as possible, and it is my hope that they will be implemented as presented or adapted as needed to make L2 learning more diverse and meaningful. Also, it is important to emphasize that the tasks can be shortened, and students do not need to work in all knowledge processes. If you are inspired (as I hope you will be) by the work described in this chapter, and/or you also want to explore other topics and develop your own tasks, here is some advice:

- *Before you do, check what is already available.*
  L2 teachers are fortunate to have access to a variety of open materials curated by resource centers such as the Center for Open Educational Resources and Language Learning and the Open Language Resource Center. Additionally, there are other non-specialized repositories that offer L2 options. I encourage you to consult the list provided by Blyth and Thoms (2021) in the Appendix of their edited book (a link to this resource is included in the reference section). I also strongly recommend having a look at the units developed by Learning for Justice, which, though developed for L1 students, can be easily adapted for use with L2 learners. And subscribe to their free magazine![19]
- *Start small.*
  Instead of attempting to create a full task integrating *L-by-D*'s eight epistemic moves, develop an activity within one or two of the knowledge processes. Use the samples in this chapter as models, and/or incorporate the questions and foci in Appendix A to guide your students' analysis of a multimodal text. Also, I recommend you start with authentic ensembles that are attractive, and provide learners with multiple elements that can aid comprehension and interpretation. I am a fan of infographics, posters, short animated videos, picture books, comics, and artistic pieces.
- *Be ready to adapt.*
  Before you start your search for open artifacts, have a topic in mind. Choose something that is not too narrow. Instead, think of five keywords that are connected to the topic. In the wise words of my colleague and OER expert,

Dr. Carl Blyth, sometimes "what you find is not exactly what you wanted, but it will show you what to do." That is, you build your content around the authentic text you've found (see the examples in my next point).

- *Find inspiration in your everyday world.*
  My eyes and ears are always open to technology developments and social trends and movements. I have a Twitter account solely for the purpose of keeping culturally and socially up-to-date. I read the *New York Times*, and I also subscribe to email lists from organizations related to L2 Spanish local communities and beyond (e.g., I get notifications from the Library of Congress, the Smithsonian, state and national museums, and world-wide non-profit organizations). I believe that most of my OER materials have originated from or have been creatively sparked by artifacts that I have found by chance. For example, I created the recipe task after I read an interview with Texas chef Adán Medrano in the *New York Times*, and I developed an L2 Spanish unit on young Latinx activists after I saw a *DemocracyNow* video segment featuring Xiye Bastida, a young climate-change advocate who is part of the Otomi Toltec nation.[20]

- *Involve your students in materials development.*
  Much of my open work relies on artifacts developed by students in my L2 Spanish classes. These materials were the result of renewable assignments; i.e., tasks "which both support an individual student's learning and result in new or improved open educational resources that provide a lasting benefit to the broader community of learners" (Wiley & Hilton, 2018, p. 137). There are many advantages to student-produced materials. For example, assignments constitute a meaningful and purposeful instance of L2 use (Glisan & Donato, 2021), as learners produce texts that are connected to their lifeworld, and for which there will be a concrete use. Also, some of my unpublished data have shown that the knowledge that their work will be incorporated into digitally published open instructional materials is a source of student motivation and investment even in required L2 classes, because learners feel legitimized as L2 users as well as meaning-makers. Other existing projects have explored learners' open contributions (e.g., Azzam et al., 2017; DeRosa, 2016) and have reported successful results for both student learning and classroom engagement.

- *Do not be afraid to use your voice and your privilege to create materials that address socially relevant issues.*
  My final piece of advice is connected to *L-by-D*'s goal of a transformative curriculum and my responsibility as a citizen of the world. I believe that, as educators, we have the human mandate to teach for social justice, and to engage our students in meaningful and critical L2 use. Therefore, I strongly encourage you to use your practice to introduce learners to socially relevant issues, and create pedagogical interventions that will result in in-depth analysis, reflection, and, possibly, local activism. I summarize the steps in my materials development cycle in Figure 5.2.

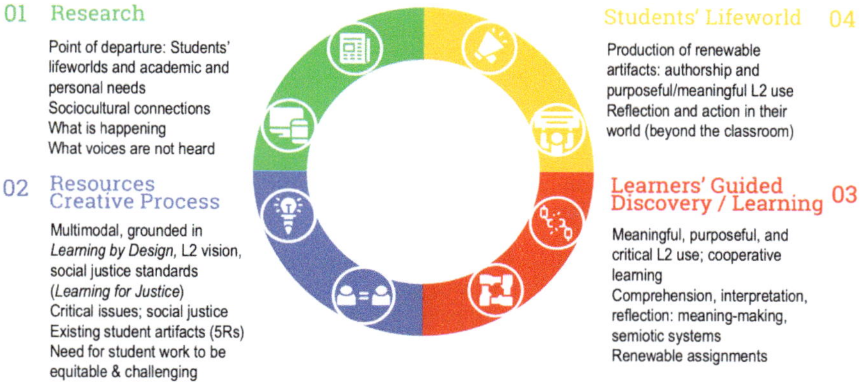

Figure 5.2 Materials development cycle relying on open resources.

Summary

My goal in this chapter was to offer L2 educators sample tasks that can be adapted for students in diverse educational contexts. Embedded in all of them are *L-by-D*'s principles of belonging and transformation, reflexive pedagogy, knowledge processes, and metafunctions, as well as the aspects of L2 learning and teaching I discussed in previous chapters. The information in each example is complemented with references to the Appendices (A, B, and C), which provide suggestions for activities in *L-by-D*'s epistemic moves, the analysis and assessment of multimodal ensembles, and links to the recommended digital tools. In the final part of the chapter, I incorporated some advice for the development of open materials with the hope that my experience can be helpful to in-service and future L2 practitioners.

Notes

1 For a similar project for elementary-school children incorporating the analysis and production of multimodal ensembles, see Zammit (2018, 2019).
2 For other ideas for L2 tasks with a critical, socially relevant focus, see Wagner et al. (2019) and Glynn et al. (2014).
3 As a starting point, L2 teachers can explore these websites: (1) Image Library, Creative Commons (http://bit.ly/ImageLibraryCC), (2) Tail & Fur Infographics (http://bit.ly/TailFurInfographics), and (3) Pinterest Animals (Infographics) (http://bit.ly/PinterestAnimals).
4 To learn more about open licenses and attributions, I recommend the comprehensive information Creative Commons offers at http://bit.ly/CCLicensesInfo and https://creativecommons.org/use-remix/attribution/.
5 For more information on the use of graphic novels/comics in L2 classes, see Bakis (2014), Cary (2004), Norton and Vanderheyden (2004), and Zapata and Ribota (2021b).
6 Yaman Ntelioglou (2011) offers ideas for implementation in her study. I also recommend Baldwin and Fleming's (2003) work, and the literature review carried out by Belliveau and Kim (2013).

148 Sample Second Language Tasks

7 A multimodal version of Anzaldúa's poem can be found at http://bit.ly/NepantlaGA. For *nepantla* examples, I suggest the following artifacts: (1) Santa Barraza's art piece *Nepantla* (https://bit.ly/SBarrazaNepantla) and the artist's video analysis of her work (https://bit.ly/SBarrazaVideo), (2) visual representations of the concept (e.g., http://bit.ly/NepantlaVisual and http://bit.ly/Nepantlas), and (3) Pat Mora's (1985) poem *Legal Alien* (http://bit.ly/LegalAlienPM).
8 This resource is available at https://yourstory.tenement.org/.
9 Recent publications focused on stories in the L2 classroom and grounded in multiliteracies approaches that can be of interest are the following: Callow (2020), Macken-Horarik (2016), Reyes-Torres and Portalés Raga (2020), Timlin et al. (2021), and Zammit (2019).
10 For a list of other possible tools for animation, see https://bit.ly/AnimationResources.
11 For another recent example of podcasts, see Allen and Gamalinda's (2021) work. In this project, L2 French university students created podcasts to narrate personal experiences similar to those featured in shows such as *This American Life*, or in the case of the study, its French equivalent, *Transfert*. This task could also be considered as another option for the development of identity texts (see section on "Identity Texts" in this chapter), and L2 instructors could use the podcast suggestions in this section to enact it.
12 Gautam et al. (2019) describe a multi-year, interdisciplinary project in which middle, high school, and university learners collaborate in the development of student-produced radio documentaries. The initiative is titled *University Laboratory High School*, and, like the example described in this section, focuses on highlighting sociocultural aspects of the local community (e.g., oral histories on community members' personal experiences). If L2 instructors have connections with colleagues in other educational settings, this could be another rich pedagogical option.
13 For information on podcast development and instructional guidelines, I recommend *PodcastInsights* (https://www.podcastinsights.com/start-a-podcast/), *Escuela Radio Ambulante* (in Spanish; https://radioambulante.org/educacion/escuela-radio-ambulante), and *NPR Teaching Podcasting* (https://n.pr/3jrWJsX).
14 For examples of the materials I use, see Module 4 (Section 4.3) of my OER book for L2 Spanish writing (Zapata, 2021), available at http://bit.ly/ModelArtifacts.
15 Another alternative is for students to create recipes from their state/regional area, and to develop a cookbook. This task offers learners the opportunity to use the L2 to share local culinary traditions with an L2 audience. An example of this type of work, created by intermediate-low L2 Spanish university students, can be found at http://bit.ly/CookbookExample.
16 Sample materials developed by my students can be found in Zapata (2021), Module 4 (Section 4.6), available at http://bit.ly/SampleStudentMat. For recent work with procedural videos, see Fadila et al. (2021).
17 Other popular brochure options are those that focus on tourism. For instance, students develop artifacts on local attractions to encourage target-language tourists to visit the area. The steps in this section could be adapted for the development of this topic. Also, see Yeh (2018) for a project in which L2 English learners created videos to highlight aspects their native Taiwan.
18 For example, this task could be combined with the activities presented in #1 and #2. Learners could go a step further, and develop short posters or infographics with calls for action.
19 Web addresses: Center for Open Educational Resources and Language Learning: https://www.coerll.utexas.edu/coerll/; Open Language Resource Center: http://olrc.ku.edu; Learning for Justice: https://www.learningforjustice.org/; Learning for Justice Magazine: https://www.learningforjustice.org/magazine.
20 The interview with chef Adán Medrano can be found at http://bit.ly/CocinaTexas, and my unit on young Latinx activists is available at http://bit.ly/ActivismoJoven. To learn more about the Otomi Toltec nation, I recommend their website: http://otomi.org/about/.

References

Works Cited

Albala, K. (Ed.). (2013). *Routledge international handbook of food studies*. Routledge.

Allen, H. W., & Gamalinda, S. (2021). Making podcasts in the collegiate French writing course. *Calico Journal*, 38(1), 1–16. https://doi.org/10.1558/cj.40912

Anderson, L., & Meribah, R. (2016). A taste of the past: Teaching Spain's culinary and cultural history. *Global Food History*, 2(1), 74–84. https://doi.org/10.1080/20549547.2016.1129594

Anstey, M., & Bull, G. (2006). *Teaching and learning multiliteracies: Changing times, changing literacies*. International Reading Association.

Anzaldúa, G. (1987). *Borderlands/La frontera: The new mestiza*. Aunt Lute Books.

Apple, M., & Christian-Smith, L. K. (1991). *The politics of the textbook*. Routledge.

Azzam, A., Bresler, D., Leon, A., Maggio, L., Whitaker, E., Heilman, J., Orlowitz, J., Swisher, V., Rasberry, L., Otoide, K., Trotter, F., Ross, W., & McCue, J. D. (2017). Why medical schools should embrace Wikipedia: Final-year medical student contributions to Wikipedia articles for academic credit at one school. *Academic Medicine: Journal of the Association of American Medical Colleges*, 92(2), 194–200. https://doi.org/10.1097/ACM.0000000000001381

Bakis, M. (2014). *The graphic novel classroom: POWerful teaching and learning with images*. Skyhorse.

Baldwin, P., & Fleming, K. (2003). *Teaching literacy through drama: Creative approaches*. Routledge/Falmer.

Belliveau, G., & Kim, W. (2013). Drama in L2 learning: A research synthesis. *Scenario*, 2013(2), 7–27. https://doi.org/10.33178/scenario.7.2.2

Bender, D., Ankeny, R., Belasco, W., Bentley, A., Mandala, E., Pilcher, J. M., & Scholliers, P. (2011). Eating in class: Gastronomy, taste, nutrition, and teaching food history. *Radical History Review* 110, 197–216. https://doi.org/10.1215/01636545-2010-035

Beucher, B., Low, D. E., & Smith, A. (2020). Memes and social messages: Teaching a critical literacies curriculum on DAPL. *International Journal of Multicultural Education*, 22(3), 24–49. https://doi.org/10.18251/ijme.v22i3.2235

Black, R. W. (2005). Access and affiliation: The literacy and composition practices of English-language learners in an online fanfiction community. *Journal of Adolescent & Adult Literacy*, 49(2), 118–128. https://www.jstor.org/stable/40017563

Black, R. W. (2006). Language, culture, and identity in online fanfiction. *E-Learning and Digital Media*, 3(2), 170–184. https://doi.org/10.2304/elea.2006.3.2.170

Black, R. W. (2008). *Adolescents and online fan fiction*. Peter Lang.

Blyler, N., & Perkins, J. (1999). Culture and the power of narrative. *Journal of Business and Technical communication*, 13(3), 245–248. https://doi.org/10.1177/105065199901300301

Blyth, C., & Thoms, J. (2021). Appendix. In C. Blyth & J. Thoms (Ed.), *Open education and second language learning and teaching: The rise of a new knowledge ecology* (pp. 266–269). Multilingual Matters. https://www.degruyter.com/document/doi/10.21832/9781800411005-014/pdf

Brown, A., & Green, T. D. (2007). Video podcasting in perspective: The history, technology, aesthetics, and instructional uses of a new medium. *Journal of Educational Technology Systems*, 36(1), 3–17. https://doi.org/10.2190/ET.36.1.b

Bueno-Alastuey, C. M., & Nemeth, K. (2020). Quizlet and podcasts: Effects on vocabulary acquisition, *Computer Assisted Language Learning*. https://doi.org/10.1080/09588221.2020.1802601

Callow, J. (2020). Visual and verbal intersections in picture books–multimodal assessment for middle years students. *Language and Education, 34*(2), 115–134. https://doi.org/10.1080/09500782.2019.1689996

Cameron, M. (n.d.). *Developing a media portfolio*. Learning for Justice. https://www.learningforjustice.org/classroom-resources/lessons/developing-a-media-portfolio

Cary, S. (2004). *Going graphic: Comics at work in the multilingual classroom*. Heinemann.

Cognard-Black, J., & Goldthwaite, M. A. (2008). Books that cook: Teaching food and food literature in the English classroom. *College English, 70*(4), 421–436. https://www.jstor.org/stable/25472279

Cross, J. (2014). Promoting autonomous listening to podcasts: A case study. *Language Teaching Research, 18*(1), 8–32. https://doi.org/10.1177/1362168813505394

Cummins, J. (2006). Identity texts: The imaginative construction of self through Multiliteracies pedagogy. In O. García, T. Skutnabb-Kangas, & M. E. Torres-Guzmán (Eds.), *Imagining multilingual schools: Language in education and globalization* (pp. 51–68). Multilingual Matters.

Cummins, J., & Early, M. (2011). Introduction. In J. Cummins & M. Early (Eds.), *Identity texts: The collaborative creation of power in multilingual schools* (pp. 3–19). Trentham Books.

Cummins, J., Bismilla, V., Chow, P., Cohen, S., Giampapa, L. L., Sandhu, P., & Sastri, P. (2005). Affirming identity in multilingual classrooms. *Educational Leadership, 63*(1), 38–43. https://bit.ly/3iEjfya

Cummins, J., Hu, S., Markus, P., & Montero, M. K. (2015). Identity texts and academic achievement: Connecting the dots in multilingual school contexts. *TESOL Quarterly, 49*(3), 555–581. https://doi.org/10.1002/tesq.241

Danzak, R. L. (2011). Defining identities through multiliteracies: EL teens narrate their immigration experiences as graphic stories. *Journal of Adolescent & Adult Literacy, 55*(3), 187–196. https://www.jstor.org/stable/41320371

DeRosa, R. (2016, May 8). *My open textbook: Pedagogy and practice*. http://robinderosa.net/uncategorized/my-open-textbook-pedagogy-and-practice/

Domínguez Romero, E., & Bobkina, J. (2021). Exploring critical and visual literacy needs in digital learning environments: The use of memes in the EFL/ESL university classroom. *Thinking Skills and Creativity, 40*. https://doi.org/10.1016/j.tsc.2020.100783

Dunlap, J. C., & Lowenthal, P. R. (2016). Getting graphic about infographics: Design lessons learned from popular infographics. *Journal of Visual Literacy, 35*(1), 42–59. https://doi.org/10.1080/1051144X.2016.1205832

Durá, L.; Salas, C.; Medina-Jerez, W.; Hill, V. (2015). De aquí y de allá: Changing perceptions of literacy through food pedagogy, asset-based narratives, and hybrid spaces. *Community Literacy Journal, 10*(1), 21–39. https://muse.jhu.edu/article/605291

Dyjur, P., Ferreira, C., & Clancy, T. (2021). Increasing accessibility and diversity by using a UDL framework in an infographics assignment. *Currents in Teaching & Learning, 12*(2), 71–83. https://www.washington.edu/doit/increasing-accessibility-and-diversity-using-udl-framework-infographics-assignment

Espinosa-Dulanto, M., Calderon-Berumen, F., & O'Donald, K. (2020). Nepantla connection: Testimonio and Anzaldúa's poetry. In M. Cantú-Sánchez, C. de León-Zepeda, & N. E. Cantú (Eds.), *Teaching Gloria E. Anzaldúa: Pedagogy and practice for our classrooms and communities* (pp. 15–32). The University of Arizona Press.

Fadila, N. N., Setyarini, S., & Gustine, G. G. (2021). Channeling multiliteracies in digital era: A case study of EFL student-made video project in vocational high school. *Journal of *English Language Teaching and Linguistics*, 6(1), 73–91. http://dx.doi.org/10.21462/jeltl.v6i1.494

Faramarzi, S., Tabrizi, H. H., & Chalak, A. (2019). The effect of vodcasting tasks on EFL listening comprehension progress in an online program. *International Journal of Instruction*, 12(1), 1263–1280. https://files.eric.ed.gov/fulltext/EJ1201185.pdf

Galda, L., Ash, G. W., & Cullinan, B. (2000). Children's literature. In M. L. Kamil, P. B. Mosenthal, P. D. Pearson, & R. Barr (Eds.), *Handbook of Reading Research, Volume III* (pp. 361–379). Lawrence Erlbaum Associates.

Gautam, A. A., Morford, J. H., & Yockey, S. H. (2019). On the air: The pedagogy of student-produced radio documentaries. *The Oral History Review*, 42(2), 311–351. https://doi.org/10.1093/ohr/ohv044

Glisan, E. W., & Donato, R. (2021). *Enacting the work of language instruction: High-leverage teaching practices* (Vol. 2). ACTFL.

Gonulal, T. (2020). Improving listening skills with extensive listening using podcasts and vodcasts. *International Journal of Contemporary Educational Research*, 7(1), 311–320. https://doi.org/10.33200/ijcer.685196

Goriunova, O. (2016). The force of digital aesthetics: On memes, hacking, and individuation. *The Nordic Journal of Aesthetics*, 24(47), 54–75. https://doi.org/10.7146/nja.v24i47.23055

Glynn, C., Wesely, P., & Wassell, B. (2014). *Words and actions: Teaching languages through the lens of social justice*. ACTFL.

Hung, H.-T., Chiu, Y.-C. J., & Yeh, H.-C. (2013). Multimodal assessment of and for learning: A theory-driven design rubric. *British Journal of Educational Technology*, 44(3), 400–409. https://doi.org/10.1111/j.1467-8535.2012.01337.x

Indahsari, D. (2020). Using podcast for EFL students in language learning. *Journal of English Educators Society*, 5(2), 103–108. https://jees.umsida.ac.id/index.php/jees/article/view/767/888

Jewell, T. (2021). *This book is anti-racist journal*. Quarto Publishing.

Jewitt, C. (2012). Technology and reception as multimodal remaking. In S. Norris (Ed.), *Multimodality in practice: Investigating theory-in-practice-through-methodology* (pp. 97–11). Routledge.

Kalantzis, M., & Cope, B. (2012). *New Learning: Elements of a science of education*. Cambridge University Press.

Kalantzis, M., Cope, B., Chan, E., & Dalley-Trim, L. (2016). *Literacies* (2nd ed.). Cambridge University Press.

Kalantzis, M., Cope, B., & the Learning by Design Project Group. (2005). *Learning by Design*. Victorian Schools Innovation Commission and Common Ground Publishing.

Kalantzis, M., Cope, B., & Zapata, G. C. (2019). *Las alfabetizaciones múltiples: Teoría y práctica*. Octaedro.

Kargozari, H. R., & Zarinkamar, N. (2014). Lexical development through podcasts. *Procedia–Social and Behavioral Sciences*, 98, 839–843. https://doi.org/10.1016/j.sbspro.2014.03.489

Karrebæk, M. S., Riley, K. C., & Cavanaugh, J. R. (2018). Food and language: Production, consumption, and circulation of meaning and value. *Annual Review of Anthropology*, 47, 17–32. https://doi.org/10.1146/annurev-anthro-102317-050109

Kelly, C., & Zak, M. (1999). Narrativity and professional communication: Folktales and community meaning. *Journal of Business and Technical Communication*, 13(3), 297–317. https://doi.org/10.1177/105065199901300304

Kress, G. (2010). *Multimodality: A social semiotic approach to contemporary communication*. Routledge.

Krishnan, J., Maamuujav, U., & Collins, P. (2020). Multiple utilities of infographics in undergraduate students' process-based writing. *Writing & Pedagogy*, *12*(2–3), 369–394. https://doi.org/10.1558/wap.18814

Krum, R. (2014). *Cool infographics: Effective communication with data visualization and design*. Wiley.

Lanyon Cluster of Schools. (n.d.). *Learning by Design*. https://newlearningonline.com/_uploads/lanyon_toolkit.pdf

Levy, M., & Kimber, K. (2009). Developing an approach for comparing students' multimodal text creations: A case study. *Australasian Journal of Educational Technology*, *25*(4), 489–508. https://doi.org/10.14742/ajet.1125

Lewis, C. (2015). Eating history: A United States history project. *Teaching History: A Journal of Methods*, *40*(2), 91–100. https://doi.org/10.33043/TH.40.2.91-100

Maamuujav, U., Krishnan, J., & Collins, P. (2020). The utility of infographics in L2 writing classes: A practical strategy to scaffold writing development. *TESOL Journal*, *11*(2), e484. https://doi.org/10.1002/tesj.484

Macken-Horarik, M. (2016). Building a metalanguage for interpreting multimodal literature: Insights from systemic functional semiotics in two case study classrooms. *English in Australia*, *51*(2), 85–99. https://www.aate.org.au/documents/item/1132

Martinez, M. G., & McGee, L. (2000). Children's literature and reading instruction: Past, present, and future. *Reading Research Quarterly*, *35*(1), 154–169. http://www.jstor.org/stable/748293

Matrix, S., & Hodson, R. (2014). Teaching with infographics: Practicing new digital competencies and visual literacies. *Journal of Pedagogic Development*, *4*(2), 17–27. https://www.beds.ac.uk/jpd/volume-4-issue-2/teaching-with-infographics

Mills, K. A., & Levido, A. (2011). Iped: Pedagogy for digital text production. *The Reading Teacher*, *65*(1), 80–91. https://doi.org/10.1598/RT.65.1.11

Mills, K. A., & Unsworth, L. (2018). iPad animations: Powerful multimodal practices for adolescent literacy and emotional language. *Journal of Adolescent & Adult Literacy*, *61*(6), 609–620. https://doi.org/10.1002/jaal.717

Moyna, M. I. (2019, February 21–23). *Students' podcasts in the Hispanic linguistics class* [Conference session]. 6th National Symposium on Spanish as a Heritage Language, University of Texas Rio Grande Valley, McAllen, TX, United States. https://nsshl2019.weebly.com/program.html

Nathanson, S. (2006). Harnessing the power of story: Using narrative reading and writing across content areas. *Reading Horizons: A Journal of Literacy and Language Arts*, *47*(1), 1–26. https://scholarworks.wmich.edu/reading_horizons/vol47/iss1/2

National Education Association (NEA). (2011). *Preparing 21st century students for a global society: An educator's guide to the "Four Cs"*. https://dl.icdst.org/pdfs/files3/0d3e72e9b873e0ef2ed780bf53a347b4.pdf

National Standards in Foreign Language Education Project. (2015). *World-readiness standards for foreign language learning*. ACTFL.

Norton, B., & Vanderheyden, K. (2004). Comic book culture and second language learners. In B. Norton & K. Toohey (Eds.), *Critical pedagogies and language learning* (pp. 201–221). Cambridge University Press.

Partnership for 21st Century Skills (P21). (2011). *21st century skills map*. https://www.actfl.org/sites/default/files/resources/21st%20Century%20Skills%20Map-World%20Languages.pdf

Osborn, T. A. (2006). *Teaching world languages for social justice: A sourcebook of principles and practices*. Routledge.

Phillips, B. (2017). Student-produced podcasts in language learning: Exploring student perceptions of podcast activities. *IAFOR Journal of Education, 5*(3), 157–171. https://files.eric.ed.gov/fulltext/EJ1162673.pdf

Reyes-Torres, A., & Portalés Raga, M. (2020). Multimodal approach to foster the multiliteracies pedagogy in the teaching of EFL through picture books: The Snow Lion. *Atlantis, Journal of the Spanish Association of Anglo-American Studies, 42*(1), 94–119. http://doi.org/10.28914/Atlantis-2020-42.1.06

Riley, K. C., & Paugh, A. L. (2019). *Food and language: Discourses and foodways across cultures*. Routledge.

Rodney, A., Cappeliez, S., Oleschuk, M., & Johnston, J. (2017). The online domestic goddess: An analysis of food blog femininities. *Food, Culture & Society, 20*(4), 685–707. https://doi.org/10.1080/15528014.2017.1357954

Saeedakhtar, A., Haqju, R., & Rouhi, A. (2021). The impact of collaborative listening to podcasts on high school learners' listening comprehension and vocabulary learning. *System, 101*(102588). https://doi.org/10.1016/j.system.2021.102588

Sauro, S., & Sundmark, B. (2016). Report from Middle-Earth: Fan fiction tasks in the EFL classroom. *ELT Journal, 70*(4), 414–423. https://doi.org/10.1093/elt/ccv075

Şendağ, S., Gedik, N., & Toker, S. (2018). Impact of repetitive listening, listening-aid and podcast length on EFL podcast listening. *Computers & Education, 125*, 273–283. https://doi.org/10.1016/j.compedu.2018.06.019

Serafini, F. (2010). Reading multimodal texts: Perceptual, structural and ideological perspectives. *Children's Literature in Education, 41*, 85–104. https://doi.org/10.1007/s10583-010-9100-5

Swift, C. L., & Wilk, R. (2015). Introduction: Teaching with and through food. In C. L. Swift, & R. Wilk (Eds.), *Teaching food and culture* (pp. 9–20). Left Coast Press.

Thorne, S. L. (2013). Digital literacies. In M. R. Hawkins (Ed.), *Framing languages and literacies: Socially situated views and perspectives* (pp. 192–218). Routledge.

Timlin, C., Warner, C., Clark, L., & Ploschnitzki, P. (2021). Living literacies in a Märchenwelt: World building and perspective taking in a fairy-tale simulation project. *Die Unterrichtspraxis/Teaching German, 54*, 5–19. https://doi.org/10.1111/tger.12151

Tobin, T. J., & Behling, K. T. (2018). *Reach everyone, teach everyone*. West Virginia University Press.

Trubek, A. B., & Belliveau, C. (2009). Cooking as pedagogy: Engaging the senses through experiential learning. *Anthropology News, 50*(4), 16. https://doi.org/10.1111/j.1556-3502.2009.50416.x

UDL-IRN. (2011). *UDL in the instructional process* (version 1.0.). UDL-IRN. https://www.learningdesigned.org/sites/default/files/UDL%20Instructional%20Planning%20Process.pdf

Wagner, M., Cardetti, F., & Byram, M. (2019). *Teaching intercultural citizenship across the curriculum: The role of language education*. ACTFL.

Wiggins, B. E. (2019). *The discursive power of memes in digital culture: Ideology, semiotics, and intertextuality*. Routledge.

Wiley, D., & Hilton III, J. L. (2018). Defining OER-enabled pedagogy. *The International Review of Research in Open and Distributed Learning, 19*(4), 133–147. https://doi.org/10.19173/irrodl.v19i4.3601

Winn, R. (2021a, August 25). *2021 podcast stats & facts (new research from Apr 2021)*. Podcast Insights. https://www.podcastinsights.com/podcast-statistics/

Winn, R. (2021b, August 26). *How to start a podcast: A complete step-by-step tutorial.* Podcast Insights. https://www.podcastinsights.com/start-a-podcast/

Yaman Ntelioglou, B. (2011). 'But why do I have to take this class?' The mandatory drama-ESL class and multiliteracies pedagogy. *Research in Drama Education: The Journal of Applied Theatre and Performance, 16*(4), 595–615. https://doi.org/10.1080/13569783.2011.617108

Yeh, H-C. (2018). Exploring the perceived benefits of the process of multimodal video making in developing multiliteracies. *Language Learning and Technology, 22*(2), 28–37. http://hdl.handle.net/10125/44642

Zammit, K. (2016). Responding to literature: iPads, apps and multimodal text creation. *Literacy Learning: The Middle Years, 24*(2), 8–16. https://link.gale.com/apps/doc/A458564953/AONE?u=txshracd2564&sid=googleScholar&xid=bc53df4d

Zammit, K. (2018). "We're all real serious filmmakers": Learning about and creating multimodal mini-documentaries. *English Teaching: Practice & Critique, 17*(4), 371–386. https://doi.org/10.1108/ETPC-11-2017-0161

Zammit, K. (2019). Pedagogy, curriculum, and assessment: Multimodal practices that engage students with and in learning. In H. de Silva Joyce & S. Feez (Eds.), *Multimodality across classrooms: Learning about and through different modalities* (pp. 49–64). Routledge. https://doi.org/10.1080/1554480X.2010.509479

Zapata, G. C. (2020). Sprinting to the finish line: The benefits and challenges of book sprints in OER faculty-graduate student collaborations. *The International Review of Research in Open and Distributed Learning, 21*(2), 1–17. http://www.irrodl.org/index.php/irrodl/article/view/4607/5315

Zapata, G. C. (2021). *Introducción a la escritura. Genre-Based writing for intermediate Spanish learners.* Pressbooks. https://intermediatespanish.pressbooks.com/

Zapata, G. C., & Ribota, A. (2021a) The instructional benefits of identity texts and learning by design for learner motivation in required second language classes. *Pedagogies: An International Journal, 16*(1), 1–18. https://doi.org/10.1080/1554480X.2020.1738937

Zapata, G. C., & Ribota, A. (2021b). Open educational resources in heritage and L2 Spanish classrooms: Design, development, and implementation. In C. Blyth & J. Thoms (Eds.), *Open education and foreign language learning and teaching: The rise of a new knowledge ecology* (pp. 25–46). Multilingual Matters. https://www.degruyter.com/document/doi/10.21832/9781800411005-003/html.

Instructional Resources Cited

Cortázar, J. (2008 [1953]). *Final del juego.* Punto de Lectura.

Gerster, M., & Dunnett, F. (2021). *Travesía: A migrant girl's cross-border journey/El viaje de una joven migrante.* Arsenal Pulp Press.

Ha, R. (2020). *Almost American girl: An illustrated memoir.* Balzer Bray.

Mora, P. (1985). *Chants.* Arte Público Press.

Tan, S. (2007). *The arrival.* Scholastic.

Yang, G. L. (2006). *American born Chinese.* First Second.

Zumbastico Studios (2020, June 15). *The night face up/La noche boca arriba* [Video]. YouTube. https://youtu.be/9HPoD6A5uO8

Appendix A: Template Questions and Foci for the Analysis of Multimodal Texts[1]

Focus on Meaning (focus on the analysis of the *reference, agency, context,* and *interest metafunctions*)

- What is this text about?
- Why would you use it?/What purposes does it serve?
- Who created the text?
- Who is the text for (intended audience)?
- What are the meaning-maker's qualifications for creating the text?
- In what social situations and/or activities could we find a text like this one?
- Where was this text published (e.g., on a website, an academic book, etc.)?
- Why has the meaning-maker chosen this medium to publish the text?
- If the medium is open source (i.e., people do not have to pay to access the text), what can we hypothesize about the meaning-maker?
- What social voices are present in the text and which ones are absent? What does this say about the meaning-maker?

Focus on Structure (focus on the analysis of the *structure metafunction*)

- What information does each part of the text convey?
- How does each part contribute to the social purpose of the text as a whole?

Focus on Semiotic Resources

- What modes are present in the text?
  - Written (linguistic)
  - Oral (linguistic)
  - Visual
  - Spatial
  - Auditory
  - Gestural

- What does each semiotic element or mode contribute to the meaning of the text?
- How does each mode achieve its purpose? (Based on the analysis of the *reference, agency, structure, context,* and *interest metafunctions*)

Categories for Analysis of Semiotic Elements in Each Mode

Guiding Question: How does each semiotic element (within a particular mode) shape the message conveyed (reference, agency, structure, context, interest)?

LINGUISTIC

- Terminology associated with theme/topic
- Register and dialect
- Parts of speech (e.g., adjectives, adverbs, conjunctions, nouns, prepositions, pronouns, verbs [mood, tense])
- Punctuation
- Phrases and clauses
- Types of sentences (simple; coordination vs. subordination)
- Cohesive devices (connections within and between paragraphs)

VISUAL AND SPATIAL (BASED ON KRESS & VAN LEEUWEN, 2021)

Analysis of:

- Information value: This refers to the way in which elements/entities are placed in an image, which "endows them with specific informational values attached to the various zones of the image: left and right, top and bottom, center and margin" (p. 181).
- Salience: "the degree to which [elements of an image] attract the viewer's attention" (van Leeuwen, 2005, p. 284), with a focus on:
  - Position: Foreground or background (with respect to other elements/entities in the image).
  - Size (with respect to other elements/entities in the image).
  - Colors
    - Value: "The grey scale from maximally light (white) to maximally dark (black) … Light and dark are fundamental [sociocultural] experiences" (p. 245).
    - Saturation: Color intensity. Meaning connection: "ability to express emotive 'temperatures,' degrees of emotional intensity" (p. 245).
    - Purity: How "pure" the color is in connection with other colors (i.e., the degree to which it is mixed with other colors or not). Pure colors (vs. hybrid) might have cultural and/or ideological connotations.

- Transparency: This refers to "the scale that runs from transparent to opaque, via translucency" (p. 246). For example, a transparent color that allows for what is in the background to be seen might indicate some type of relationship between the things depicted.
- Luminosity: This describes a color's "ability to glow from within" (p. 246), which conveys the idea of a certain aura or special quality emanating from the depicted object/entity.
- Differentiation: This defines "the scale that runs from monochrome to the use of a maximally varied palette, and its very diversity or exuberance is the key to its meaning potential, as is the restraint involved in its opposite, lack of differentiation" (p. 247).

• Point of view: Relationship between the element/entity depicted and the viewer (e.g., eye level, bottom up, top down). For example, "the gaze at the viewer[s] [i.e., eye level] … creates a visual form of direct address, [and] it acknowledges [them] explicitly, addressing them with a visual 'you'." Also, the meaning-maker "uses the image to *do* something to the viewer" (pp. 116–117, emphasis in original).

• Framing: The placement of elements in relationship to other elements as determined by "the presence of framing devices (realized by elements which create dividing lines, or by actual frames), [which] disconnects elements of the image, signifying that they are, in some sense, to be understood as separate elements" (p. 182).

AUDITORY

Analysis of:

- Intonation
- Pace (as denoted by pauses, silences, and string of sounds/phrases)
- Pitch (high, low)
- Stress
- Volume

GESTURAL

Analysis of:

- Appearance: Clothing, hair style, make-up
- Facial expressions and body movement
- Posture
- Position and orientation of body (as a separate entity and in connection with other elements/bodies)

Note

1 The information in this section has been adapted from Anstey and Bull (2006, 2018) and Hyland (2014).

References

Anstey, M., & Bull, G. (2006). *Teaching and learning multiliteracies: Changing times, changing literacies*. Australian Literacy Educators' Association and International Reading Association.

Anstey, M., & Bull, G. (2018). *Foundations of multiliteracies: Reading, writing and talking in the 21st century*. Routledge.

Hyland, K. (2014). *Genre and second language writing*. The University of Michigan Press.

Kress, G., & van Leeuwen, T. (2021). *Reading images: The grammar of visual design* (3rd ed.). Routledge.

Van Leeuwen, T. (2005). *Introducing social semiotics*. Routledge.

Appendix B: Recommended Websites and Digital Tools

Name of Tool/Website	URL	Pedagogical Uses
Adobe Spark	https://www.adobe.com/	Platform for the development of webpages, multimodal stories, posters, collages, graphics, and short videos
Anchor	https://anchor.fm/	Platform for podcast development and distribution
Animation Creator HD	https://apple.co/2ZVIDcB	App for the development of animations
Animation Desk Draw & Animate	https://www.kdanmobile.com/animation-desk	App for the development of animations
Animoto	https://animoto.com/education/classroom	Platform for video development
Archive of Our Own	https://archiveofourown.org/	Repository of fan fiction stories
Audacity	https://www.audacityteam.org/	Software to produce and edit audio
Blogger	https://www.blogger.com/about/	Platform for creating and publishing multimodal blogs
Buzzsprout	https://www.buzzsprout.com/	Platform for podcast hosting
Canva	https://www.canva.com/	Platform for the development of multimodal posters, collages, short videos, infographics, storyboards, graphs, etc.
Canva (brochures)	https://www.canva.com/brochures/	Platform for the development of multimodal brochures
Comic Life	https://plasq.com/education/take-comic-life-to-school/	App for the development of multimodal comics
Creative Commons Search (Images)	https://search.creativecommons.org/	Search platform to find copyright-free photos and videos
Creative Commons Search	https://oldsearch.creativecommons.org/	Search platform to find copyright-free materials (e.g., articles, webpages, etc.)
FanFiction.net	https://www.fanfiction.net/	Repository of fan fiction stories and platform for writing and publishing this type of text

(*Continued*)

(*Continued*)

Name of Tool/Website	URL	Pedagogical Uses
Flaticon	https://www.flaticon.com/	Repository of copyright-free icons and vectors
FlipaClip	https://flipaclip.us/	App for the development of animations
Flipgrid	https://flipgrid.com/	Platform with a variety of pedagogical tools, including those for video production and publishing
Flipsnack	https://www.flipsnack.com/edu.html	Platform for digital publication (e.g., magazines)
Free Music Archive	https://freemusicarchive.org/	Repository of royalty-free music
Google Sites	https://sites.google.com/	Platform for the development of webpages/websites
Google Slides	https://www.google.com/slides	Platform for the development of multimodal presentations
hypothes.is	https://web.hypothes.is/	Platform for social reading
Incompetech	https://incompetech.com/music/	Repository of royalty-free music
issuu	https://issuu.com/	Platform for the publication of digital magazines
Jamboard	https://jamboard.google.com/	Platform for students to work in a collaborative canvas/board
Lucidchart	https://www.lucidchart.com/pages/	Platform for the development of collaborative conceptual/spider maps
Lucidpress (brochures)	https://www.lucidpress.com/pages/examples/free-brochure-maker-online	Platform for the development of multimodal brochures
Make Beliefs Comix	https://makebeliefscomix.com/	Platform for the development of comics
makeStoryboard	https://makestoryboard.com/	Platform for the development of storyboards
Milanote	https://milanote.com/	Platform for students to work in a collaborative canvas/board
MindMeister	https://www.mindmeister.com/	Platform for the development of collaborative conceptual/spider maps
Moovly	https://www.moovly.com/	Platform for animation development
Noun Project	https://thenounproject.com/	Repository of copyright-free icons and vectors
Office Timeline	https://bit.ly/3CGbBeS	Microsoft-developed tool for the creation of timelines
Padlet	https://padlet.com	Platform for students to work in a collaborative canvas/board
Perusall	https://perusall.com/	Platform for social reading
PicsArt Animator	http://bit.ly/PicsArtAnimator	App for the development of animations

(*Continued*)

(*Continued*)

Name of Tool/Website	URL	Pedagogical Uses
Pixton	https://www.pixton.com/	Platform for the development of multimodal comics
PodBean	https://www.podbean.com/	Platform for podcast development and distribution
Popplet	https://www.popplet.com/	Platform/app for the development of collaborative, multimodal conceptual/spider maps
Preceden	https://www.preceden.com/	Platform for the development of multimodal timelines
Prezi	https://prezi.com/education/	Platform for the development of multimodal presentations
Renderforest	https://www.renderforest.com/video-animation	Platform for animation/video development
Silverman Sound Studios	https://www.silvermansound.com/free-music	Repository of royalty-free music
Snappa	https://snappa.com/	Platform for the development of multimodal posters, collages, infographics, blogs, etc.
Spreaker	https://www.spreaker.com/	Platform for podcast development and distribution
Storyboarder	https://wonderunit.com/storyboarder/	App for the development of storyboards
Sutori	https://www.sutori.com/en/teachers	Platform for the development of multimodal timelines and presentations
Timetoast	https://www.timetoast.com/	Platform for the development of multimodal timelines
Unsplash	https://unsplash.com/	Repository of copyright-free photos
Venngage	https://venngage.com/	Platform for the development of infographics
Venngage (brochures)	https://venngage.com/features/brochure-maker	Platform for the development of multimodal brochures
Visme	https://www.visme.co/	Platform for the development of infographics, multimodal brochures, and graphs
Wattpad	https://www.wattpad.com/	Repository of fan fiction stories and platform for writing and publishing this type of text
WavePad	https://www.nch.com.au/index.html	Software to produce and edit audio
Wix	https://www.wix.com/	Platform for the development of webpages/websites and multimodal blogs
Word Art	https://wordart.com/	Platform for the development of word clouds

(*Continued*)

(*Continued*)

Name of Tool/Website	URL	Pedagogical Uses
WordClouds	https://www.wordclouds.com/	Platform for the development of word clouds
WordItOut	https://worditout.com/	Platform for the development of word clouds
YouTube	https://www.youtube.com/	Platform for the development and distribution of videos

Appendix C: Multimodal Product Assessment

Guiding Assessment Questions

Content

- To what extent does the content reveal depth/breadth of knowledge and/or concept understanding?
- To what extent is the content appropriate for the intended audience?
- To what extent does the content reveal the meaning-maker's capacity to process/seek/express multiple sources/perspectives?
- To what extent has the meaning-maker incorporated all the required content elements into their products? Are elements missing? Are elements incomplete?
- To what extent is the content synthesized?
- To what extent are sources acknowledged? (Adapted from Levy & Kimber, 2009, p. 496.)

Use and Cohesion of Semiotic Elements

- Linguistic elements (use of the L2)
    - To what extent is the linguistic content comprehensible?
    - To what extent is the linguistic content appropriate for the intended audience (e.g., in terms of register)?
    - How do the linguistic elements in the multimodal text enable, limit, or hinder the message the meaning-maker is trying to convey?
- Visual elements
    - Has the meaning-maker adopted a visual theme?
    - If so, to what extent are visual choices (e.g., use of color, salience, typology) compatible with the visual theme and/or other semiotic elements in the text?
    - How do the visual elements in the multimodal text enable, limit, or hinder the message the meaning-maker is trying to convey?

- Gestural elements
  - Has the meaning-maker made use of any animated, gestural elements (e.g., clothing), or special effects to incorporate a dynamic sequencing to the content?
  - If so, to what extent are gestural elements used to purposefully and meaningfully complement or supplement other semiotic resources for meaning construction in a cohesive manner?
  - How do the gestural elements in the multimodal text enable, limit, or hinder the message the meaning-maker is trying to convey?
- Auditory elements
  - Has the meaning-maker made use of any auditory elements, such as music, sound effects, or narration?
  - If so, to what extent are auditory elements used to purposefully and meaningfully complement or supplement other semiotic resources for meaning construction in a cohesive manner?
  - How do the auditory elements in the multimodal text enable, limit, or hinder the message the meaning-maker is trying to convey?
- Spatial elements
  - Has the meaning-maker adopted a specific layout to structure semiotic elements?
  - If so, to what extent does the meaning-maker make use of spatial elements (e.g., text alignment, framing, point of view) to purposefully and meaningfully complement or supplement other semiotic resources for meaning construction in a cohesive manner?
  - How does the spatial design of the multimodal text enable, limit, or hinder the message the meaning-maker is trying to convey? (Adapted from Hung et al., 2013, p. 402.)

Assessment Categories

1. *Does not meet expectations* (poor/incomplete content and cohesion): Student's performance is unsatisfactory with respect to the outcomes and goals set for the task. For example, most required elements are absent from the artifact.
2. *Almost meets expectations* (weak/average content and cohesion): Student has almost achieved the outcomes and goals set for the task, but there are elements missing or not effective either in terms of content and/or the use of semiotic resources.
3. *Meets expectations* (good/very good content and cohesion): Student has successfully achieved the outcomes and goals set for the task.
4. *Exceeds expectations* (excellent content and cohesion): Student's performance exceeds expectations with regards to the outcomes and goals set for the task.

References

Hung, H.-T., Chiu, Y.-C. J., & Yeh, H.-C. (2013). Multimodal assessment of and for learning: A theory-driven design rubric. *British Journal of Educational Technology, 44*(3), 400–409. https://doi.org/10.1111/j.1467-8535.2012.01337.x

Levy, M., & Kimber, K. (2009). Developing an approach for comparing students' multimodal text creations: A case study. *Australasian Journal of Educational Technology, 25*(4), 489–508. https://doi.org/10.14742/ajet.1125

Index

Note: Page numbers in *italics* indicate figures, **bold** indicate tables in the text, and references following "n" refer endnotes

academic learning 8, 17
American Council on the Teaching of Foreign Languages (ACTFL) 22
   Learning for Justice 23, 27
   Performance Descriptors for Language Learners 23, 50
   second language educator 33
   second language teachers' organizations 102
   standards for language learning 23
   World-Readiness Standards for Foreign Language Learning 43, 92
analyzing critically epistemic move 12, 15
analyzing epistemic move 12, 17, 42, 86, 111
analyzing functionally epistemic move 12
analyzing knowledge processes 111
Anderson, L. 133
Anstey, M. 3
Anzaldúa, G. 113
applying appropriately knowledge process 13, 42, 97, 98, 101, 110–111
applying creatively knowledge process 13, 42, 98, 110–111
applying epistemic move 42, 111
applying knowledge process 13, 17, 40
assessment/assessment plan 23, 43, 44, 46, 49–50, 67–68
Available Designs 4, 5

backward design 24, 30, 44–45
belonging, principle of 6, 9, 15, 20, 29, 39, 45–46, 49, 53, 69, 147
Beucher, B. 122
Blogger, learners tool 112
Blyth, C. 31, 145, 146
Bobkina, J. 123

Bosworth, K. 64
Buck Institute of Education, scholars in 84
Bull, G. 3

Canva, learners tool 112
Center for Open Educational Resources 78, 145
Chan, P. E. 67
CLT *see* Communicative Language Teaching (CLT)
Cognard-Black, J. 133
cognitive/learning process dimensions 11–13
cohesion 93
   of semiotic elements 163–164
collaborative competence 61
collaborative construction of knowledge 31, 42, 50
collaborative learning 61–67, 69, 75, 84
communication modes 2
Communicative Language Teaching (CLT) 21
community development 93, 95–98
computer-mediated communications 2
conceptualizing knowledge processes **7**, 8, 11, 17, 43, **51–52, 55, 60, 80, 82,** 86, **88–89, 94,** 111
content 93, 163
   academic content 9, 10, 24, 30
   curricular content 6, 9, 20, 24, 26, 40, 49
   learning content 7
   multimodal content 9, 33
   novel content 11
Cope, B. 5–6, 8, 9, 15, 16, 30, 39, 44, 61, 67–68, 83
Cortázar, J. 124

Creative Commons license 102, 137, 142
Critical Framing 4, 5, 15
critical inquiry 25–27, 30, 33, 34, 48, **64**, 84–85, 93
curricular content 6, 9, 20, 24, 26, 30, 40, 49
curriculum barriers 46
Cutts, S. 31

Danzak, R. L. 111, 113
Derewianka, B. 75
design (or designing) 4–5
diagnostic assessment 68
digital tools 1, 6, 13, 23, 24, 29–31, 85, 111, 115, 116, 159–162
Domínguez Romero, E. 123
Donato, R. 24, 84
Douglas Fir Group 21–23, 29
drama-based identity texts 112–113

eComma 31, 34n3, 41–42
educational contexts 3–5, 8, 27, 48, 62, 92, 133
educators 5, 24, 25, 27, 41, 46, 50, 53, 70n1
enactment of practices 24
epistemic moves 7, 15, 16, 31, 41, 43, 53, 57–58, 67, 83, 86
evidence-based practices 33, 92
evidence of learning 24
experiencing process **7**, 9–10, 17, 43, **51–52, 54, 59, 80, 82**, 85–86, **88–89, 94**, 111
expository texts 98–103

fan fiction (or *fanfic*) 103–107
feedback, IPA 67–68
Feez, S. 83
formal instructional contexts 42
formal learning 6, 8, 17, 30, **51**, 136; *see also* informal learning
formative assessment 43, 49, 68, 75
Four Cs 22, 23, 33, 42, 45, 61, 85, 99, 108
functional models 76
funds of knowledge 6, 9, 17, 29, 43, 46, 53, 79

Gautam, A. A. 148n12
genre-based instruction (GBI) 31, 50, 75
    activities **80–82**
    fundamental basis of 76–77
    implementation of 83
    instructional sequence *vs.* knowledge processes and metafunctions 83
    integration of 78
    objectives of 77
    pedagogical sequence 79
    into second language teaching 77–78
Glisan, E. W. 24, 84
Goldthwaite, M. A. 133
grammar of multimodal transposition 15
graphic novels/comics 111
group processing 64–67, **64, 65**

Halliday, M. A. K. 3
Hanauer, D. I. 40
heritage language (HL) 20
human cognition 17
Hyland, K. 17n1, 77, 83

ideational metafunction 4
identity blogs 112
identity dimensions 9, 26, 27, **28**, 30, 47, 49, 107–**117**, 148n11
identity texts 107–111
Independent Construction of the Text stage 79
individual and group accountability 62
infographics 98–103
informal learning 6, 8, 9, 13, 17, 29, 30, 43, 45, **51**, 79; *see also* formal learning
instructional moves 24, 49–50, 53, 57
instructional outcomes 24, 30
instructional resources 29
instructional tools 11, 53
instructors 24
    reflection and new understandings 53, 57
Integrated Performance Assessment (IPA) 50, 67
integrated theory 15
interpersonal and small-group collaborative skills **64**
interpersonal mode of communication 23, 31, 33, 43, 49, 50, **54–57**, 59, 61, 68, 84, 86, **88–89**, 95, 99, 103, 104, 108, 111, 118, 129, 130, 134, 139
interpretive mode of communication 23, 31, 33, 43, 49, 50, **54–57**, 59, 61, 68, 84, 86, **88–89**, 95, 99, 104, 108, 111, 118, 125, 129, 130, 134, 139
IPA *see* Integrated Performance Assessment (IPA)

Jewell, T. 46
Jewitt, C. 124
Johnson, D. W. 62, 64, 66
Joint Construction of the Text 78, 79, 101, 105–106, 136–137, 141

Index

Kalantzis, M. 5–9, 15, 16, 30, 33, 39, 44, 50, 57, 61, 67–68, 83
knowledge creators 39–40
knowledge-making process 39
knowledge processes 7–9, 43
  Learning by Design 9–14
knowledge sharing 61
Kress, G. 5, 103
Krum, R. 98
K–12 educational contexts 27
Kubota, R. 26, 30

learners 79, 96, 98, 100, 126
  academic content and 9
  activities 112
  applying appropriately 13
  applying creatively 13
  artifacts 112
  cooperative work 42
  educational experiences 68
  experiences and texts 17
  Four Cs 85
  identities and personal experiences 20, 25
  identity texts task 112
  meaning-making 5
  multiliteracies 6, 7, 29, 41
  work 40, 42
Learning by Design (L-by-D) 6
  of *belonging* and *transformation* 20, 39
  and components 6–9
  eight knowledge processes 31, 50
  epistemic moves 147
  genre-based instruction (GBI) 31, 50, 75–79, **80–82**, 83, 83
  instruction based on 9, *10*, *16*
  knowledge processes *see* knowledge processes
  metafunctions 4, 14–15, *16*, 45, 46, 49, **54–56**, **59**, **80–82**, 83, 85, 86
  and open education 29
  and pedagogical vision 22
  project-based learning (PBL) 83–86, 86, 90
  reflexive pedagogy 39–44, 68, 70
  sample project grounded in **87–89**
  sample second language tasks *see* sample second language tasks
  second language instruction *see* second language instruction
  second language social reading task in *32*
  second language teaching *see* second language teaching

  theoretical and pedagogical bases 1–6, 14–15
  transformative curriculum 29, 42, 44, 68, 146
  UDL and *see* Universal Design for Learning (UDL)
Learning for Justice 27, 29, 33, 34, 50, 92, 145
Levido, A. 112
Lewis, C. 133
Lister, M. 2
literacy 21, 77, 92, 134
  technology 23, 24, 45
  traditional concept of 2

materials development cycle *147*
meaning-making metafunctions 83, 86
  community development 96–98
  expository texts and infographics 99–103
  fan fiction (or *fanfic*) 104–107
  identity texts 107–111
  media collection (critical analysis) 118–122
  multimodal stories 125–129
  nepantla 114–115
  podcasts and vodcasts 130–133
  recipes and procedural texts 134–138
  school brochures 138–143
meaning-making process 3–5, 12, 75, 77
media collection (critical analysis) 117–124
Medrano, A. 146
memes 122–124
Meribah, R. 133
meta-cognitive monitoring activities 41
metacognitive strategies 41
metafunctions 4, 14–15
Michaelsen, L. K. 65
Mills, K. A. 112, 124, 127
Modelling and Deconstructing the Text 79
modes of communication 50
Moll, L. C. 6
Moyna, M. I. 129, 132
multiliteracies 2–6, 15, 30, 41, 57, 108
  vs. Learning by Design (L-by-D) **7**
multiliterate meaning-makers 107, 111
multimodal artifacts 93, 111, 128
multimodal blogs 112
multimodal content 9, 33
multimodal meaning-making 2–4, 15, 103
multimodal stories 124–129
multimodal texts 10, 155–157

multiple means of action and expression 44
multiple means of engagement 44
multiple means of representation 44

Nathanson, S. 124
National Education Association (NEA) 22, 92, 98–103
National Research Council 41, 42, 53
NCSSFL-ACTFL Can-Do Statements 50
NEA *see* National Education Association (NEA)
nepantla 113–115
New London Group (NLG) scholars 1–6
  pedagogy of multiliteracies 57
Nieto, S. 26, 30
NLG scholars *see* New London Group (NLG) scholars
Norton, B. 20

OERs *see* Open Educational Resources (OERs)
Open Educational Resources (OERs) 25, 26, 29, 78, 102, 138, 145, 146
Open Language Resource Center 78, 145
open practices 25, 26, 29, 39, 78–79, 102, 145–146
open resources 102, 136, 137, *147*
Osborn, T. A. 27, 30, 85, 93
  cycle of critical inquiry 34
  proposed pillars 26, 49
Overt Instruction 5, 15

Partnership for 21st Century Learning (P21) 22, 23, 29
PBL *see* project-based learning (PBL)
pedagogical planning 45–49
performance-based instruction 23, 34n2, 70
persuasive infographic *144*
Pittaway, D. S. 20
podcasts 129–133
positive interdependence 62
presentational mode of communication 23, 31, 33, 49, 50, **54–57**, 59, 61, 68, 84, **88–89**, 95, 99, 104, 108, 111, 118, 125, 130, 134, 139
procedural texts 133–138
professional development opportunities 27
project-based learning (PBL): educators, planning and developing 83–86
  grounded in *L-by-D* **87–89**
  instructional phases for 85, 86
  teaching method 83–84
promotive interaction 64

recipes 133–138
reflexive pedagogy 39–44, 49, 68–70, 75, 76, 92
resource centers 79, 145
Ribota, A. 108

sample second language tasks 92–93
  community development 93, 95–98
  expository texts and infographics 98–103
  fan fiction (or *fanfic*) 103–107
  identity texts 107–117
  L-by-D's knowledge processes, activities for **94, 95**
  media collection (critical analysis) 117–124
  multimodal stories 124–129
  podcasts and vodcasts 129–133
  recipes and procedural texts 133–138
  school brochures 138–143
second language instruction: checkpoints and assessment 67–69
  collaborative learning 61–67
  instructional objectives 58, 61
  knowledge processes 57–58
second language teaching 39
  contexts 21, 23
  curriculum 30
  educators 25, 27, 30, 33, 43, 45, 85, 147
  everyday practices for instruction 57–58, **59–60**, 61–69, **63, 65, 66**
  GBI, instruction based on 78
  instructors *see* instructors
  learners *see* learners
  and learning 20, 26, 27, 29–31, 33, 50, 68, 69, 77, 78
  practices 29–31, 33
  reflexive pedagogy 39–44
  social reading task *32*
  universal design, instruction based on *see* Universal Design for Learning (UDL)
semiotic systems 2, 3, 93, 99, 128
Serafini, F. 17n2, 123
SFL *see* Systemic Functional Linguistics (SFL)
Situated Practice 5, 15
social identity 47–48
social justice: second language teaching for 49
  standards and outcomes **28**
social-reading platforms and tools 31
social-reading task 42–43

students' group and self-assessment, sample template for **63**
Systemic Functional Linguistics (SFL) 3, 75
   situational features and metafunctions 4, 14

target language 24
   development of 42
   and Four Cs 42
   knowledge and 11
   modes of communication 23–24, 31, 33
   sample model texts in 103
teachers 100, 106, 122, 135, 143
   and learners 7, 10
   second language 45, 46, 49, 50, 53, 62, 67, 70, 93
   and students 26
teaching method 83
text comparison stage 78, 82, 102, 107, 138, 143
textual metafunction 4, 14
This Book Is Anti-Racist Journal (Jewell) 46
Thoms, J. 145
transduction process 103, 107, 138
transformative curriculum 8–9, 15, 29, 30, 42, 44–46, 49, 53, 68, 69, 92, 146
transformed practice 4, 5, 15, 34
Troyan, F. J. 77, 78
21st Century Skills Map **22**, 22–23, 29

UDL *see* Universal Design for Learning (UDL)

UDL-IRN *see* Universal Design for Learning Implementation and Research Network (UDL-IRN)
Universal Design for Learning (UDL) 43–44
   instructional moves 49–50, 53, 57
   and *Learning by Design (L-by-D)* 44–45, 53
   pedagogical planning 45–49
   principles 61
Universal Design for Learning Implementation and Research Network (UDL-IRN) 44–45, 49, 50, 75
Unsworth, L. 124, 127

visible pedagogy 76, 77
vodcasts 129–133
Vygotsky, L. S. 40, 42

Watson, W. E. 65
"weaving" of knowledge processes 8
websites 159–162
Wiggins, B. E. 122
Winn, R. 129
Wix, learners tool 112
World-Readiness Standards for Foreign Language Learning (W-RSFLL) 23, 78

Yaman Ntelioglou, B. 113

Zammit, K. 124, 128, 138
Zapata, G. C. 108
Zone of Proximal Development 40, 42